BAR British Series 166
1987

J. D. Richards

The Significance of
Form and Decoration
of Anglo-Saxon
Cremation Urns

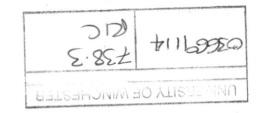
B.A.R.

5, Centremead, Osney Mead, Oxford OX2 0DQ, England.

GENERAL EDITORS

A.R. Hands, B.Sc., M.A., D.Phil.
D.R. Walker, M.A.

B.A.R. 166, 1987: 'The Significance of Form and Decoration of Anglo-Saxon Cremation Urns'.

Price £13.00 post free throughout the world. Payments made in dollars must be calculated at the current rate of exchange and $8.00 added to cover exchange charges. Cheques should be made payable to B.A.R. and sent to the above address.

ISBN 0 86054 439 7

For details of all new B.A.R. publications in print please write to the above address. Information on new titles is sent regularly on request, with no obligation to purchase.

Volumes are distributed from the publisher. All B.A.R. prices are inclusive of postage by surface mail anywhere in the world.

Printed in Great Britain

CONTENTS

BIBLIOGRAPHY

APPENDICES

ACKNOWLEDGMENTS

The text of this volume is substantially the same as that presented for a Ph.D. to the Council for National Academic Awards in November 1985 (and awarded in May 1986). It was felt then that the work was of sufficient theoretical and methodological interest to justify wider circulation, and that the results tables, which formed the core of the thesis, should be available for further investigation. British Archaeological Reports kindly agreed to take the complete work as it stood, although comments by Tania Dickinson and Peter Addyman, as external examiners of the thesis, have been taken into account in some of the amendments for this volume.

A large number of people contributed to the research, without whose assistance it would have been impossible. My first acknowledgment must be to those whom have excavated and published the Anglo-Saxon cremation vessels incorporated in the study. They are too numerous to name individually, but one man, J.N.L.Myres, must be singled out. His <u>Corpus</u> remains the starting point for anyone studying Anglo-Saxon pottery.

A further debt is due to those archaeologists who have allowed me to draw freely upon excavated material which is currently being prepared for publication. Firstly, I must thank the Spong Hill Project, namely Catherine Hills, Kenneth Penn and Robert Rickett. At Mucking Post-Excavation, Margaret and Tom Jones and their colleagues gave me every assistance. For Elsham, I am indebted to Freda Berisford and Chris Knowles; for Newark to Gavin Kinsley; for Sancton to Nicholas Reynolds; for Illington to Barbara Green and Bill Milligan; and for Worthy Park to Sonia Hawkes. In addition, I am grateful to Mary Harman and Keith Manchester for allowing me to use their unpublished skeletal reports.

A substantial amount of computer time has been used in the course of the investigation, both in terms of the central processor, and the human operator. The facilities of two organisations have been extensively used. Most of the number-crunching was done at Stafford, where the staff of the Computing Services Department of North Staffordshire Polytechnic are to be thanked. The former deputy director, Tony Whitehouse, and the chief operator, Eric Halliday, deserve especial mention. The research was completed at Leeds University, where the Computing Service was equally generous in its allocation of resources.

The Science and Engineering Research Council provided financial support for the project (studentship 80802863), and Catherine Hills and John Wilcock have had the task of supervising the research. To Catherine Hills, I also owe a personal debt for introducing me to Anglo-Saxon archaeology. Of my other university teachers, Ian Hodder should be singled out for introducing me to archaeological theory.

Many friends and colleagues also gave freely of their time, and I have benefited greatly from their discussion and intellectual stimulation. In particular, I would like to thank Chris Arnold, Janet Bagg, Mike Fletcher, Dan Smith, Paul Reilly, Nick Ryan, and Martin

Walsh.

Finally, to Linda, especial thanks are due, for help and support whilst these results were recorded.

All of the above have provided help, but this research is necessarily my own work, and the shortcomings which remain are my own responsibility.

"I have been engaged in a series of structural analyses, all of which are concerned to define a number of extra-linguistic languages" (R.Barthes, <u>Essais Critiques,</u> Paris; Seiul 1964, 155).

CHAPTER 1

THEORY

This essay is the result of the fusion, or more accurately collision, of three areas of archaeological research: funerary ritual, artefact typology, and Anglo-Saxons. Put briefly, the thesis presented here is that aspects of the form and decoration of Early Anglo-Saxon cremation vessels are related to the social identity of the occupant(s). Before proceeding towards an expansion of this hypothesis in section 1.5, it will be necessary to outline the separate threads which will hopefully be woven together in the synthesis. To use a metaphor adopted from computer programming, the approach will be 'top-down', working from the general to the particular (fig.1).

Figure 1 Schematic diagram illustrating relationship of sections

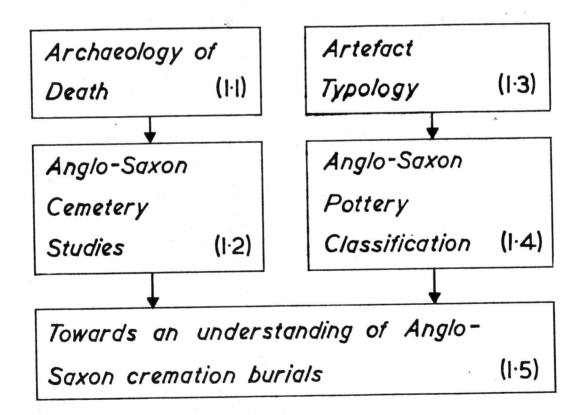

1.1 The archaeology of death

The study of the material remains of funerary behaviour has played a central role in the development of explanatory models in archaeology. Chapman and Randsborg have recently presented an historical overview (1981), so only a few general points will be made here, in order to place the present work in context. Mortuary practices have also been a major concern of ethnographers, who began to search for patterning in the variety of human response to death from an early date. Bartel (1982) and Cogbill (1982) have both recently summarised the development of anthropological thought relating to death.

As Huntington and Metcalf note:

> The diversity of cultural reaction is a measure of the universal impact of death. But it is not a random reaction; always it is meaningful and expressive (1979,1).

For the archaeologist, only a small fraction of the total behaviour relating to death survives (see Bartel, ibid fig.1). Nothing normally remains of elaborate mourning, funeral processions or grave-side rituals. All that survives is the disposal of the corpse itself, if that involves burial underground. On the other hand, as the residue of one of the few deliberate acts of deposition, funerary remains are often regarded as one of the "purest" forms of the archaeological record. Admittedly, they suffer from the same post-depositional distortions resulting from differential preservation as does all archaeological evidence, and inevitably they suffer from the same distortions due to differential recovery. Nevertheless, a grave and its contents are the result of conscious selection and deposition, unlike the majority of artefacts found in archaeological contexts.

Despite the great void between the archaeological and anthropological records of mortuary behaviour, the development of interpretative models in archaeology has closely followed that in anthropology. From our present position it is possible to identify four broad phases: a pre-scientific era in the eighteenth and nineteenth centuries (section 1.11), an early twentieth century phase dominated by the culture historical school (section 1.12), followed by a post-1960 functionalist stance (section 1.13), itself questioned in the 1980's by the structuralist position (section 1.14). By telescoping the more distant past and separating out more recent trends it may well be that undue emphasis is being placed on recent developments. In Kuhn's terms (1962) it may be that we are still groping in a pre-paradigmatic phase and have not quite lost our innocence (cf. Clarke 1973). Nevertheless, the rival schools appear to be well enough established in anthropology to justify their extrapolation into archaeology, and the division will be followed as being empirically useful!

1.11 The eighteenth and nineteenth centuries

From an early date antiquarians were interested in barrows and other visible forms of burial, and subsequently these have always constituted a major proportion of the observed archaeological record. In the pre-scientific age speculation centred on the identity of the builders and occupants of tombs.

In the late eighteenth and early nineteenth centuries burials were the subject of the first systematic excavations. Thomas Jefferson in Virginia, Colt-Hoare, Bateman, Mortimer and Greenwell in England, and Worsaae in Denmark excavated hundreds of burial mounds, recovering vast quantities of material (Chapman and Randsborg 1981, 2). Although these excavations were still concerned with the identity of the mound-builders, they also became interested in chronological problems. The Three Age System provided an appropriate chronological framework.

Early anthropological work was based on pseudo-psychological principles relating to the universal occurrence of religious beliefs.

Following Bastian (1860), anthropologists examined beliefs about the afterlife and ancestor worship in primitive societies, and sought to place them within an evolutionary framework. Tylor (1865, 1871) emphasised the association of beliefs about the afterlife with the universal body-soul dichotomy. Just as the soul was supposed to leave the body during dreams, so it was permanently released at death. Therefore animism, or belief in spirits, was seen as being one of the most primitive forms of religion, frequently taking the form of ancestor worship. Offerings to the dead were regarded as prototypes of sacrifices to ancestors.

As Bartel (1982, 35) has noted, Tylor did not present much relevant information concerning the patterning of cultural activity related to death and burial, and so his work is of little value to archaeologists. Tylor used single examples of burial types for each society, and did not discuss differences in burials relating to age, sex, or status.

Discussion of archaeological material was included in early syntheses by John Lubbock. Lubbock (1865) described burial treatment for each stage of religious belief, and discussed how the amount and types of grave-goods associated with the corpse differed. He also reported that burial treatment differed with age, sex and social status of individuals. Lubbock believed that:

> the size of the tumulus may be taken as a rough indication of the estimation in which the deceased was held (1865, 123).

From an early statistical analysis of 297 British barrows Lubbock concluded that where grave-goods were found they could be taken as evidence for belief in an after-life:

> The care with which the dead were interred, and the custom of burying implements with them, may fairly be regarded as indicating the existence of a belief in the immortality of the soul, and in material existence after death (1865, 133).

This assumption continues to permeate the archaeological literature to the present day.

1.12 The early twentieth century

Three aspects of the archaeological study of death may be identified in the early twentieth century. The first feature is the continued interest in chronological approaches, and the use of cemetery material to study changes in artefacts through time and space.

The second is the domination of the cultural or normative approach. The large amount of material from burial sites has played an integral part in the recognition of regional and chronological variations in material culture. The cultural approach has been traced to the Austro-German school of anthropological geographers (1880-1900), who were concerned with the mapping of cultural attributes and the correlation of the distributions with environmental variables. It was then taken up by those such as Kossinna (1911, 1926) who linked cultural distributions with racial groups (see Hodder 1982a, 2ff). However, the culture concept has really become associated with Gordon Childe. Although rejecting any simple racial or linguistic interpretation of cultures, Childe retained the idea that a culture represented what he called a "people".

> We find certain types of remains - pots, implements, ornaments, burial rites, house forms - constantly recurring together. Such a complex of regularly associated traits we shall term a "cultural group" or just a "culture". We assume that such a complex is the material expression of what would today be called a "people". Only where the complex in question is regularly and exclusively associated with skeletal remains of a specific physical type would we venture to replace "people" by the term "race" (1929, v-vi).

The normative view of culture is that common patterns of behaviour, or "norms" produce spatial regularities in material remains, including mortuary evidence:

> Community of tradition imposes on all members of the society in question a common pattern of behaviour. This must result in the production of standard types, which, if they be artifacts, burial rites or remains of repasts, archaeology can identify (Childe 1956, 9-10).

Similarities and differences between cultures in attributes such as cremation versus inhumation rites, single versus collective burial, and types of grave-goods, were interpreted in terms of diffusion or population movement. This allows the production of "cultural-history". Binford (1971, 9) summarises the assumption behind this approach as being that:

> the degree of formal similarity observed among independent sociocultural units is a direct measure of the degree of genetic or affiliational cultural relationship among the units being compared.

Mortuary practices were integral to Childe's cultural framework. Changes in burial rite were interpreted as invasions by new peoples, and measurements of cranial types were used as supporting evidence. The validity of the model may be questioned, however, where a total change in burial rite appears to be unrelated to any historically documented invasion, such as the widespread adoption of inhumation without grave-goods in seventh century England.

Childe's definition demanded that cultures should be described in terms of several aspects of life, but in practice many, such as the Bell Beaker people, were known solely from their burial rite. As Chapman and Randsborg (1981, 4) point out, the subsequent excavation of settlement sites has thrown doubt on many cultural discontinuities. In the anthropological literature, the degree to which distributionally studied burial practices were as useful for historical inquiries as other cultural features was already being questioned. Kroeber (1927) observed that distributions of mortuary traits did not conform to boundaries of cultural areas as defined by other traits. Recently, there has been increasing criticism of the cultural normative approach within archaeology, from several quarters (e.g. Binford 1965, Renfrew 1977, Hodder 1977, 1978b).

The third area of archaeological interest in mortuary practices in the early part of this century has been the continued focus on social and socio-religious aspects. Some of this work is in direct descent from the evolutionary approach established by Tylor and Lubbock (e.g. Childe 1945). Indeed in Soviet archaeology the evolutionary perspective is still dominant (see Alekshin 1983), although it has been given a Marxist slant. Childe and others also used burial evidence to infer social differences within cultures, often focusing on the identification of "chiefs" or "aristocrats". For example, the large barrows and rich furnishings of Wessex barrows were used as evidence for Wessex "chiefdoms" (Childe 1957).

1.13 Post-1960's functionalism

In the early twentieth century there was a major revision in anthropological interpretations of funerary ritual, explained by Bartel (1982) as being derived from the influence of the French school of sociology: Durkheim (1915), Hertz (1907) and Van Gennep (1908). Instead of interpreting religious beliefs in isolation, methodological emphasis shifted towards correlating religious practices with other aspects of the social system. There was a focus on the ceremonial, with an attempt to observe what purpose it served within society. Ritual was seen as an adaptive mechanism, rather than being explained in terms of pre-conceived notions of the afterlife.

This view of funerary ritual was maintained by British social anthropologists of the structural-functionalist school, and hence was influential in functionalist interpretations in archaeology. Radcliffe-Brown re-emphasised the belief that funerary ritual is a group expression of solidarity. Death is seen as the loss of one of the constituent parts of the social system:

> A person occupies a definite position in society, has a certain share in the social life, is one of the supports of the network

of social relations. His death constitutes a partial destruction of the social cohesion, the normal social life is disorganised, the social equilibrium is disturbed. After the death the society has to organise itself anew and reach a new condition of equilibrium (Radcliffe-Brown 1922, 285).

Psychological phenomena have also been integrated within this holistic interpretation of mortuary practices. Bendann (1930) has examined social organisation and mortuary practices in a wide range of ethnographic contexts. She identified several common features, including beliefs about cause of death, spirits, significance of burial, and mourning rites. A more recent ethnography of the LoDagaa of West Africa (Goody 1962) attempts to merge social relationships with their psychological context. Goody confirms that differences in mourning practices within LoDagaa society are related to social relationships, which are themselves related to inheritance and authority structures. Most recently Bloch (1971) has given an important account of mortuary practice among the Merina of Madagascar. Death-related behaviour is interpreted in terms of the promotion of group solidarity, and the beneficial psychological effects on the participants.

Functionalist interpretations in archaeology were linked with systems theory and the desire for scientific testability under the banner of the "New Archaeology". In the United States they were associated especially with Lewis Binford (1972), in the United Kingdom with David Clarke (1968).

Among the central tenets of the New Archaeology was the denial of any basic limitations to our knowledge of the past. Binford argued against the pessimistic view prevalent in the 1950's (e.g. Hawkes 1954) that archaeologists could only come to reliable conclusions about the technology and economy of past societies, whilst social organisation and religion were beyond the frame of reference. Binford believed that "new archaeologists" should develop theories examining the relationship between material culture and other parts of the socio-cultural system. Analysis of mortuary practices was central to this position (see also Chapman 1977).

Binford (1971) criticised the cultural-history method of deducing relationships between societies on the basis of similarities in burial form. He argued instead that disposal of the dead must be studied within the context of the individual society. Two components of the social system might be symbolised in mortuary behaviour: the social persona of the deceased, and the composition and size of the social group recognising responsibilities to the deceased. The social persona is a composite of the social identities which the individual held during life, and which were recognised as appropriate for consideration in death. Binford identified the main dimensions recognised as age, sex, social position, social affiliation, conditions of death, and location of death. He then tested these hypotheses on forty non-state societies taken from the HRAF (Human Resources Area Files), and claimed that the data supported his initial assertions. He found that with increases in social complexity, the dimensions of social position and social affiliation assumed greater importance and were increasingly represented in the burial rite. Binford concluded that it was possible to relate the form of mortuary practices to the form of society. Therefore mortuary practices should no longer be seen as indicators of cultural diffusion, but rather they should be analysed within the context of variations in society and social complexity. Amongst the Nyakyusa of Tanzania, for example:

> Differences in ritual are directly connected by the people themselves with differences in lineage, and the principle is maintained that every individual follows the ritual of his or her father's lineage, though a married woman will follow that of her husband when at her husband's home (Wilson 1957, 10).

Binford's work was followed by many allied analyses (see papers in Brown 1971). Saxe (1970) related the existence of formal disposal areas, i.e. cemeteries, to the existence of corporate groups, each justifying their claims to land by their direct descent from ancestors who occupied the same land. Tainter (1975, 1978) linked energy expenditure in mortuary practices to the rank of the deceased. Several papers (e.g. Randsborg 1974, Shennan 1975) have examined ranking within cemeteries or regions through "wealth scores" derived from the quantity or quality of grave-goods. Most analyses, however, have concentrated on recognising the social persona of the deceased, rather than on the social group owing responsibilities to the deceased. Attention has focused on the buried, rather than the buriers, and grave-goods have been taken to be a direct reflection of the status of the deceased, not of those attending the funeral and perhaps wishing to impress others with their generosity.

Consequently, such approaches have met with some scepticism. Leach has observed:

> If graves are in any way an indication of social status it is the social status of the funeral organisers as much as the social status of the deceased that is involved (1979, 122).

There has been unease that ethnographic data does not support the assumption, regarded as simplistic, that cemetery organisation can be equated with social organisation. Sceptics have drawn support from a cautionary paper by Ucko (1969). From a wide ranging survey of the ethnographic literature Ucko concluded that burial practices are not necessarily indicative of afterworld beliefs, that grave-goods do not always reach the grave, that the absence of grave-goods does not necessarily imply low status or poverty, and that large funerary structures do not always reflect rulers or chiefs. Leach (1977) has reiterated many of these criticisms, emphasising for example, that the grandest monuments in Asia originated as memorial cairns erected over the relics of an impoverished saint.

However, as Chapman and Randsborg (1981) are at pains to stress, in at least one respect Ucko echos the conclusions of Binford and Saxe:

> in the vast majority of cases known ethnographically, a culture or society is not characterised by one type of burial only, but ... on the contrary, one society will undertake several

different forms of burial, and ... these forms will often be correlated with the status of the deceased (Ucko 1969, 270).

Most of the papers in the recent collected volume (Chapman, Kinnes and Randsborg 1981) take this simple relationship between cemetery and social organisation for granted. Consequently the collection has been criticised by some:

> many of the interpretations offered rely on a reductive form of functionalist analysis which fails to provide an adequate penetration of the form, content and context of mortuary practices and the relationship between these practices and social strategies and social actions (Tilley 1982, 139).

If the functionalist assumption of a direct relationship between artefact style and social identity is misplaced, then the real nature of this relationship must be established. Cemeteries provide ideal data sets for this purpose because of the direct association between people and objects:

> If there is no automatic equation between style and social identity, it will be important to study symbolism, and where better to do so than in cemeteries? (Bradley 1980, 172).

As Jones (1980, 179) has noted, cemeteries also have certain characteristics which make them ideal for computer analysis. They consist of easily definable entities, or graves, which can be described in terms of obvious attributes such as the presence or absence of particular grave-goods. The "New Archaeology" has made a lasting contribution to mortuary studies in the quantification of cemetery analyses. Through the use of computer simulation and multivariate analyses the examination and classification of cemetery material has been placed on a rigorous and testable footing (cf. Doran and Hodson 1975, 309ff).

1.14 Structuralism and archaeology in the 1980's

In the second half of this century structural-functionalism tended to go out of fashion in anthropology. One of the most influential schools of thought to replace it was the structuralist movement (Levi-Strauss 1958, 1962).

The philosophical roots of structuralism can be identified in the work of the eighteenth century thinker, Immanuel Kant. Kant believed that man confers a structure upon the world through his concepts and categories. Whilst these ideas have been developed in different ways, all brands of structuralism share some basic generalities. Firstly, that there is structure underlying all human behaviour and mental functioning; secondly, that this structure can be discovered by orderly analysis; thirdly, that it has cohesiveness and meaning; and fourthly, that structures extend across all cultural sub-systems. Beyond these four general statements there is a great variety of structuralist viewpoints, largely stemming from whether the structures are seen as physical or cultural. As Bartel (1982) notes, structuralism acts as more of an anthropological philosophy than an operational methodology. But as he goes on to say:

> It has great potential for developing into a new methodology related to religion in general, and to mortuary practice in particular (1982, 43).

There are few examples of structuralist analysis of mortuary ritual in the anthropological literature. Levi-Strauss himself analysed life-death dualism in the Zuni and western Pueblo mythology (1958), although he did not extend this to cover mortuary practices. Two recently published papers have attempted to analyse mortuary practices within a structuralist framework (De Coppett 1981, Barley 1981). Barley (1983) has also presented an extended version of this work which is significant for the stress it places on the role of material culture within the ritual. Battaglia (1983) has discussed the use of artefacts in encoding fundamental concepts of person among the Sabarl of Papua New Guinea. These objects are further employed as symbolic substitutes for persons in mortuary ritual and exchanges. Generally, anthropologists have neglected the role of material culture in society.

Functionalist approaches have also been criticised within archaeology (see Hodder 1982c for a summary), and as Leach (1973) predicted, there have been attempts to incorporate some of the major tenets of structuralism within archaeological analyses. Structuralism is seen as offering a less mechanistic explanation of human behaviour, in which primacy is given to the human mind. Material culture represents one transformation of the underlying structural grammar and so archaeology must play a central role in the humanities, documenting changes in this grammar through time. Despite some early attempts at "high" structuralist interpretations (e.g. McGhee 1977), most archaeological applications have blended aspects of structuralism with structural-marxism to produce a model of material culture in which artefacts form part of a communication system which is actively manipulated in the process of social interaction, instead of merely being a passive reflection of social relationships (see Deetz 1977, Hodder 1982a, 1982b, Leone 1982).

Several archaeologists working on ethnographic data have justified the need for interpretative models of mortuary practices which place more emphasis on the ideology of the particular context (e.g. Hodder 1980, Parker-Pearson 1982). Hodder has shown how the burial practices of the Mesakin Nuba represent an idealised social system, rather than the existing one (cf. Bloch 1971), refuting, in this instance, the Binford-Saxe hypothesis about corporate cemeteries. However, there have been few archaeological studies of mortuary practices which have incorporated elements of this new approach, Van de Velde (1979a) and Shanks and Tilley (1982) being rare exceptions.

1.2 Anglo-Saxon cemetery studies

The study of Anglo-Saxon cemeteries must be seen as an integral part of Anglo-Saxon archaeology. Indeed, until post World War II developments in survey and excavation techniques led to the recognition of settlement sites, the archaeology of Anglo-Saxon England was the archaeology of its cemeteries. Burials are still numerically predominant; compare for instance the respective size of the gazetteers of burials (Meaney 1964) and settlements (Rahtz 1976). Distribution maps of the area of Anglo-Saxon settlement (e.g. Morris 1973; 59, 107) are really maps of areas of adoption of the Anglo-Saxon burial rite. Typologies of artefacts, upon which chronologies are based, depend upon objects deposited in graves.

The history of the study of Anglo-Saxon cemeteries can be seen as a microcosm of the history of mortuary studies in general, reflecting, after a time-lag, developments in interpretative models in prehistoric archaeology, themselves related to changes in anthropology and other related disciplines. It is therefore possible to see the four phases identified in section 1.1 in Anglo-Saxon archaeology. Commencing in the late eighteenth and early nineteenth century with a pre-scientific phase (section 1.21), the sub-discipline was then dominated for much of the twentieth century by a cultural-history model (section 1.22). This approach was tinged with a few attempts to infer social distinctions, and these have been more rigorously developed under the percolated influence of the so-called "New Archaeology" (section 1.23). At the same time, the criticisms of functionalism advanced in other areas have also been put forward within Anglo-Saxon archaeology (section 1.24).

1.21 The pre-scientific age

The beginnings of Anglo-Saxon archaeology are generally dated to the late eighteenth century, when James Douglas identified certain Kentish burials as Anglo-Saxon (Jessup 1975). In 1846, however, Henslow could still describe Anglian pots as "having been deposited by the aboriginal Britons", and in the same year, Anglo-Saxon ceramics from Kingston were merely attributed to the "Primeval Period" (cited in Laing 1979). In this period interest focused on the identity of the people buried, from a racial standpoint.

The main breakthrough came in 1855 with the publication of Kemble's Burial and cremation. Kemble drew attention to the similarity between cremation urns from eastern England and those from Hanover, hence confirming that they were the burials of Anglo-Saxons:

> Comparison of data, capable of being tested by known and ascertained facts of history, now enables us to bring them within fixed limits of space and time; to assign various phenomena to various periods, and to reason with some security upon the races to which such phenomena are to be referred (1855, 309).

Kemble also discussed the religious beliefs of the Anglo-Saxons. Drawing parallels with ethnographic situations he concluded that cremation was a heathen custom, whilst inhumations must be the graves of early Christian converts.

1.22 Twentieth century Anglo-Saxon cemetery studies

The cultural-history model has come to dominate twentieth century Anglo-Saxon archaeology, principally through the work of two men: J.N.L.Myres and E.T.Leeds. Both wished to contribute to the history of the period, for which a chronological and geographical framework became necessary. Therefore both treated cemeteries as quarries of material which they used in two ways. Firstly grave-goods became the basis of typological dating, and secondly they served as dots on a distribution map. By comparing distributions of classes of grave-good the growth and spread of archaeological cultures could be traced, with the added advantage that these could be related to the historically named peoples of Bede's Ecclesiastical History (Colgrave and Mynors 1969): Angles, Saxons and Jutes.

Leeds laid the foundations for this approach in the early part of this century, defining the respective cultural metalwork assemblages (Leeds 1913). In two further articles he later elaborated the typology for particular metalwork groups: square-headed brooches (Leeds 1949), and florid cruciform brooches (Leeds and Pocock 1971). In separate papers he related the chronological and spatial development of Anglo-Saxon metalwork to historically attested events (Leeds 1912, 1933, 1945).

Publication of the basic material from cremation cemeteries, i.e. the pottery, has had to wait until relatively recently, and the two companion works by Myres (1969, 1977a). Both Myres and Leeds viewed cemeteries, not as entities in their own right, but as sources of datable objects from which a history of the period might be written.

This tradition has been continued by other scholars, both with the publication of comparable corpora for other groups of material e.g. shield bosses (Evison 1963), spearheads (Swanton 1973, 1974), disc brooches (Avent 1975), and wheel-thrown pottery (Evison 1979); and with the production of general works of historical synthesis, based upon cemetery material, e.g. for Kent, Hawkes (1956) and Evison (1965).

Research upon the third strand of twentieth century cemetery studies, namely the social aspects, has been relatively small scale and patchy, as were the first attempts in the prehistoric field. It has focused especially on the identification and discussion of very rich graves, notably Sutton Hoo (for a bibliography see Bruce-Mitford 1972). There have also been individual attempts to infer social distinctions from the identification of structures within some graves (Hogarth 1973, Reynolds 1976, Hills 1977a). Generally Anglo-Saxon archaeologists have followed the minimalist stance advanced by Hawkes (1954), that social structure and religion are rarely observable archaeologically. This position is followed by Wilson when he remarks that:

Occasionally a very rich grave may give an idea of social structure and the wealth of a particular person, but such indications are rare (1976, 3).

One or two papers have seen the cemetery as an entity in its own right, looking both at the organisation of graves within it (Faull 1977), and the relationship of the cemetery and the landscape (Faull 1976). Kirk (1956) attempted to define the organisation of burial from the distribution of cemeteries in a localised area. Others have tackled the vexed question of grave orientation (see Rahtz 1978 and Kendall 1982). However, these attempts often hark back to the earliest stages of cemetery investigation and the speculative statements about religious beliefs made by early antiquarians (cf. Wells and Green 1970, Hawkes 1977). In a similar vein, conclusions based upon single anomalous graves have been used as a basis for speculation about Anglo-Saxon ideology (cf. Hawkes and Wells 1975). In the last decade the state of Anglo-Saxon cemetery studies was such that Hope-Taylor wrote that:

> our so-called Anglo-Saxon archaeology is today still blinkered by antiquarian pre-occupation with grave-goods. Every year we see Anglo-Saxon cemeteries used as convenient quarries to provide raw material for the perpetuation of an habitual and unquestioning academic activity (itself not without a curiously ritual aspect). The Anglo-Saxon cemetery in Britain has never been studied as a complete phenomenon, as the deeply revealing local entity it certainly is. It ought by now to have been recognised as an unwritten form of historical document roughly equivalent (though at once broader in scope and less exact) to the parish register of later times, and investigated as such (1977, 262).

1.23 Functionalism in Anglo-Saxon cemetery studies

The impact of the "New Archaeology" on the study of the Early Medieval period has been less, and later, than for Prehistory, perhaps because of the buffering effect of historical scholarship. However, its influence may be identified in two respects, namely in the adoption of quantitative analyses, and in approaches to the study of social organisation. Rahtz (1983) has assessed the influence of the New Archaeology on the study of the proto-historic and historic periods, but two papers deserve individual mention because of their concern with cemetery analysis. Both Shephard (1979) and Arnold (1980) have produced functionalist style wealth-score applications to Anglo-Saxon cemeteries.

Shephard notes the increasing diversification in form of burial in the sixth and seventh centuries, with the appearance of both barrow cemeteries and large isolated barrows in the early seventh century. He distinguishes between these burial types on the basis of the associated grave-goods, using multivariate statistical techniques including clustering and principal coordinates analysis to isolate grave-good groupings. He notes that males generally have a more restricted range of grave-goods than females, paralleling Shennan's findings for the Bronze Age (1975). Males in isolated barrows, however, are apparently less constrained in their choice of grave-goods than males in cemeteries. In addition, sex differences count for less in the provision of grave-goods for burials in isolated barrows than for those in cemeteries. Applying Binford's (1971) hypothesis that the more complex the society, the less likely it is that age and sex should be recognised in burial rite, Shephard concludes that the isolated barrows represent the increasing hierarchisation of society, although he acknowledges the difficulty of recognising and defining status archaeologically.

It may be noted that by their very nature isolated barrows are necessarily socially distinct, as they do not represent the burials of a whole community. In addition, barrow graves in flat cemeteries must also be regarded as different from the surrounding burials in at least one sense (of having a mound erected over them), even if they are indistinguishable in terms of grave-goods. Furthermore, Shephard's statistical results might be questioned on the grounds that the lower cumulative variance (accounted for by his first six principal coordinates) for isolated barrows rather than for cemeteries (indicating wider variability in grave-goods), might be the result of small sample size, as he acknowledges. Alternatively, bearing in mind that the barrow group incorporates burials from all over the country, the wider variability might be a consequence of regional differentiation. The variation for cemeteries is assessed in terms of variability within cemeteries. Nevertheless, Shephard's paper represents a significant attempt to infer social distinctions from archaeological data in a rigorous manner.

Arnold's examination of the social structure of Kent and Wessex (1980) proceeds from the basic assumption that there is a direct relationship between the system of status-grading in Anglo-Saxon society, and the nature of the archaeological assemblage; that is, that an Anglo-Saxon burial accurately reflects the occupant's position in society. Arnold predicts that with the emergence of the Anglo-Saxon kingdoms the distribution of wealth in graves should become disproportionate with time. Scores are allocated to graves, firstly on the basis of the rarity of the objects within them, and secondly according to the number of different object types within the grave. Both methods have problems. The first technique will produce distorted results if there is regional variation in wealth between cemeteries. Rich and poor cemeteries cannot be compared, since rarity is measured on an individual cemetery basis. The second method gives inadequate weight to exceptional single items.

Nevertheless, Arnold argues that patterning does emerge. In the early cemeteries most graves are low status; in an intermediate phase in the mid-sixth century there are one or two separate wealth groups, and in the late cemeteries there are a few very rich groups removed from the low status groups. One might question how far the dating evidence can support such conclusions. In particular, since the richer graves tend to be those which are best dated (because of the number of objects), and later objects are more easily datable, whilst graves without grave-goods are undatable, there is a danger of circularity in the argument.

However, the major problem must be that which is shared by all attempts to identify ranking through wealth scores. Orton and Hodson (1981) have shown that none of the archaeological attempts to distinguish ranking are based on a large enough sample of graves. Where distinct ranks are claimed, the real situation could be one of continuous grading of wealth. They demonstrate that in order to identify four ranks at the 10% confidence level it would be necessary to have at least 300 graves. Unfortunately, none of Arnold's cemeteries meets this requirement.

Several other papers (e.g. Welch 1980, Alcock 1981) have adopted aspects of the New Archaeology and even some of the concerns with social structure, but may be seen to be still traditionally rooted in typological studies.

1.24 The influence of structuralism on Anglo-Saxon cemetery studies

At the same time as functionalist explorations of Anglo-Saxon cemetery material were being advanced, the same objections were raised to these approaches as had been generated in anthropology and later in prehistoric archaeology[1]. Indeed, in the same conference proceedings in which Arnold's paper was published, other papers challenged the central assumption that social organisation is mirrored in cemetery organisation (Hodder 1980, Pader 1980). Pader's research, which attempted to take into account some of the structuralist criticisms of functionalism, later appeared in full (1982).

Pader's work owed its theoretical framework to Giddens (1979) rather than Levi-Strauss. She argued that one must look at the symbolic function of artefacts, including not just what is used, but how it is used as well. Symbols are ambiguous, and have many possible meanings. The actual meaning comes from the specific context. Pader cites the straw hat as an example. In different situations, of Eton college, a butcher's shop, a Venetian canal, and a music hall, the same artefact can have different meanings. Symbolic codes are acquired through the repeated use of artefacts in context. Therefore although the archaeologist cannot reconstruct the "world view" of the Anglo-Saxon, it may be possible to recognise symbolic codes by close examination of graves. Hence one may understand the relations on which society is based, and appreciate, for example, the relative importance of age distinctions in structuring society.

Pader argues that one must look at the symbolic function of

NOTE

[1] In fact Barley, an anthropologist, had already adopted a structuralist approach to three aspects of Anglo-Saxon symbolism studied from written sources: naming systems, colour systems, and kinship terminology, but his work (1974) has not been widely acknowledged in archaeological circles.

artefacts, examining not only what is used, but how it is used as well. She investigates material from three Anglo-Saxon inhumation cemeteries: Bergh Apton, Holywell Row, and Westgarth Gardens. In constructing social groupings she takes into account not only the presence or absence of specific objects, but also their position within the grave, and the way in which the body was laid out. Pader finds that whilst there is no direct correlation between an artefact type and its position within the cemetery, once the positions of artefacts and skeletons are included, then spatial groupings appear. At Holywell Row, for example, whilst both the females in Sector 1 and those in Sector 2 were buried with knives, those in Sector 1 have the knife on their right, whilst in Sector 2 it was placed on their left. Rather than explaining such variation in terms of chronological developments, following traditional models, Pader prefers to interpret the clusters as social groupings.

In some respects Pader's work is similar to that of Arnold and Shephard. In terms of the development of Anglo-Saxon cemetery studies the structuralist criticisms of functionalism are peripheral, to the extent that both functionalism and structuralism are concerned with explanatory hypotheses about society, in contrast to the previous typologically dominated schools. Pader's work does not deny that social organisation is reflected in cemetery organisation. She merely extends the parameters by which social organisation is represented, and shows that simplistic wealth scores are inadequate. Regrettably, Pader is hampered by her choice of data sets. The cemeteries used were neither completely excavated, nor apparently completely recorded. All are small, and this problem cannot be overcome by the impressive array of quantitative techniques utilised. Pader's conclusions cannot therefore be applied more widely, although her work can be seen as a pointer to the direction in which Anglo-Saxon cemetery analysis might proceed.

1.3 Artefact typology

The hypothesis under examination in the present work is that aspects of the form and design of Anglo-Saxon funerary vessels are associated with the identity of the people buried in them. In order to quantify such associations it is necessary to isolate individual attributes of form and decoration. Existing classifications of Anglo-Saxon pottery will be considered in section 1.4, but it is first essential to review the literature concerning artefact typology in general. Most of this has originated in the United States. It is also predominantly concerned with prehistoric material, but in the absence of literary or historical references to Anglo-Saxon pottery, the issues discussed are just as relevant to Pagan Anglo-Saxon pottery.

1.31 Do artefact types exist?

The classic definition of an artefact type was established by Krieger (1944) as a consistently recurring combination of attributes. The same definition reappears in Clarke's more recent and more wordy classic, Analytical Archaeology, where an artefact type is defined as:

an homogeneous population of __artefacts__ which share a consistently
recurrent range of attribute states within a given polythetic set
(1968, 188).

This definition has been widely applied, both before and since
Krieger, whenever archaeologists have sought to organise the material
under study. A few papers (Spaulding 1953; Whallon 1972) have
attempted to apply statistical techniques, and particularly the
chi-square test, in order to identify types. However, considerable
debate has focused on whether types defined in this manner - whether
intuitively or by the use of statistics - may be regarded as natural
types which have any objective reality (see, for example, Ford 1954).
Krieger's original formulation stressed that a type should have
meaning in terms of the cognition of the people under study:

> Each type should approximate as closely as possible that
> combination of mechanical and aesthetic executions which formed a
> definite structural pattern in the minds of a number of workers,
> who attained this pattern with varying degrees of success and
> interpretation (1944, 278).

Following Krieger and Clarke, an archaeological classification only
has meaning in so far as it corresponds with the perception of the
artefact makers. Eggert (1977) has denied the feasibility and utility
of discovering cognitive structures underlying patterning in
artefacts. His argument rests upon the belief that there is a reality
independent of both the archaeological typology, and of the native
cognition, although it is unclear where this reality resides.

Hill and Evans (1972) argue that there may be several equally
correct typologies. The native description of an artefact is
dependent on the context of the inquiry. Artefacts may be grouped
according to material, form, function, or any one of a large number of
attributes. Many archaeologists, including Deetz (1967), whilst
questioning the feasibility of discovering the native classification,
have defended the artefact type description as a convenient means by
which assemblages may be compared. A typology is merely regarded as a
useful archaeological tool for organising and presenting material.
Therefore it is not important that it is:

> the creation of the archaeologist and not necessarily of the
> makers of the artifacts being analysed (1967,51).

However, the question of whether types are real or invented is of
importance to the present work. If the makers and users of
Anglo-Saxon pottery recognised distinct pottery types then it becomes
helpful to identify these in order that possible associations between
types and contents may be examined.

1.311 Mental templates

It is frequently suggested that artefact makers have a norm or mental
template of the object which they wish to produce (e.g. Deetz 1967,
45-9). The range of variation about the norm exhibited by the

finished product reflects their degree of success in giving material expression to their ideas. If such templates exist then they might form the basis of an objective classification, and would give support to those who argue that real artefact types may be discovered.

A great deal of ethnographic work substantiates this view. Ruth Bunzel's classic analysis of the Pueblo potter (1929) revealed a communal idea of the "correct" forms and of the designs considered appropriate to them. Judy Birmingham writes of potters in the Kathmandu:

> there is a recognisable ideal template ... which both potters and consumers are aware of (1975, 377).

Hardin (1979) reports that potters in San Jose have no mental picture of the finished product before they start; instead they go from decision to decision in the painting process. Yet each decision must be taken according to a template of the possible options at each stage. Kempton (1981) has made a study of folk classification of ceramics, and also concludes that potters work according to fixed prototypes. He stresses the psychological importance of a stable classification within a society, and notes (1981, 53) how those adults he interviewed vehemently defended their classification against doubting children, and how they strove for mutually exclusive classes.

Cognitive psychology may also be able to contribute to the search for mental templates. In particular, the work of Eleanor Rosch (1973, 1975) suggests that perception of colour and form is based upon non-arbitrary categories which develop around natural prototypes. If such natural categories exist then they might be expected to form the basis of mental templates, and hence artefact types.

1.312 Identifying artefact types

If natural artefact types exist, based upon mental templates, is it possible for the archaeologist to discover them? Every artefact consists of a very large number of attributes, very few of which may have been deliberately selected by human action. As well as those reflecting the mental template of the type to be made, there are many attributes which are really background "noise", due to such things as the physical properties of the material used. Others may be accidental by-products of attributes which were selected. What is accidental and what is intentional is not always obvious:

> We can guess that a handaxe pebble was not selected for radioactivity or its refractive index; we reasonably guess that size and weight were selected for, probably the material also, but what about colour and all the other possible attributes? (Clarke 1968,15)

Initially, it may appear that in many cases, such as coins or Samian pottery for example, artefacts naturally fall into discrete well-defined types. In practice, even such obvious types may have had little meaning for the people under study. Samian was not purchased from a pattern book with Dragendorf catalogue numbers, and careful study reveals a continuum of forms. Coins are just as likely to have been grouped according to how much they were worth, which may have borne a minimal relationship to their size and decoration. Sometimes historical sources may be used to identify artefact types. Occasionally, analysis of organic residue or micro-wear studies may identify functional categories with which to check a typological sequence. More usually, however, there is a continual gradation of artefacts on which type boundaries are arbitrarily imposed by the classifier.

A one-to-one correspondence between an archaeological typology and a past cognitive system may not be assumed. Even twenty English educated people, each with an archaeological background, are unlikely to classify a series of pot shapes consistently (Chantrey, Wilcock and Celoria 1975). The difference between an imposed and a native classification can only be greater when other periods and other cultures are involved. In anthropology it is generally held that each society conceptualises its environment in a different manner (e.g. Levi-Strauss 1962). One cannot impose twentieth century western liberal conceptions of shape and design upon other societies without practising cultural imperialism.

1.32 Pottery classification

Shepard (1957) may still be regarded as the classic discussion of pottery typology. Her ceramic classificatory scheme gives prominence to vessel shape, which is described in terms of proportion and contour. Vessel proportions are expressed by a series of ratios of measurements, and contour is described in terms of "characteristic points" derived from Birkhoff (1933). Vessel design is classified according to the layout and symmetry of the decoration. The resultant typology is apparently intended to be of universal application, and whilst Shepard stresses the importance of examining the potter's technique, her scheme ignores the native classification. Several subsequent works have followed Shepard in attempting to produce a classificatory scheme which might be universally applied (e.g. Ericson and Stickel 1973, Llanos and Vegas 1974, Hole 1984, Washburn 1983c).

Archaeological classifications inevitably reflect the aims of the classifier. Despite claims of objectivity, the generalised schemes of pottery description make certain assumptions. Their aim has been to provide an objective means of comparison of pottery assemblages, on the assumption that the more alike two assemblages, then the greater the degree of interaction between the two groups of pottery users.

However, there may be other explanations for the variability between artefacts. Plog (1980, 115ff) has distinguished between five sets of theories:

    (1) normative theory
    (2) stylistic drift
    (3) social interaction

(4) motor habit variation
(5) information exchange

The first three rest on the approach described above, and stress the importance of interaction between individuals in the transmission of ideas through space. They differ in what they regard as the locus of stylistic behaviour.

The normative approach is based on the idea that broad culture areas are characterised by a single norm or idea. This approach lies at the root of most cultural historical interpretations. The stylistic drift approach believes that social units of different size may act as the loci. Finally, the social interaction approach sees the individual as the locus of stylistic variation (see Lathrap 1983).

The difference between the first three theories lies mainly in the level on which cultural norms are seen to operate. The motor habit variation school takes another view. Variation in stylistic attributes is seen to be determined by differences in the "motor habits" of individuals. The relative heights and numbers of lines, and the distances between them, are the result of subconscious variation in the execution of designs by individual potters. Finally, there is the information exchange theory, favoured by Plog. Stylistic behaviour is seen as fulfilling a communicative function. Decoration encodes information about the identity of the maker and user, including group membership, wealth, status, religious beliefs, and political ideology. From a study of the pottery of the American South West, Plog concludes that ceramic design:

> may have served as a means of communicating information concerning social group affiliation, thus aiding social integration by making social intercourse more predictable and less stressful (1980, 138).

The approach adopted in the present study is similar to Plog's in that it places emphasis on the communicative potential of pottery (see also Pollock 1983, Wiessner 1984).

Universal pottery classifications are unsuitable for categorising Early Anglo-Saxon pottery. They place virtually all Anglo-Saxon cremation vessels in one category. Existing classifications of Anglo-Saxon pottery are also seen as inadequate (section 1.4). It is necessary to devise an alternative classificatory scheme which is in accordance with the theoretical aims of the project. Since the pottery is seen as communicating information to the users, a successful scheme should attempt to take account of the native classification. The classification should be specific to the Early Anglo-Saxon context and must reflect the variability within the specific artefact type. Therefore it must emphasise the alternative choices made by the potter at the different stages of making the vessel. The hierarchical scheme used by Plog (1980) in classifying Chevelon Creek ceramics provides an example of a successful application of this principle.

An appropriate classification must also identify the individual design elements used to build up the overall design. The major problem is to identify those design elements which are significant to the people under study.

An archaeological typology may not necessarily be the same as the native classification. Some means of identifying significant design elements must be sought. Clarke offers one solution to the identification of artefact types. He observes that intentional attributes are regularly selected for, and notes that:

> the term "regularly selected-for" reveals the statistical aid that can be sought when dealing with aggregates of similar artefacts (1968, 15).

Generally, if an attribute is unintentional it will be randomly distributed throughout the artefacts and will not be correlated with other attributes. The null hypothesis, therefore, is that there is no correlation between attributes. If there are no "types" the frequency of combination is expected to be a simple function of the relative frequencies of the component attributes. Where two or more attributes are correlated to a higher degree than could result from sampling error, then it may be concluded that there was a genuine tendency for the artefact makers to combine the attributes in question, and that the existence of a type has been demonstrated.

Longacre provides a demonstration of this principle in his study of the pottery at the Carter Ranch site:

> It was decided to work first with the smallest units of design and to combine units later if statistically significant ... we hoped to isolate the smallest units of design that would be non-consciously selected based upon learning patterns within the social frame (1964, 162).

Clarke has also applied the approach to his own study of Beaker pottery (1962; 1970). He identified four major classes of variable, concerning shape, decorative motifs, position of decoration, and paste and firing. The latter were seen to be largely a matter of local geology so this factor was omitted. Shape was expressed by twenty-three variables, decoration by ten, and position of decoration by a further six. Matrix analysis was then applied to identify groupings of variables. In this case a continuous spectrum was found, with groupings around certain properties, rather than discrete groupings. The large number of variables involved in such analyses means that computer aid becomes essential. In her foreword to the fifth printing of Ceramics for the Archaeologist written in 1965, Anna Shepard had already noted the aid which might be sought from machine-based methods in the analysis of pottery design:

> the speed of operation of computers opens undreamed-of possibilities for studying correlations of features (1965, xii).

Shepard follows Clarke, however, in emphasising that in order to obtain meaningful answers from the computer, questions must have meaning in anthropological terms.

Subsequently, Gaines (1970) has applied computers to the classification of Hohokam pottery, again working from the hypothesis that a statistically significant relation exists between the frequency of occurrence of various diagnostic attributes. Indeed, amongst prehistoric researchers such projects have multiplied, although those working in Anglo-Saxon archaeology have responded with characteristic reluctance. In her 1979 review of the state of Anglo-Saxon cemetery studies, Tania Dickinson could still write:

> The varieties of quantitative analysis, which include types utilising computer programmes, have been current in archaeology for well over a decade (Doran and Hodson 1975), but they have not yet been made the explicit basis for the classification of a major group of Anglo-Saxon artefacts (1980, 18).

1.4 The study of Anglo-Saxon pottery

Early, or "Pagan" Anglo-Saxon pottery is conventionally dated circa 400 - 650 A.D. It includes fragmentary material found in domestic refuse on settlement sites, plus more complete vessels used as cremation urns, or as accessory vessels in inhumation burials. It is debated how much these classes overlap (see section 2.11). All the pottery is hand-made and is apparently coil-built in most cases, although there are a few examples of "thumb" pots. Some of the finer vessels are of such regular shape and thickness that they may have been turned on a slow wheel. The pottery was apparently manufactured from local clays, with the addition of various mineral, vegetable, and occasionally grog tempering (but see section 1.43). At West Stow, the remains of a stockpile of unfired clay have been found (West 1969a, 11), and at Sutton Courtenay Leeds interpreted one of the sunken buildings as a potter's workshop complete with clay-puddling hole (1947, 83). Otherwise little survives of the production process. Many vessels were fired undecorated, but others were embellished with one or more of various classes of incised, impressed, stamped and applied decoration. Twelve dies used to stamp designs on pots are all that remains of this stage of the manufacturing process (see Briscoe 1981, 22). Some vessels were evidently burnished, and in at least one instance (from Loveden Hill), differential oxidisation may have been deliberately controlled to produce a mixed red and black colouring (Nigel Kerr, paper presented to Early Anglo-Saxon Pottery Group 22/5/82). The firing itself was to a fairly low temperature (below 1000 degC), and would not be inconsistent with temperatures reached on a bonfire. Indeed, one might speculate that cremation vessels may have been fired on the same funeral pyres which cremated their future occupants. However, two primitive kilns consisting of double hollows were excavated at Purwell Farm, Cassington, and there may have been a further at Buckden, Hunts. (Arthur and Jope 1961). Experimental work has also suggested that a shallow hollow would reduce the amount of fuel required (Mike Stokes, paper presented to Early Anglo-Saxon Pottery Group 7/4/84).

Anglo-Saxon pottery (or at least those vessels used as cremation urns) was first identified as such in the nineteenth century (see section 1.21). Since then, most studies have concentrated on the funerary wares, where the field has been dominated by J.N.L.Myres's cultural-history. Two recent works of synthesis (Hurst 1976, 1977; Kennett 1978) have accepted Myres's classification as standard. There has been little methodological discussion of artefact typology compared to that concerning prehistoric pottery (see section 1.32). Consideration of Myres's contribution is now necessary.

1.41 Anglo-Saxon Pottery and the settlement of England

In 1931 J.N.L. Myres was asked to prepare a section on the Anglo-Saxon settlements for the Oxford History of England. This immediately provides an insight into his later work for he was:

> urged to include in this all the information that a historian could properly derive from the current state of Anglo-Saxon archaeology (Myres 1969, 1).

Thus Myres was concerned with the historical implications of archaeological data. He goes on to say that:

> When I came to survey the state of the archaeological evidence for the Anglo-Saxon settlements in 1931 I was impressed at once by the absence of any recent work of consequence on the pottery of the pagan period (1969,1).

Myres decided that three things needed to be done. Firstly, a "type" site should be excavated in order to understand the relationship between groups of pots. This was fulfilled when Caistor-by-Norwich was dug between 1932 and 1937, although the site was not to be published until much later (Myres and Green 1973). Secondly, it was necessary to gain an appreciation of the relationship between the English and Continental material. This was aided by the publication of some of the great Elbe-Weser cemeteries, especially Westerwanna (Zimmer-Linnfeld et al 1960). Thirdly, it would be important to prepare a corpus of the English material. It was not until 1977 that this last aim was fulfilled, making the material available for future study (Myres 1977a).

When Myres first examined the material the only published work was a scheme of classification for the continental pottery prepared by Plettke (1921). This was to influence Myres's own approach, both in the manner in which Plettke tried to produce a systematic classification of distinct numbered and lettered categories, and in his choice of diagnostic features used to distinguish between categories.

One of Myres's first papers on Anglo-Saxon pottery took the form of a discussion of three styles of decoration: panels, multiple shoulder bosses and vertical fluting, each of which he compared with parallels from the continent. He concluded that by disentangling the various classes of decoration:

may come also a surer understanding of the historical forces
which lie behind (1937a, 437).

At the same time Myres published (1937b) a discussion of a series of
vessels which because of similarities in decorative motifs, and in
particular of the stamps used, he concluded must have been made by the
same potter.   Three of the pots from Girton were of very different
types. Ironically, for Myres was later to be criticised for this
himself (see Dickinson 1978), he noted that the contemporaneity of the
three urns:

> illustrates the danger, into which some scholars have fallen, of
> attaching dates to the varieties of pottery in this period on a
> rigid classification of forms (1937b, 397-8).

Myres went on to produce a series of papers in which the styles of
pottery were used to throw light on the history of the Anglo-Saxon
settlement of England, and on the origins of the settlers.   In his
next paper (Myres 1941) he discussed the significance of the pottery
from Norfolk for illuminating the origins of the East Anglians, and
the date of their settlement. Ten years later (Myres 1951)
Lincolnshire was given similar treatment. In 1954 Myres used two urns
from Ickwell Bury in Bedfordshire to examine the extent of Saxon
penetration of the East Midlands (Myres 1954).   An earlier paper
(Myres 1948) had also discussed the significance of the Frisian
contribution, noting parallels between pots in England and those in
Holland and Belgium.

Myres also wrote several general syntheses of the history of the
migrations, drawing especially on ceramic evidence to support his
arguments. Latterly, however, descriptions of pottery from individual
sites, often requested as specialist contributions to excavation
reports (Myres 1968, 1973a, 1973b, 1974), were the most characteristic
output although particular classes of urns were also discussed
(1977b). In these Myres would discuss the continental parallels for
particular pieces, drawing upon his knowledge of the foreign material,
and would make deductions about date and racial affinities.

At the same time, his life's work reached its fruition with the
publication of <u>Anglo-Saxon</u> <u>Pottery</u> <u>and</u> <u>the</u> <u>Settlement</u> <u>of</u> <u>England</u>
(1969) and the <u>Corpus</u> (1977a), which must be regarded as companion
works.

The first publication commences with a discussion of the typology,
but is largely taken up with an account of the Anglo-Saxon settlement.
Myres divided this into five phases, following Bede's <u>Ecclesiastical</u>
<u>History</u> (Colgrave and Mynors 1969):

(i)   overlap and controlled settlement
(ii)   transition
(iii) uncontrolled settlement
(iv)   British recovery
(v)   Anglo-Saxon consolidation

He then seeks to use the pottery distributions to illuminate these phases, although the distribution maps do not always seem to back up the conclusions, such as his distribution of stamped panel-style pottery (pendant triangles without bosses), purporting to illustrate the age of Ceawlin of Wessex (map 9, 118). Myres concludes with a short chapter on the social and economic aspects of the settlement.

In the Corpus Myres published all the primary English material on which he had based his discussion, along with an extended description of the typology.

Much of the subsequent debate has focused on Myres's interpretation of the continental material and his view of the nature of the English settlement. The issue which has perhaps aroused most controversy is his early dating of the first Anglo-Saxon pottery in England. He first advanced this view in the Caistor report (Myres and Green 1973), for which he was critically reviewed (Morris 1974).

Some assessment of Myres's work is called for. Rather than take issue with specific points of historical interpretation, I shall question whether Anglo-Saxon pottery can be used to dot historical 'i's.

1.411 Historical interpretation

Myres writes in his introduction to Anglo-Saxon Pottery and the Settlement of England that one should be able to extract information from Anglo-Saxon pottery on:

> the origin and distribution of the settlers, their relationship to the pre-existing population, their social and economic development, and their notions of religion and decorative art (1969, 11).

However, as Arnold (1981, 243) has pointed out, it is only the first of these potential topics that Myres has really pursued. In order to use archaeological evidence to provide the sort of historical information required by Myres (on rates of movement of ethnic groups) one must have a secure chronology. Myres's chronology for Anglo-Saxon pottery rests upon the assumption that those features which are also found in the "Continental homeland" are early, whilst those traits found exclusively in England must be indigenous developments after the migration. This rests in turn upon a tacit invasionist hypothesis, prevalent throughout archaeology in the post-war years (see Clark 1966), that changes in material culture represent invasions or migrations of incoming peoples. Applied to the Anglo-Saxon period, the model works as follows. At some fixed point in time, either in the late fourth or early fifth centuries, the Germanic peoples inhabiting the North Sea coastline of Europe loaded their possessions, including pottery, into boats and sailed to England, where they settled along the south and east coasts. At first they continued to manufacture pottery in traditional styles, but as time went on local experimentation led to divergence from cultural norms, and as there

was no contact with the homeland, or so the model goes, local styles
developed. According to this hypothesis, the growth of new indigenous
styles may thus be used to trace the expansion of Anglo-Saxon settlers
into British areas. With alarming anthropomorphism Myres describes
the march of Germanic wares up the British valleys. The distribution
of Buckelurnen with feet, for example:

> seems to fan out from the Humbrensian area over the northern
> Midlands (1969, 101)

whilst those without feet:

> appear to spread rather from East Anglia south-westward through
> Middle Anglia to the upper Thames valley and to have penetrated
> at quite an early stage as far as such Berkshire sites as Harwell
> and East Shefford (1969, 102).

The typology also rests upon a further assumption of unilinear
evolution of styles. There can be no oscillation in the development
of types, although many studies (cf. Clarke 1968, 184ff) show
regression and fluctuation in stylistic developments. Furthermore, in
the absence of any fixed dating points, in order to pin the relative
sequence of styles onto an absolute chronology one must assume a
fairly constant and regular development of style. In actual fact
there might be periods of rapid change, followed by stagnation.
Moreover, if there was little contact between regions, then localised
developments might be expected to proceed at different rates.

Myres has been criticised for being over-selective in his choice of
continental parallels (see Kidd 1976), and for basing his chronology
upon too few examples. Arnold has calculated (1981, 243) that of the
3471 vessels in the Corpus only about 130 are dated to 360-410 AD, 154
to 410-550 AD, and thereafter very few vessels can be dated with any
precision.

For the period following the migration the only dating tool which
might be used to tie down the chronology is the association of pottery
with datable metalwork. However, Myres has selected which associated
objects to include in the Corpus which leaves him open to the charge
of fixing the evidence (see Dickinson 1978 for a full discussion).
Only about 100 vessels are listed with associated "datable" objects,
including both cremation urns (where the objects are usually
fragmentary) and inhumation accessory vessels. Furthermore, only
about half of these are decorated vessels. Moreover, Wilson (1959)
has drawn to our attention the problems of relying on associated
objects for dating, suggesting that because of the practice of
depositing heirlooms and worn objects in graves, we may not be able to
achieve a resolution better than a century. All this must lead one to
conclude that the dating of Anglo-Saxon pottery rests upon very
insecure foundations (see also Kidd 1977 for discussion). Indeed, one
might conclude that the material is undatable, and several scholars
have questioned whether it is appropriate to ask historical questions
of the archaeological evidence. Hills has commented that:

> Fitting the archaeological evidence into a pre-existing

historical framework can reduce the archaeology to illustrations for the history and does not produce essentially independent new information (1979a, 325).

1.412 Typology

The major problem in classifying Anglo-Saxon pottery is its tremendous variety of style with no discrete boundaries defining individual types:

> There is no other group of primitive hand-made pottery in Europe which displays anything approaching the imagination, variety, and spontaneity of the ornamental designs devised by Anglo-Saxon potters during the first two centuries of the settlement in Britain (Myres 1969, 23).

Existing continental classifications (cf. Plettke 1921) had emphasised form rather than decoration. Myres argued, however, that it would be unsatisfactory to classify the English material by form alone. He unkindly describes the English potters as "a chance assortment of uprooted amateurs" (1969, 24) who would be most likely:

> to imitate the simpler schemes of decoration familiar in their former homes and to apply them to vessels of any shape that might emerge from their unskilled efforts (1969, 24).

It is not clear why the channel crossing was so traumatic that ceramic skills were lost overnight; nor why the ability to produce pots of specific form should be lost any more than the ability to decorate vessels. Nevertheless Myres continues that with time:

> it is likely that both forms and ornamental schemes should develop in their own way, the former on conservative lines and paying less attention to precision of contour than on the Continent, the latter increasing in originality and complexity, as confidence and competence returned, and diverging even further from continental fashions (1969, 24).

Again it is unclear why form should stagnate whilst decoration flourished, apart from some intuitive idea that barbaric peoples should decorate their pottery exuberantly whilst rejecting the standardisation of forms associated with Roman civilisation. Myres argues (1969, 25) that in the earlier period a considerable range of forms carry the same general type of decoration, although one suspects a circularity of dating. One might equally argue that one form was the earliest and since it carries different decorative schemes it must be the latter that was the ill-remembered aspect.

Nevertheless, Myres uses these arguments as grounds for basing his classification upon decoration, except for plain pots which are not susceptible to this approach. In the case of plain vessels grouping by form is attempted, immediately introducing an inconsistency. However, he tends to neglect the plain forms anyway, regarding them as undiagnostic, and they are under-represented in the Corpus. Six

vessel forms are distinguished in the Corpus although Myres admits
that there is really a continuum of form: biconical, sub-biconical,
shouldered, globular, sub-globular, and low-bulbous. The only type
which had been rigorously defined in the earlier work were bowls,
distinguished by a rim diameter which is equal to, or greater than,
the height. However, by 1977 even this had been abandoned on the
grounds that it overlapped with the other groups. Consequently types
are vaguely described and defining features must be deduced from the
illustrations. There is considerable variation within classes and
identical forms appear in different classes. Therefore terms have
been inconsistently applied by subsequent workers, each with their own
ideas of what, for example, is a typical sub-biconical urn.

The crucial difficulty stems from trying to impose a unilinear
classification system in order that urns might be organised in a
one-dimensional book. A more workable approach rests upon the
realisation that urns have several attributes, including size, form,
and the different aspects of decoration, and cannot be slotted into a
unilinear framework (see section 1.32).

The same basic problem underlies the classification of decoration.
As Hills (1979b) has pointed out, most groupings are based on an
overall pattern, combining several motifs, although some, such as
stehende Bogen or Buckelurnen take one detail only. Particular
importance is placed on certain features, often on an arbitrary basis.
Dickinson (1978) notes, for example, that the presence of a footring
is used to draw together a selection of otherwise very different pots.

This is not to devalue the Corpus as a catalogue of the material.
However, even here there are problems, principally in the
standardisation of illustrations. Myres has always maintained that
one should draw what the potter intended, rather than what was
achieved:

> It is always necessary in drawing Anglo-Saxon pottery to keep
> these blunders and mistakes as far as possible in the background,
> and always to hold in the forefront of one's mind the question:
> what did the potter intend this pot to look like? (1951, 70)

Myres argues that:

> Anglo-Saxon potters hardly ever spaced their designs (especially
> repetitive ones) before beginning to draw them on the pot: hence
> there is very often a point where the intended design does not
> fit the space allowed for it, being either too wide or too
> narrow. There is generally no point in emphasising these muddles
> in the drawing, and it may even be positively misleading to do
> so, by giving a distorted impression of what was in the potter's
> mind (letter 6/12/83, Early Anglo-Saxon Pottery Group files).

Whilst it may be true that asymmetrical designs may represent accident
rather than intention, this is a very ethnocentric assumption, and it
is difficult to guess at what the potter really intended. By drawing
pots as he believed they ought to appear, Myres has misrepresented the
evidence; compare, for example, the unstandardised drawings of the

Sancton urns in Myres and Southern (1973) with those in Myres (1977). This has serious implications for the value of the Corpus for any studies which attempt to examine potters' styles, including the present one.

1.42 Other classificatory studies

Dissatisfaction with Myres's undefined descriptive terms has led other researchers to follow more rigorous approaches. Three unpublished doctoral theses have each attempted to produce more systematic classifications: Fennell (1964), Wilson (1972), and Hills (1976).

Fennell, in a study of the material from Loveden Hill (1964), was faced with the problem of organising over 400 urns from his excavations. His answer was to follow the approach proposed by Shepard (1957) in her seminal work on pottery classification (see section 1.32). Fennell took a sample of 216 urns and sorted then initially into three decorative classes, according to whether they were plain, had linear decoration, or had stamped decoration. He then used two of the ratios proposed by Shepard - rim diameter/ diameter, and height/diameter - to classify the vessels, followed by visual sorting to determine the position of the maximum diameter. By an elaborate process of manual over-drawing Fennell then compared the forms of the three decorative classes. He found certain differences between classes, such as that wide-mouthed urns were more often plain than decorated.

Fennell uses ratio values as cut-off points between classes, thus providing a more rigorous definition of Myres's terms, although he does not say why particular values were chosen. A vessel is a wide-mouthed bowl, for example, if it has a height ratio of less than or equal to 0.8, and a mouth ratio of more than or equal to 0.7. Similarly, it is a jar if it has a height ratio of more than or equal to 0.9 and is not a bowl or tall vase. Thus it can be seen that Fennell is trying to produce by statistical sorting the same groups of urns that Myres arrived at intuitively. This causes some problems as the same criteria cannot be consistently applied. Furthermore, Fennell follows Myres in attempting to fit each urn into a single category, whilst using several attributes as the diagnostic criteria. In his final classification Fennell produces thirteen groups of urns. Urns are allotted to groups by a hierarchical method. Thus all plain urns are categorised first; then urns with just linear designs are taken out; then stamped urns are removed. Of course, this means that urns with stamped designs might also have the same linear schemes as vessels already allocated to a different group. Fennell does not make it clear why linear decoration should have a higher place in the hierarchy than stamped decoration, although this assumption does determine the resulting classification. Similarly it is unclear why bossed urns are treated as sub-groups rather than as another major group. The more complex the decoration, the more problems posed for Fennell's simple unilinear classification.

The remaining sections of Fennell's thesis are taken up with a traditional approach to the dating of the pottery groups , followed by a discussion of the development of the cemetery.

Wilson is also concerned with traditional goals, such as the delineation of culture areas, and the identification of cultural linkages, in her study of the archaeological evidence of the Hwiccian area (1972). She uses later diocesan boundaries to define her study area and then uses the similarity of artefacts between areas as a measure of the strength of cultural linkages. However, rather than measuring similarity intuitively, she uses a powerful clustering package, CLUSTAN IA, and a computer, to produce groupings of various artefacts, including pottery. It is with her treatment of the pottery that I shall be concerned here.

Wilson's work is restricted to a relatively small sample of 128 vessels (although for brooches she includes material outside the study area in order to give a representative range, and it is not clear why this could not also have been done for the pottery). For these vessels she identifies 70 presence/absence attributes, which seems rather excessive given the number of cases. Indeed, the list of attributes reveals that most of these "attributes" are not really attributes at all, but are rather alternative attribute states of a more restricted number of actual attributes. Thus, for example, five mutually exclusive "attributes" describe the base, although any vessel could only take one of these states, (see Richards and Ryan 1985, 17-8). This has serious implications for the clustering results, since although Wilson writes that each attribute is given equal weighting, in practice it will be given a weighting related to the number of states into which it is divided. In fact, selective weighting of attributes might have produced more useful results as intuitively the attributes chosen are certainly not of equal significance. Furthermore, in order that quantitative measurements might be directly comparable with decorative and other qualitative attributes, the values for continuous variables, such as maximum diameter, are broken into a few presence/absence variables. The divisions chosen are apparently purely arbitrary, with an attendant loss of information.

The actual choice of attributes used to describe the form of urns is again largely derived from Shepard (1957). Fabric surface texture and paste consistency are assessed visually, rather than by fabric analysis. Colour and evenness of firing are also described.

The clustering results are as good as could be expected given the data definition. Since there are almost as many variables as cases discrete clusters would be unlikely to stand out. Indeed, the values for the fusion coefficient at the various clustering levels do not immediately suggest what is the appropriate number of clusters. There are small breaks at three and six clusters, but Wilson decides that seventeen clusters gives the best results (apparently on the basis of which pots are in which groups, rather than the coefficient levels). This includes thirteen plain pot types and four decorated ones (as might be anticipated as only 15 of the 70 "attributes" are concerned with decoration). Wilson contrasts this result with Myres' stress on decorated urns, although since her sample only included 27 decorated urns, it may be regarded as untypical of Anglo-Saxon pottery assemblages. Wilson discusses the distribution of the 17 types within the region and attempts to give date ranges. Some are widespread whilst others have a more localised distribution, which Wilson ascribes to the work of a local potter. Her plain types bear some resemblance to those of Myres, which may mean no more than that she uses some attributes which Myres had intuitively applied. As Wilson admits, the lack of correspondence for the decorated urns is merely a reflection of the small sample size.

Hills (1976) also considers Anglo-Saxon pottery typology, as part of her discussion of the cremation cemetery at Spong Hill. Like Fennell, her concern with classification is dictated by the need to impose ordering on the material under study, namely 355 urns with reconstructible profiles from the 1972-4 excavations. Hills's approach follows on from Myres's classification but she attempts to give his types more rigorous definition. She also treats size, shape, and decoration as three independent variables, which leads to a more logical system. Sizes are arbitrarily split into three groups. Small urns are defined as those with a diameter of less than 20cm and a height of less than 15cm. Large urns have a diameter of 25cm or more and a height of 20cm or more. The third intermediate class, comprising the bulk of the material, are described as "normal" urns.

The terms used to describe urn shape are largely derived from Myres, although the largest group, which Myres would probably class as sub-biconical, are described as "normal". These are urns whose maximum diameter is approximately at mid-height, and whose height is less than or equal to their diameter. Urns with a maximum diameter above mid-height are shouldered, whilst those few which have a maximum diameter below mid height are baggy. Those with a carination at mid height are biconical, and those with no clear angle and with a convex profile and short neck and rim are globular. Bowls are defined as being shorter than they are wide and having a mouth diameter greater than two-thirds of their maximum diameter. Finally, jars are those urns with a diameter greater or equal to their height and whose maximum diameter is at the mouth.

Hills's definitions represent a significant attempt to combine objectivity with the attributes intuitively selected by Myres. The classification of decoration is less developed; urns are categorised according to whether they are plain, or have linear, plastic or indented decoration.

1.43 Anglo-Saxon potters

With one exception, Myres was more concerned with the cultural and historical affinities of the finished products than with the process of manufacture of Anglo-Saxon pottery. Early in his study, however, he did become aware of the possibility of finding identical stamps and designs on different vessels (1937b), and so identifying individual potters or workshops of potters. By 1977 he was able to list 157 such groups, and a catalogue of stamp-linked pottery has become a standard feature of Anglo-Saxon cremation cemetery excavation reports (e.g. Hills 1977b, Hills and Penn 1981, Williams 1983).

In 1937 Myres was hesitant to ascribe stamp-linked groups of urns to professional potters. He assumed that potting was a female task and suggested that similar pots from two areas might be the result of intermarriage, "the lady taking her pottery stamps and her taste in decoration with her to her new home?" (1937b, 396). In his 1969 synthesis, Myres maintains that plain, supposedly domestic wares are the product of a female domestic industry, but suggests that decorated pottery with a "professional touch" may represent the "early stages of a specialised industry" (1969, 127), and the potters are now described as craftsmen[1]. In the Corpus Myres identifies four distinct types of distributions of potter's work. Firstly, where two or more pots by the same potter are found in the same cemetery, this need be no more than domestic manufacture serving the interests of one community, or even one household. Secondly, where pots are found in two or more neighbouring cemeteries, as in the Cambridge region, then Myres suggests they may be grouped around a common market centre. Thirdly, where products of a single workshop, such as the Illington-Lackford group, are found further afield, they may reflect the loose association of small political units, with demand confined to these areas by political boundaries. Finally, where the distribution is more widespread, such as in the case of the Sancton-Baston potter, Myres suggests we may be dealing with itinerant potters.

As Myres recognised, fabric analysis might offer one an important means of testing if stamp-linked groups originated from the same clay source, and in 1962 he instigated a very limited spectrographic analysis of sherds of the Illington-Lackford potter, the results of which were "not conclusive" (1969, 136). Subsequently, more extensive characterisation has been undertaken, including a macroscopic examination of the Illington-Lackford potter (Green, Milligan and West 1981), followed by a full petrological analysis (Russel 1984), a study of undecorated pottery from settlement sites in Northamptonshire (Walker 1978), and extensive grain size and heavy mineral analysis of pottery from Spong Hill (Brisbane 1980, 1981). However, the full appreciation of such work requires the clarification of several unresolved assumptions. These are, firstly, how many clay sources did a potter (or school of potters) use, and how tightly controlled were the proportions of various tempering agents going into the clay? Was the clay varied, for instance, according to local firing conditions? How homogeneous was the fabric of a batch of pots, or even the fabric of a single vessel? Secondly, if potters were itinerant, did they carry their clay supply with them, or use whatever local sources were available? Thirdly, can we assume that vessels were always eventually buried close to their place of production? Itinerant potters may have

NOTE

[1] See Kidd (1977) for a discussion of the case that Anglo-Saxon potters were professionally organised craftsmen.

carried their finished products rather than do their potting on the
spot, or alternatively, it may be the consumers rather than the
suppliers who moved. As Arnold has reminded us, many cremation
cemeteries have a large catchment area and so:

> burial pattern may be a stronger force in determining the
> dispersal patterns than the system of exchange (1981, 246).

Putnam (1981b) has added the interesting speculation that as a
migrating people, Anglo-Saxons may have carried their ancestral
cremation urns with them, with the implication that potter's groups
represent patterns of population movement rather than marketing
systems. Support for this hypothesis may be found in the ethnographic
literature. The Nahua of Central America, for example, are said to
have burned their chiefs so as to be able to carry their ashes about
with them in their migrations (James 1928, 227).

1.44 Symbolic interpretations of Anglo-Saxon pottery

If Myres pays little attention to the production of Anglo-Saxon
pottery, then he gives even less consideration to ritual, symbolism
and iconography. Certainly he appears to have recognised the
potential for symbolic interpretations of the material:

> At first sight it may seem obvious that a purely decorative
> intent was uppermost in a craftsman's mind in devising the
> pattern of his stamps.... But some of the designs, even such
> simple and common forms as concentric circles and rosettes,
> certainly represent objects of ritual or magical significance
> familiar in northern mythology, and sometimes associated with the
> worship of particular gods (1969, 136-7).

Nevertheless, only four pages at the end of Anglo-Saxon Pottery and
the Settlement of England are given over to discussion of possible
symbolism, and one is aware that Myres regards this as an area "over
which it is easy for the imagination to run riot" (1969, 136),
preferring to be on the safer ground of cultural affinities. Myres
does draw attention to the portrayal of swastikas and serpents on
vessels of the Sancton-Elkington potter, which he associates with the
cult of Thor. He also notes the use of the serpent or "wyrm" motif to
safeguard a vessel and its contents against disturbance, and admits:

> It is more than probable that other types of stamps carried some
> similar significance which is no longer apparent to us (1969,
> 139).

In particular, Myres discusses the use of freehand or stamped runic or
pseudo-runic symbols, including the rune indicating the god Tiw.

There has been surprisingly little research undertaken to examine
other possible cases of symbolism. Brown (1981) has examined the use
of swastika patterns on pottery and metalwork, but he avoids any
discussion of their significance. Hills (1983) catalogues the animal
stamps found on pottery in East Anglia. She acknowledges that they

may have a symbolic significance, but does not speculate on what it
might be. Reynolds (1980, 236) discusses the association of a
whetstone and a swastika design at Sancton as perhaps being symbolic
of the god Thor, opening up the possibility that grave-goods may be
linked with decorative motifs. Myres had recognised that particular
grave-goods were often found with certain decorative motifs:

> with the simpler types of unstamped stehende Bogen urns, bone
> combs of various forms are often associated (1977, 29).

Discussing those urns with massed linear or corrugated decoration
Myres notes:

> There is a marked tendency for urns of this type to contain iron
> manicure sets comprising small tweezers, shears, knives etc., or
> individual items of such sets; some also contain plano-convex
> counters or other evidence of gaming.... Combs and bronze
> objects are by contrast less commonly found in urns of this type
> (1977, 38).

Finally, he remarks (1977, 52) on the positive association of ivory
"bag rings" with chevrons and pendant triangles on simple linear
decorated forms. Nevertheless, there is no discussion of the possible
significance of these associations. One must assume that Myres was
not surprised to find objects which he regarded as being culturally
diagnostic in pots which he also regarded as being culturally
diagnostic i.e. Anglian miniatures in Anglian pots, even when some of
the objects, such as combs, had not previously been suspected to be
culturally diagnostic, and when objects of several cultures were found
on the same site.

Reynolds suggests that the iconography of an Anglo-Saxon burial may
be:

> a combination of symbols particularly relevant to the personality
> or status of the person concerned, or to the gods involved in the
> manner or timing of his death; or there may be intentions of
> extraordinary complexity or subtlety, of whose real meaning we
> can only ever hope to catch a glimpse (1980, 236).

He notes however that the link between swastika and whetstone at
Sancton is just a single association, and that:

> a catalogue of all associations, osteological and artifactual, is
> an essential preliminary if we wish to search these corners of
> the pagan Anglo-Saxon mind (1980, 236).

Finally, Arnold (1983) has recently put forward a rival interpretation
of potter's groups which implies a symbolic significance for stamped
designs. Examining vessels of the Sancton-Baston potter, Arnold
claims that whilst being very similar, the stamp impressions were not
struck from the same die. If this is the case, and Arnold's 1983
paper merely reports the results of a pilot study for further
research, then the stamped designs must have been selected to have
particular form and dimensions. This, Arnold suggests, may have been

due to the designs having a heraldic or totemic significance.

1.5 Towards an understanding of Anglo-Saxon cremation vessels

Work on Anglo-Saxon cemeteries and cremation urns has concentrated on cultural-history and artefact typology; symbolism and social structure have been relatively ignored. It is proposed that Anglo-Saxon cremation urns should be studied as symbolic artefacts, capable of communicating information about mortuary behaviour and the people associated with them.

1.51 Artefact groups as symbolic systems

It has been proposed that as a means of classifying Anglo-Saxon pottery an attempt should be made to isolate individual units of form and decoration, and so derive the grammar of their construction. We have thus applied a linguistic analogy to material culture. Such a position is not really alien to traditional archaeological thinking. Indeed, writing On the Evolution of Culture in 1875, Pitt-Rivers noted that:

> implements are but outward signs or symbols of particular ideas in the mind .... It is the mind we study by means of these symbols (Myres 1906, 23).

Pitt-Rivers believed that artefacts reflect the mind as language does, and that it should be possible to trace the evolution of the mind through changes in material culture:

> Words are ideas expressed by sounds, whilst tools are ideas expressed by hands (Myres 1906, 25).

These sentiments are also echoed by Childe when he stresses that archaeologists only record and classify objects because they express human thoughts (1956, 4), and lie behind Wheeler's exhortation that archaeologists should dig up people rather than things (1954, 13).

However, having accepted the potential for symbolism which exists in artefact groups, it becomes necessary to identify the levels on which they operate, and to determine what they are saying. Here there is considerable room for disagreement. Bourdieu (1979) has identified three functions of a symbolic system:

(i) as a means of communication.

(ii) as an instrument for the knowledge and construction of the world.

(iii) as an instrument of domination.

Not everyone would accept that material culture can operate on each of these levels. Most people would agree that objects can work as symbols which communicate ideas, if we define symbol vaguely, as something that indicates something else. A crown, for example, is frequently seen as a symbol of royalty. Leach emphasises that:

> all the various non-verbal dimensions of culture .... are
> organised in patterned sets so as to incorporate coded
> information in a manner analogous to the sounds and words of a
> natural language (1976, 10).

However, not all archaeologists would agree that all artefacts can communicate. Those of the functionalist school usually see artefacts which symbolise things as belonging to a special class, whereas others believe that all artefacts must be part of the symbolic system.

In the United States, Lewis Binford has been a champion of functionalist archaeology. In a seminal work (1962), Binford distinguished between three classes of artefact:

(i) Technomic, whose primary functional context is in coping directly with the physical environment, such as tools.

(ii) Sociotechnic, whose primary context is in the social sub-system, such as grave-goods.

(iii) Ideotechnic, whose primary context is in the ideological sub-system, such as deity figures.

It may be more realistic to regard these as different levels of function, each of which may operate in different circumstances. Thus there is the potential for each in a single artefact, and meaning has to be derived from context. Thus Deetz (1977, 51) describes how a candle may function on a technomic level when it is simply used for lighting, on a sociotechnic level at the dinner table, and on an ideotechnic level in a Catholic church. Symbols do not function in isolation. They must take their meaning as part of patterned sets:

> A symbol only has meaning from its relation to other symbols in a
> pattern. The pattern gives the meaning. Therefore no item in
> the pattern can carry meaning by itself isolated from the rest
> (Douglas 1973, 11).

Therefore one cannot study particular designs in isolation. One must examine the total set of possible designs. Nordbladh (1978) has emphasised that all artefacts are part of a total symbolic system. He proposes the use of a "semiotic approach", arguing that society is only intelligible through the messages and the communication structures which it comprises.

This brings us to Bourdieu's second function of a symbolic system, that as an instrument of knowledge and construction of the objective world. Symbols are:

> attempts to provide orientation for an organism which cannot live
> in a world it is unable to understand (Geertz 1973, 140-1).

In other words, symbolic systems operate to categorise information as an aid to the regulation and direction of appropriate behaviour (see Washburn 1983b, 3). Structuralist theory developed partly out of linguistics, where Chomsky (1957) noted the underlying structure, or transformational grammar, present in all languages. In order to explain how children were able to acquire language, Chomsky postulated that there must be innate cognitive capacities. Certain structures within the brain accounted for grammatical constructions and explained why cultures share similar words and grammars. Structuralism represents the systematic extension of linguistic concepts to non-linguistic fields. Structuralist anthropologists (e.g. Levi-Strauss 1958, Leach 1976) interpreted primitive mythology as a way of thinking about the real world. Similarly, folk taxonomies reveal the structure of aspects of the cultural world. Those archaeologists who follow a structuralist approach (see, for example, papers in Hodder 1982b) interpret material culture as another transformation of the underlying structure. The structure exists partly independent of the observable data, having generated and produced that data. Artefacts are seen as tools for thinking about the world.

Many of the papers in Hodder (1982b) also see the symbolic structure as functioning on Bourdieu's third level, as an instrument of domination. Hodder notes that:

> the meaning of an object resides not merely in its contrast to others within a set. Meaning also derives from the associations and use of an object (Hodder 1982c, 9).

Because material culture is a non-discursive mode of communication it may be used to "say" things which cannot be "said" verbally (Hodder 1982e, 176). Thus artefacts are not only a passive symbolic reflection of the world, but act to constitute and change it. Bourdieu writes that symbolism establishes and legitimates, through its ideological effect, the dominant culture. Thus structuralism is frequently integrated with a Marxist or Neo-Marxist philosophy.

The contrast between these rival interpretations of material culture might also be viewed as follows. According to functionalism, culture is seen as a system which functions to integrate society and the environment. Material culture is something other than, and outside of, the society which generates it. According to structuralist and structural-marxist views, material culture is seen as the result of actions which are at once articulated through social relationships, and also as a means by which social relationships are constructed:

> Material culture is thus an active participant in the construction of the social system, and its meaning is internal to that system (Barrett 1981, 206).

1.52 Symbolism and ceramics

Pottery provides a particularly appropriate medium for the presentation of visual symbols. The clay can be worked into a variety of shapes. The surface can then be decorated in a variety of ways, providing a large potential fund of symbols. If mistakes are made they can frequently be smoothed over and the process begun anew. Designs can thus be precisely executed, and once fired, they become permanent. Pots are produced by what Miller (1982, 17) decribes as an additive process, being built up from relatively homogeneous clays, unlike flint tools which are produced by a subtractive strategy, removing parts of a pebble. Consequently the finished product may be expected to bear a closer relationship to the original intention, or mental template, of the maker, who has had the opportunity to correct any errors.

There have been several studies of the overt symbolic nature of pottery assemblages, most taking Boas (1927) as their starting point. Bunzel (1929), for example, notes how designs on Zuni pottery are associated with ideas of religious character. Two early works focused on the decoration of mortuary ceramics. Rydh (1929) made a cross-cultural survey of decorative motifs on funerary wares, highlighting similarities between urns as widely separated as the Danish Bronze Age and the Chinese Neolithic. Palmgren (1934) concentrated on the Kansu mortuary urns of China.

More recently, there have been several examples of explicitly structuralist approaches to the analysis of ceramic design. Dean Arnold (1983) borrows the idea that the same structural principles responsible for patterning social organisation may also be reflected in artefact design from Adams's work (1973) on textile design on the Island of Sumba. He argues that the organisation of environmental and social space in Quinua, Peru, is also reflected symbolically in the organisation of decorative space on pottery:

> the basic principles of organising and utilising environmental and social space in Quinua, Peru, are reflected in the organisation and utilisation of decorative space on four of the most frequently utilized painted vessels produced in the community (1983, 57).

Van de Velde (1979a, 1979b) has presented what he describes as a structuralist analysis of the Bandkeramik cemetery at Elsloo, which includes an analysis of the pottery and a discussion of the links between pottery types and age and sex of the burials.

The majority of studies, however, have sought to demonstrate that ceramic design plays an active role in structuring society, rather than just reflecting its organisation. Hodder (1982d) has taken Van de Velde's work a stage further by distinguishing between two phases and attempting to demonstrate a structural change between them[1]. During the first phase there is little expansion and pottery design shows little concern with contrasts and oppositions. In the second

NOTE

[1] Van de Velde had also put forward a possible Neo-Marxist interpretation (1979a).

phase there is expansion and more dispersed settlement. This is matched with concern with oppositions in the pottery decoration, with a large number of vessel forms and large amounts of decoration. Hodder argues that:

> material culture helps to form and legitimate the social categories in a period of increasing contradictions (1982d, 162).

Tilley (1984) has incorporated an analysis of pottery design in his study of the legitimation of power in the Middle Neolithic in Southern Sweden. It is argued that the change from the Funnel Neck Beaker to the Battle-Axe/Corded-Ware tradition was the manifestation of the collapse of the social order.

Unfortunately, as Hodder (1986, 41-4) has admitted, there is a common flaw shared by all these studies, for no where is one presented with enough information to justify why there should be any relationship between pottery decoration and aspects of social organisation. Hodder (ibid) has argued that one needs to consider the context of the pottery usage in order to link design structure with social functions.

In some cases ethnographic data may be used to provide the necessary contextual information relating ideology and material culture. Braithwaite (1982) has examined the use of pottery amongst the Azande of Sudan. Cooking pots are seen as female artefacts, but are transferred to men for eating; all are decorated. Water pots, on the other hand, are only ever used by men; they are undecorated. Braithwaite suggests that:

> decoration may function as a ritual marker of particular breaches of the conceptual order in contexts where covert expression of the messages or concepts involved is necessary or advantageous given the social order (1982, 81).

Welbourn (1984) describes the forms of pottery used amongst the Endo of Kenya. She argues that the central role played by some pots in the wedding ceremony may explain the decoration. Pottery serves both to separate and to mediate between the spheres of activity associated with male and female roles:

> The pottery forms can thus be related to the assimilation and ritual legitimation of the social order, and in particular, of male dominance (1984, 17).

It will be argued below, however, that one does not necessarily need contemporary ethnographic observations in order to understand the context of use, and that the approach is also applicable to purely archaeological situations. Specifically, it is suggested that we do have enough contextual information about Anglo-Saxon funerary ceramics to justify a deeper interpretation of their form and decoration.

1.53 Symbolism and Anglo-Saxon pottery

There is considerable potential for the analysis of the design structure of Anglo-Saxon pottery as a means of understanding social questions.

It has been argued that the majority of cremation vessels were manufactured specifically for the disposal of the dead (section 2.112). In most societies mortuary behaviour is highly charged with ritual and symbolism. A number of archaeological sources for the early Anglo-Saxon period, ranging from sacrificial executions such as that at Sewerby (Hirst 1985) to royal barrows such as Sutton Hoo, each suggest a particular emphasis upon ritualised treatment of the dead at this period. This is further corroborated in our few surviving literary sources, such as the early epic poem Beowulf. Hodder has suggested that whether pottery decoration should be viewed as purely decorative, or whether it should be seen as a symbolic code, depends upon the social context of its use:

> the symbolic codes in the pottery decoration and shapes may be related to codes within the social structure. But the relationships between the different codes depend very much on the position and function of decoration within the particular society concerned (1982e, 182).

In a non-literate society, such as Pagan Anglo-Saxon England, pictorial symbolism is likely to have played an important communicative role. As far as we can tell, decoration is less common in a domestic context, on loomweights or cooking pottery for example, but is found on other categories of artefact which accompany burials. Cruciform brooches from inhumations, for instance, are frequently decorated with the same stamped motifs which occur on cremation urns.

This use of symbolism may continue into the Christian period, although now transformed into decoration of the grave monument, rather than the grave-goods. Butler notes, for example, that:

> The carving of symbols upon a coffin-lid indicated to an illiterate populace the rank or profession of the deceased, often serving to identify him in his generation (1964, 133).

Being hand-made and non-standardised there is an enormous range of styles of Anglo-Saxon pottery. In one sense, every vessel is unique, varying slightly in shape, or in the use of a stamp, or in the number of lines in a chevron, from its nearest match. Yet there is considerable repetition in the range of forms and decorative motifs so that common styles may be identified. Anglo-Saxon potters were working according to a very rigidly defined cultural model of the type of pot that could be produced (section 3.11). If there was a symbolic system, then it is likely to have been well-understood.

Several aspects of the pottery design reinforce the idea that it is more than purely decorative. Some of the motifs are overtly symbolic, even to modern eyes. We have already noted that Myres (1969) comments on the use of swastikas and serpents amongst others (section 1.44).

Figure 2 Pseudo-runic pottery decoration: Spong Hill urn number 2067
(after Hills and Penn 1981 fig.50)

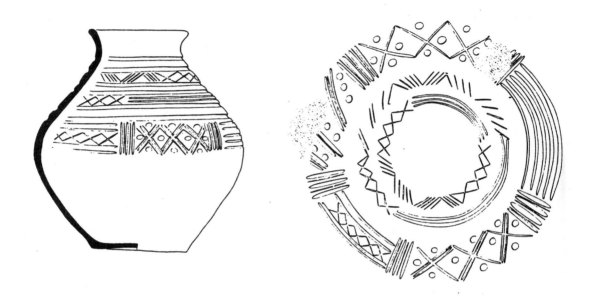

Figure 3 Pseudo-runic Scandinavian rock carving motifs (after Elliot
1959 text-fig.2)

In addition, we might note the use of runes and pseudo-runic symbols, sometimes spelling out the name of a northern god. Several funerary urns have the runic "t" form incised or stamped upon them, perhaps invoking the protection of the god Tiw (see Page 1973, 93; Hills 1974). Many of the other linear designs might also be interpreted as pseudo-runic, although indecipherable to us (fig.2). If the intention was purely decorative, then one might expect geometrical and symmetrical patterns, rather than the deliberate asymmetry that is frequently encountered. If we can identify some aspects of design as containing representational symbols, on the basis of folk tradition and literary sources which have survived to the present, then surely it is likely that other aspects of the design are also symbolic, although their meaning is no longer understood, and their interpretation evades us?

The large number of stamped motifs are another decorative class which tend to evoke ideas of symbolism (Briscoe 1983, 59). Many bear striking similarity to motifs executed on rock carvings in Scandinavia (see Elliott 1959, Storms 1978 and fig.3). Elliott notes the association between picture runes and ideas such as fertility and the sun. The common north European culture running through the Scandinavian and Germanic Iron Age may have been remembered in some elements of Anglo-Saxon tradition. Many are simple geometric designs, and their use may be coincidence, or as Lethbridge (1951) suggests, derived from Roman stamped pottery. On the other hand, it is likely that the Roman stamped motifs were themselves derived from Germanic models or could have had a native Iron Age ancestry (see Elsdon 1975). Certainly, many motifs seem too peculiar to have been chance decoration, and their use has to be explained. The footprint, or planta pedis motif, for example, is seen by Storms (1978, 319) as denoting the invisible presence of the gods.

The study of Anglo-Saxon symbolism has hitherto been neglected. There have been discussions of particular instances of the more obvious examples, but there has been no attempt to view all the possible designs of Anglo-Saxon pottery as a patterned set, the understanding of which is essential if one is to comprehend the significance of individual motifs.

1.54 A possible means of understanding Anglo-Saxon cremation vessels

In summary, the aim of the present work is to apply some of the theories and methodologies current in prehistoric archaeology and anthropology to an area of historic, or at least proto-historic, archaeology. This should combine some of the advantages of the two, with none of the drawbacks. From the former may be borrowed:

i) the use of quantitative techniques which lead to a more rigorous analysis of the data.

ii) a concern with social rather than historical questions.

iii) a concern with the general rather than the particular.

From the latter may be taken:

i) a degree of chronological resolution lacking in prehistory, which allows one to study a group of several thousand objects which were made within 200 years of each other.

ii) a knowledge of the people involved (derived from written sources) which is missing but is commonly assumed for the prehistoric period (e.g. belief in an afterlife).

Anglo-Saxon cremation vessels may be understood as a potential set of communicating symbols. On one level the form and decoration of the vessels reflects the social identity of the occupant. People were buried in vessels which, through aspects of their size, shape and decoration, were individually suited to them.

It is not possible to resolve whether people were consciously aware of this symbolism, nor is it presently apparent how this question can be resolved. Cremation urns may have been designed with a specific individual in mind, or they may simply have been selected as somehow appropriate. Alternatively, and perhaps more likely, they may have been chosen through a combination of these two factors, in much the same way as a modern headstone contains some elements (such as the inscription of name and date of birth) which are personal to the individual, and some elements, such as poetic epitaph and style of ornamentation which pertain to the culture rather than to the individual. Certainly it is proposed that it should be possible to "read" a cremation vessel, in an analogous fashion to that in which a tombstone may be read.

Neither can we be certain whether the symbolic system is a passive reflection of the Anglo-Saxon world, or whether it is actively involved in its construction. Most studies of pottery design have taken the latter stance (cf. section 1.52). One suspects that except where the study was conducted in a contemporary ethnographic situation, this rests upon faith rather than evidence. The critics of functionalism have themselves been criticised for their failure to offer testable alternatives. Wylie (1982) has argued that this is only a flaw in so far as one accepts a model of science and scientific testing which is itself outmoded and thus inappropriate. On one level the hypothesis under examination in the present study is amenable to testing. It will be possible to establish if the internal contents of cremation urns are correlated with their external designs. It is not obvious how one might determine if symbols were consciously manipulated by Anglo-Saxons in a bid to alter social reality, although it should be possible to establish if the totality of the design of Anglo-Saxon cremation pottery represents a patterned set, rather than individual symbols. The reasons determining the specific choice of symbolic motifs are always likely to remain obscure. Indeed, within the structural linguistics of Saussure (1959) the sign itself is seen as arbitrary. Thus any symbol (a chevron, a cross, a circle) could be used to signify a warrior, for instance, and there is no necessary relationship between the symbol chosen and the role signified. The purpose of analysis, therefore, must be to examine the pattern or form, not the content.

Similarly, what exactly is reflected must remain loosely defined. Precisely what is meant by social identity? Social identity at time of death is a multi-dimensional phenomenon, representing the combination of a number of roles. These may include:

i) **Sex**

ii) **Age at death**

iii) **Ethnic affiliation**

iv) Group affiliation, including both kinship and/or moiety or clan allegiances.

v) Status, including both wealth, and the number of individuals owing allegiance to the deceased, and covering both ascribed and achieved status.

vi) Circumstances of death, including place and cause.

Each of these roles may be reflected in single or combined attributes of cremation vessel design, complicated by the fact that each cremation may contain the remains of more than one individual. For the present these roles will be loosely grouped as social identity, but in section 4 some general distinctions will be made.

Our knowledge of the social identity of the occupants of Anglo-Saxon cremation vessels must rest upon three sources of information:

i) the cremated skeletal remains.

ii) the burnt objects cremated with the deceased on the pyre, mainly comprising items of personal dress.

iii) the unburnt grave-goods placed in the urn with the ashes.

From the skeletal remains information can be derived about age, sex, and number of individuals. From the objects we can again learn about age and sex distinctions, but these artefacts may also reflect other aspects of social identity, including the status of the deceased. The nature of the objects suggests the idea of an "after-life", although we should beware of imposing our own idea of what this might entail on another society. Certainly amongst the items of personal dress and adornment included in the burials are objects which appear to be for the "use" of the deceased, such as spears and swords, combs and manicure sets, buckets and glass vessels etc. Accessory vessels, presumably carrying provisions, were also frequently buried with the inhumations, and occasionally with the cremations. Further support for this interpretation of Anglo-Saxon grave-goods may be derived from later Anglo-Saxon literature. The Beowulf poet, describing death as a journey, relates:

I have not heard of a ship more splendidly bedecked with weopons of war and battle garments, swords and mail-coats. Amidships lay a multitude of treasures which were to travel far away with him into the possession of the ocean (Bradley 1982, 412).

Snorri Sturluson relates, in the first book of Heimskringla, that Odin made a law that all the dead should be burnt and their possessions placed on the pyre (Adalbjarnarson 1941). It is not unreasonable to suppose that this remembers a common Germanic tradition, and confirms that grave-goods were the personal possessions of the deceased.

In order to test if form and decoration of the urns reflect the social identity of the occupant it is necessary to check for correlations between these variables. Firstly form and decoration must be broken down into the individual attributes which had meaning to the makers and users of the vessels, in order to identify the elements of the symbolic language. The approach adopted was inspired by Clarke's study of Beaker pottery (1970), and involves working upwards from the smallest possible units, as described in section 1.32.

Secondly, one must then search for associations between those attributes which describe the urn, and those which describe the social identity of the occupant. The approach is basically inductive and involves cross-tabulating all attributes of pottery form and decoration with all attributes of social identity. It is assumed that where a "pottery attribute" is associated with an "identity attribute" to a higher degree than would be expected by chance, then that aspect of pottery style must have been selected for the individual. For instance, if a particular grave-good is found in vessels bearing a particular decorative motif more times than could reasonably be expected by chance then a positive association must exist. The decorative motif may then be taken to symbolise the same aspect of social identity as represented by the grave-good, be that age, sex, or any other aspect of social persona. Where the correlation is with a skeletal attribute, then the meaning of the association may become clearer.

On the other hand, if grave-goods and skeletal attributes are found to be randomly distributed throughout pots of all designs, then the hypothesis is refuted, and we must at least conclude that the pottery attributes do not signify the same aspects of social identity which are accessible to us through grave-goods and skeletal evidence. This does not preclude the fact that they may represent aspects of social identity not accessible to us, such as moiety membership perhaps. In general, however, the ethnographic evidence suggests that several features of mortuary behaviour may reflect the same aspect of social identity. Bartel (1982, 55) in particular, has commented on what he describes as the large amount of "redundant signification" involved in mortuary behaviour. Therefore the loss to archaeology of several stages of mortuary practices may not be so severe a problem as it at first appears.

1.541 Significance levels

In order to establish if the degree of association between pottery
attributes and social identity attributes was greater than could have
been expected by chance appropriate statistical tests were used
throughout. For discrete data, such as presence or absence of
particular decorative motifs, the chi-square test has been used.
Generally a four cell contingency table would be produced, using the
SPSS CROSSTABS procedure (Nie et al 1975, 1981). For example, to test
for links between tweezers and standing arches, urns with and without
standing arches would be cross-tabulated against those with and
without tweezers (see Appendix A). The figures would then be examined
to test if tweezers were found in pots with standing arches according
to an expected random distribution. If tweezers were distributed
randomly throughout all vessels, then the proportion of tweezers in
pots with standing arches should be equal to the proportion of pots
with standing arches. If 25% of vessels are decorated with standing
arches, then 25% of tweezers should be in these vessels. Differences
from this figure represent the degree of negative or positive
correlation between the respective attributes. The significance of
the correlation is found by consulting the appropriate statistical
tables.

For continuous data, such as the dimensions of pottery, the
Kolmogorov-Smirnov test was employed (see Siegel 1956). The
theoretical frequency distribution, against which other distributions
were tested, was produced for the appropriate total sample using the
SPSS FREQUENCIES procedure. For example, to test for links between
urn size and tweezers, the cumulative frequency curve for heights of
urns with tweezers would be tested against that for heights of all
urns (see Appendix B). If tweezers were randomly distributed
throughout urns of all sizes then both curves should be the same. The
significance of differences between curves was checked in the
appropriate tables.

For both the chi-square and Kolmogorov-Smirnov tests the 10%
significance level was chosen. In other words, any link which could
have happened by chance in more than one sample in ten, was rejected.
Cowgill (1977) has pointed out the dangers of reading too much into
significance levels. Statistical results cannot be directly converted
into the probabilities of hypotheses being true. Significance levels
should not be seen as magical numbers which lead one to reject or
affirm an hypothesis. Firstly, there is a logical assymmetry between
accepting the null hypothesis and rejecting it, which means that there
is a greater danger of accepting the null hypothesis when the result
is really significant, than the other way around. This is especially
true when the difference from random is not large. Secondly, the
larger the sample, the smaller the deviation from random required to
yield a significant result. Therefore, as Cowgill suggests, a level
of 10% or even 20% might be suitable for small samples, while 1% or
even lower might be required for large samples.

For this reason, in section 3, rather than just list those results
significant at the 10% level, significance level and sample size for
all cross-tabulations will be noted wherever possible. In addition to

observing the major correlations, readers and future researchers will therefore also be able to note those correlations, which whilst not judged significant in the present sample, might be worthy of future study.

A few of the links described as significant in section 3 are at levels of significance close to 10%, and could have occurred by chance. However, the low significance level is generally at least partly the result of small sample size. Whilst the total number of pots examined is large, the number of some of the rarer grave-goods available for study may be fairly small. The weak correlations may be strengthened by further examination of larger samples. They are noted, therefore, in order that future researchers may test them. Nevertheless, the majority of the links described in section 3 are significant at fairly high levels, generally 1% or more, implying that they could only have occurred by chance in one sample in 100, or sometimes in one sample in 1000. There can be no question that these represent positive links between pottery attributes and identity attributes.

On the other hand, none of the links examined are exclusive links. For example, there are no cases where a grave-good is found only in vessels with a particular pottery attribute. If the hypothesis that urn form and decoration symbolise the occupant is correct, then some explanation is necessary. The answer is likely to be that a number of factors are operating to lessen the strength of links. The following factors can be identified:

1) Depositional

   a) Incomplete collection. Not all cremated bones and grave-goods may have been collected in all cases. Excavation of pyres at Liebenau suggests that collection of bone was generally deliberate and careful, although some grave-goods were left on the pyre (Cosack 1982, Hassler 1983).

   b) Accidental mixing of material from two or more cremations at the time of collection. This may be caused by inadequate cleaning of the site after the previous cremation, or by the cremation of more than one individual at a time.

   c) Multiple burials. If more than one individual is buried in a pot (see Putnam 1980; Wilkinson 1980) then complications are likely. PCA was employed as a possible means of resolving these difficulties (see section 2.224). Recent work on over 1300 of the cremations from Spong Hill has, in fact, suggested that the number of multiple burials has previously been overestimated. A maximum of 5% of these vessels contained the remains of more than one individual (McKinley pers comm).

2) Post-depositional

   a) Decay of bones and grave-goods due to local burial conditions.

b) Disturbance by animals and by plough action may have resulted in the loss of some evidence. Although only complete and reconstructable vessels were used in the study, many of these had still been damaged and grave-goods may have been scattered.

3) Recovery

a) Incomplete recording of material, particularly from earlier excavations, including the deliberate disposal of "uninteresting" or "undiagnostic" material will have compounded the loss of data.

b) Inaccurate identification of material, even from recent excavations. This applies particularly to the cremated skeletal remains, which may only be identified with a given degree of certainty, but also to the grave-goods, where the difficulty of distinguishing between cremated glass beads and glass vessels, for instance, has been highlighted. In addition, there are obvious difficulties in picking out cremated bone combs, or ivory rings, for instance, from fragments of burnt human skeleton.

c) Lack of standardisation of recording terms exacerbates the problems above. Again it applies particularly to the analysis of cremated bone, but also to the grave-goods, where there is disagreement, for instance, on when a fragment of bronze is a bronze sheet, when it is a bronze fitting, and when it is just a bronze fragment.

4) Analysis

Unlike the grave-good and skeletal identifications, which relied upon information from a number of previous workers, the pottery, at least, was classified according to first principles, and by one system. However, it is here, one suspects, that the major reasons for the lack of 100% correlations must lie. Whilst typological specialists might argue about the exact classification of brooches and combs, they at least agree about what is a brooch and what is a comb. We can also safely assume that the distinction was relevant to the Anglo-Saxons. With the pottery, however, the continuous gradation of forms means that types must be arbitrarily defined. Although a Clarkeian approach was followed in an attempt to identify units significant to makers and users (see section 1.3), it must be admitted that there is considerable room for subjectivity in this area. The potter's grammar may have been misunderstood and the units picked for analysis may only be partially related to those important to the Anglo-Saxons. For example, the class "chevron" may mask several types of chevron, each with individual meanings, but indistinguishable by the analyst. Therefore, by cross-tabulating chevrons and tweezers one may be combining a 100% link between one type of chevron and tweezers, with a zero link, or even a negative link between other chevron types and tweezers, thus reducing the strength of the correlation. Similarly, it may be that it is particular combinations of motifs out of the infinite number of possible combinations which are significant, rather than individual motifs. Again the problem is one of definition of basic grammatical units.

In conclusion, bearing in mind all the factors itemised above, it is not surprising that there are no 100% links between pottery attributes and identity attributes. Rather, it is surprising that any links can be demonstrated at all, giving extra confidence in those which have been discovered.

1.542 Alternative explanations and counter-arguments

In section 3 it will be demonstrated that there are significant links between pottery and identity attributes. As always, however, the interpretation of such links may be questioned. Whilst it is contended here that pottery form and decoration and social identity are causally related, it might be argued that this is just a statistical relationship, reflecting other underlying causal factors. For example, the cultural history school might contend that both pottery attributes and grave-goods are reflections of underlying cultural identity. For example, tweezers are said to be Anglian grave-goods and so it is only to be expected that they should be found in "Anglian style" pottery. It is accepted that culture/race/ethnicity may be one of the roles incorporated within social identity and reflected in pottery attributes. However, it is argued that this is not the only social role reflected, on three grounds. Firstly, on examination, the pottery and identity attributes which are linked are not always those which would be expected, according to traditional cultural models. Secondly, a range of links is found in each cemetery, both for Anglian and Saxon areas. If the links were reflections of different ethnic practices, then this would imply that a mixture of Angles, Saxons and other Germanic, and perhaps native Sub-Roman, people were buried in each cemetery. Whilst some degree of racial intermixture is now generally accepted (see, for example, Hills 1979a, 316), regional differences in material imply that it was not on the scale required for this interpretation to be valid. Thirdly, a cultural historical interpretation does not explain the fact that the links are not solely with grave-goods, but are also with skeletal attributes such as age and sex, which are hardly culturally determined.

Brisbane (paper presented to Early Anglo-Saxon Pottery Group 27/10/1984), has also suggested that both pottery and choice of grave-goods may reflect different local practices. At Spong Hill he found that toilet sets were linked with a particular fabric, leading him to conclude that a specific group using pottery produced from one clay source, and perhaps in a particular style, were also practising a burial rite involving the deposition of toilet sets, which was not being practised by other groups. However, if so, then they were not using a particular area of the cemetery, as there are no localised fabric groupings. Furthermore, since the links between pottery attributes and grave-good attributes occur on all sites, then this interpretation would again suppose that different peoples using the same cemeteries were maintaining distinctive burial rites throughout the country, for several hundred years. Instead, the link between fabric and toilet sets may again be seen as a link reflecting social identity, with particular clays, (perhaps of higher quality), being chosen for those of a particular status, or as being the result of only certain potters producing vessels for those of particular status.

Finally, it might be argued that the link between pottery and identity attributes may simply reflect the fact that both pottery and grave-good types change with time. Again, this can easily be countered as a complete explanation. Whilst pottery styles may have changed over the 200-300 years of the study period, it is argued that most of the design attributes isolated in section 2 would have remained in use throughout the period. To some extent this is an argument of convenience. In the absence of any secure chronology for Anglo-Saxon pottery their chronological development will be ignored in the present study. However, this position is supported by the fact that the same range of types is found on most of the sites in the sample, despite the variations in the starting date of the cemeteries, and differences in the length of period of use (cf. section 3.1). Furthermore, this interpretation is again supported by the links with skeletal as well as grave-good attributes.

By section 4, the hypothesis presented here will have been supported by detailed data and argument. However, the broad range of the study, bringing together several classes of data sheds light not only upon Anglo-Saxon symbolism, but also upon several other issues along the way. Firstly, it will be necessary to quantify the range of variation within and between each cemetery, providing information on regional groupings. Secondly, it will be essential to examine correlations between grave-goods and skeletal attributes, providing a quantitative basis for estimating the age and sex on the basis of grave-goods. Thirdly, the skeletal data will provide information about demography and Anglo-Saxon population structure. Finally, the grave-good data will provide similar information about Anglo-Saxon social structure, yielding figures for the relative frequency of grave-goods, and hence the proportion of the population within each social grouping.

CHAPTER 2

METHODOLOGY

Chapter Two describes how the theory outlined in Chapter One was put into practice. It commences with a discussion of how the sample was chosen (section 2.1), followed by an account of the research programme (section 2.2), including a description of the method of coding and recording the data.

2.1 The research data base

Archaeologists must inevitably base their conclusions about a class of material upon a study of a sample of that class (fig.4). Not only will those individuals selected for study be a subset of those available ("the study population"), but the study population will itself be a subset of those about which information is required ("the target population").

Figure 4 The relationship of research sample to target population

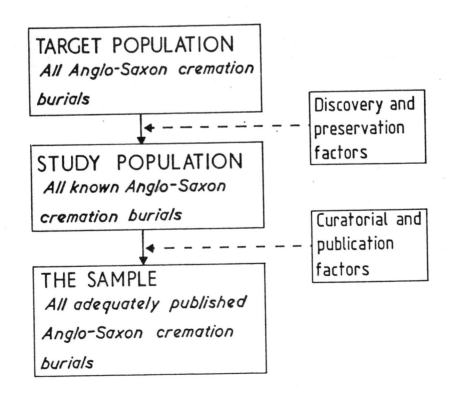

2.11 The target population

In this case the target population comprises all early Anglo-Saxon cremation vessels buried in the British Isles. It was decided at a preliminary stage that inhumation vessels should be excluded from the analysis, as should settlement pottery, and all Continental pottery. The reasons for these decisions were largely practical ones of accessibility of material, but the first two exclusions may also be justified on theoretical grounds.

2.111 Inhumation accessory vessels

Inhumation vessels belong to a rite which is clearly distinct from cremation ritual, and play a different role. Rather than being directly linked with the human remains they play a secondary function as containers, presumably for foodstuffs. A different range of grave-goods is found in inhumation burials, making it impossible to compare them directly with cremations. In addition, accessory vessels are only found in a minority of graves and appear to be generally smaller than cremation vessels. On a practical level, inhumation vessels are not found in sufficiently large numbers to constitute a statistically valid sample, and apart from those brought together in Myres (1977a) they are published in a wide range of incomparable sources.

2.112 Settlement pottery

Pottery found in the course of excavations of Anglo-Saxon settlement sites may immediately be separated from cremation vessels on the grounds that it is found in a domestic rather than a funerary context. Of course, this does not necessarily mean that it was regarded by Anglo-Saxons as a separate category of artefact. Certainly, some pottery types found in domestic refuse are rarely found as cremation vessels. Flat platters and small cups, for example, are never used as cremation vessels, for they are naturally physically unsuitable as containers. Jones (1979, 29) tabulates some further differences between cemetery and settlement assemblages at Mucking, including the absence of various forms of surface treatment in the cemetery, such as rustication, combing, and schlickung.

Brisbane (1981, 240) concludes that there are differences in method of manufacture and fabric between domestic and funerary pottery, corresponding to different modes and levels of production. Of the four fabric groups recovered from domestic contexts at Spong Hill, only one overlaps with the groups in the cemetery (Mark Brisbane, paper presented to Early Anglo-Saxon Pottery Group, 27/10/84). There would nevertheless appear to be considerable overlap between domestic and funerary styles. Many of the decorated sherds from the hut fills at Mucking (cf. Myres 1968, Jones 1969, 1979) would not be out of place in a funerary assemblage. West (1969b, 177) concludes that decorated pots were not intended purely for funerary use, although the proportions of decorated vessels are higher in cemeteries. At West Stow (West 1969a, 1969b) the decorated pottery makes up only five

percent of the total sherd count of some 12,000 sherds. Whilst even
the most highly decorated funerary urn is still likely to yield a
large number of plain sherds once broken it would appear that
decorated urns make up a smaller proportion of domestic assemblages
than funerary assemblages. Of course the decorated pottery from
settlement contexts may be derived from funerary vessels which have
been broken during manufacture, or whilst the urns have been held at
the settlement prior to burial. It has been suggested, for example,
that the Illington/Lackford potter may have been operating from West
Stow (Green, Milligan and West 1981, 210), in which case many of the
sherds from his or her work found in the domestic refuse may be
wasters from funerary urn production.

In practice, regardless of whether or not settlement pottery is
distinct from funerary pottery it has to be excluded from this study.
Pottery from domestic refuse is divorced of any associations with
individuals, and therefore cannot be examined from the point of view
of the social significance of the urn form and decoration. Whilst it
might nevertheless be worthwhile to include settlement pottery in
order that proportions of types might be quantitatively compared with
funerary pottery, in practice this is not feasible. Firstly, at the
time of embarking upon the research, there were not sufficient
domestic assemblages available for study which were large enough to
make such comparisons statistically meaningful. Secondly, such an
exercise would be of doubtful value owing to the different factors
affecting burial and preservation in a domestic context as opposed to
a cemetery context. Very few complete vessels survive on settlement
sites and most of the pottery consists of small sherds. Until
techniques are developed that allow comparisons to be made between
these different assemblages and allow one to determine whether they
might have stemmed from the same population such comparisons would not
appear to be very productive. Factors such as differential survival
according to sherd thickness and weight would have to be taken into
account in any such formulation.

2.113 Continental pottery

Pottery from late Iron Age cemeteries on the Continent was also
excluded from the study. The similarity of pottery from several North
German and Danish cemeteries, such as Issendorf (Janssen 1972) and
Westerwanna (Zimmer-Linnfeld et al 1960), to material in England is
recognised, and it might well have been useful to compare English and
Continental styles in a quantitative fashion, and to examine if the
same patterns of association found in the English material were also
present on the Continent. However, this was not possible for
practical reasons. To take just one Continental site would have been
of limited value, neither allowing one to locate regions of greatest
similarity of material, nor to discover if any patterns discovered
were valid for more than a single site. Nevertheless, to take more
than one site would have been impossible in the time available,
especially since it would have involved a great deal of research from
primary material because of problems of availabilty of published data.
Therefore, whilst it would be valuable to examine continental material
in a similar manner to that carried out here for the English material,

it must be postponed until some future study. It was thus decided to limit the present work to Anglo-Saxon material from the British Isles.

2.12 The study population

Whilst the target population was defined as all early Anglo-Saxon cremation vessels buried in the British Isles, the study population is all those that are available for study. Therefore it is immediately limited to those which have been found. Whilst we can never be certain of the relationship between study and target populations it seems safe to assume that the study population is representative of the target population. Although there may be an inbuilt bias against recovering unurned cremations it seems unlikely that we are more likely to find one type of urn in preference to another. Of course the sites which have been found and excavated have largely been dictated by the activities of gravel quarries, and to a lesser extent by the location of particularly active archaeologists. Nevertheless there is no reason to suppose that if Anglo-Saxon cemeteries were found elsewhere they would yield a completely different range of pottery types.

However, the study population is further limited because not all those urns which have been found have been published, or even saved. As long as the interest in Anglo-Saxon pottery was principally in those "diagnostic" decorated pieces which could be dated, many plain pots were not considered worth publishing, or were even discarded on excavation if they did not contain grave-goods. As recently as 1951 it was possible for Lethbridge to write:

> It seems quite unnecessary to give a detailed description of each pot. Not only would this be tedious to read and costly to publish, but when there is nothing in the contents of a particular vessel to give any information as to its possible date, its description appears to be of small importance (1951,7)

and:

> In theory one should illustrate every pot. In practice this is more trouble than it is worth ... I have therefore attempted to draw every pot which I feel may be of value to other students. This means every early pot which may have some bearing on the origins of the early settlers; every pot which contained some recognisable object; every pot associated with another pot; groups of vessels by the same hand; and all pots of late date (1951, 14).

2.2 The research programme

It was considered important to conduct a pilot study first (henceforth Phase One) in order to test if correlations existed between urn form, decoration, and contents, and to indicate which variables should be recorded in the main study (henceforth Phase Two). In order to avoid making any assumptions about which variables were significant the aim

Figure 5 Sites in the Phase One sample

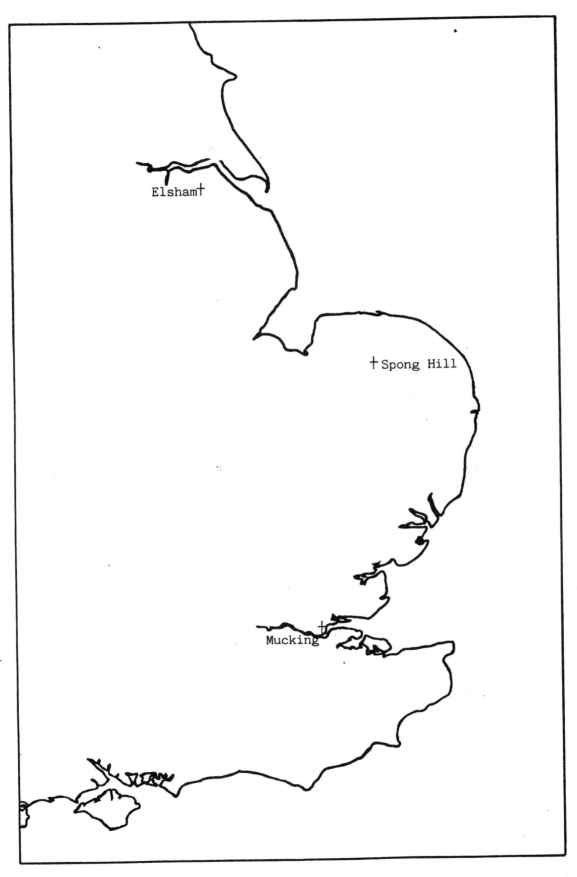

Figure 6 Sites in the Phase Two sample

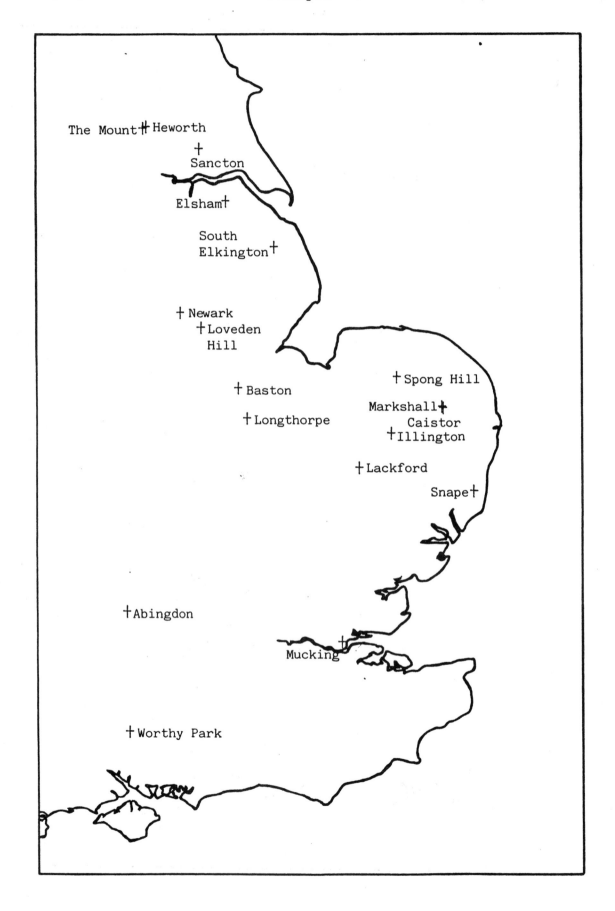

was to record urns in as much detail as possible in Phase One and to use the computer to discover which variables exhibited correlations. It was decided that the Phase One sample should incorporate material from more than one site, in case of local factors in urn symbolism, and the possibility that variables which were significant on one site might not be important on another. To increase the reliability of the Phase One results only recently excavated and well recorded sites were considered. Three data sets were available for study, giving a reasonable geographical spread (fig.5). These were urns excavated between 1965-77 from Cemetery Two at Mucking, Essex; urns excavated between 1968-77 at Spong Hill, Norfolk (Hills 1977b; Hills and Penn 1981); and urns excavated in 1975-6 from the path of the M180 - Humber Bridge link road at Elsham, South Humberside.

The physical attributes for the urns in the Phase One sample were then cross-tabulated with the urn contents, and statistically significant correlations noted. Phase One indicated that relating urn form and decoration to contents appeared to be fruitful and it was considered worthwhile to continue with Phase Two. Only those attributes which had yielded significant correlations in Phase One were now selected as it was considered that these were the aspects of urn form and decoration which were significant to the makers and users of the urns. By limiting the number of variables recorded it now became possible to investigate a much larger number of urns in Phase Two. Fortunately the variables which were believed to be significant were generally recorded in the published cemetery reports. Therefore, during Phase Two it was possible to work directly from published material, rather than from an examination of the actual urns as in Phase One. Although this demanded relying upon the accuracy of the published records it was felt that any inaccuracies would not distort the sample in any particular direction, and should eventually cancel each other out. All urns from available sites where associated grave-goods had been recorded were incorporated in Phase Two, including all such urns illustrated in Myres (1978), and several unpublished sites. These provided a good geographical spread, reflecting the distribution of Anglo-Saxon cremation cemeteries (fig.6). The additional sites examined in Phase Two were Abingdon, Berks; Baston, Lincs; Caistor-by-Norwich, Norfolk; Illington, Norfolk; Lackford, Suffolk; Longthorpe, Hunts; Loveden Hill, Lincs; Markshall, Norfolk; Newark, Notts; Sancton, Yorks; South Elkington, Lincs; Snape, Suffolk; Worthy Park, Hants; and Heworth and The Mount, both in York. In addition, it was now possible to include further urns from the Phase One sites, hitherto excluded because not all the Phase One variables could be measured for them.

The total sample comprised 2440 Anglo-Saxon cremation urns from 18 sites (table 1). These urns may be considered as a single cultural assemblage of Anglo-Saxon cremation urns from England, or they may be sub-divided according to site, and the sites compared against each other. However, there are difficulties in comparing site assemblages arising from the variable quality of excavation recording and publication, compounded by incompletely excavated assemblages. Therefore it will be necessary to discuss the quality of the sample from each site in turn. Nevertheless, unless stated otherwise, there is generally no reason for believing that the study sample for any one site is not representative of the site as a whole.

Table 1 Composition of sample

Site name	Number of urns
Abingdon	36
Baston	15
Caistor-by-Norwich	227
Elsham	205
Illington	94
Lackford	286
Longthorpe	14
Loveden Hill	251
Markshall	7
Mucking	77
Newark	142
Sancton	243
Snape	5
South Elkington	91
Spong Hill	675
Worthy Park	22
York – Heworth	42
York – The Mount	8
TOTAL	2440

Abingdon The 36 urns in the sample are all the complete or reconstructible vessels drawn from a total of 82 cremations excavated in 1934-5 from the mixed cemetery at Abingdon (Leeds and Harden 1936). These excavations explored between one half and two-thirds of the total cemetery. The excavation catalogue gives a full description of the vessels and associated grave-goods, but there is no mention of the skeletal remains. The vessels are reproduced at a scale of one to nine; therefore the drawings in Myres (1977a) were used to provide additional information not furnished in the descriptions.

Baston The excavation at Baston in 1966 produced evidence for a small mixed cemetery, dated by the excavators to the mid-fifth or late-sixth century (Mayes and Dean 1976). 44 vessels are illustrated, but most came from the ploughsoil and only 15 were usable. It is unlikely that the vessels found represent the full extent of the site, but should provide a representative sample. The report gives a complete description of vessels and contents, with an appendix on the human remains by Manchester.

Caistor-by-Norwich The mixed cemetery at Caistor was excavated between 1932-7 by F.R.Mann, and the report published by Myres and Green (1973). This includes 227 usable urns of an estimated total of 700 excavated cremations. This probably represents most of the original cemetery, but some urns had been eroded to the North and

West, and others lie deeper to the East and South. The urns and
grave-goods are fully illustrated and described. Mann identified
several child cremations, and retained bones from a small proportion
of the vessels. Wells produced a report on these, but in his own
words:

> any conclusions reached must be handled with the greatest caution
> (Myres and Green 1973, 120).

In particular, the bias towards child burials should be noted.

Elsham Excavations at Elsham took place between 1975-6, and the
report is in progress (Berisford and Knowles, in preparation). 630
cremation burials were identified in a complete excavation of the
cemetery, yielding a sample of 205 usable vessels. Publication
drawings provided details of the urns, which were examined for further
information. The excavation catalogue provided a full listing of
grave-goods and skeletal remains, (extracted from a report by Harman),
including the presence of cremated animal bones.

Illington During 1949, G.M.Knocker excavated 204 urns at Illington,
of which 94 were usable. Knocker dug a single transect across the
site, which one presumes provides a random sample, although the full
extent of the cemetery is unknown. The site is still unpublished, but
Green and Milligan kindly provided copies of Knocker's typescript
report, a corrected list of grave-goods, a human bone report by Wells,
and an animal bone report by King. Further information on the vessel
decoration was derived from Myres (1977a).

Lackford In 1947 Lethbridge excavated some 500 cremations at
Lackford, which he estimated represented half of the total cemetery.
The report (Lethbridge 1951) consists of crude drawings and
descriptions of those vessels which he regarded as having datable
contents, plus some other complete vessels. Additional vessels and
further details are included in Myres (1977a), giving a total of 286
usable vessels. Unfortunately, the grave-good lists are incomplete,
containing no references to glass, and few to bronze fragments, which
Lethbridge regarded as undiagnostic. Therefore the grave-good data
must be used with caution. There is no skeletal data.

Longthorpe A small mixed cemetery dated to the fifth and sixth
centuries was found in 1968, in the course of excavation of the Roman
fort at Longthorpe. 22 cremations were found within the trenches.
These are probably representative of a larger total number of burials.
The report includes a full description of the pottery by Myres (1974),
and all vessels are illustrated. All contents are listed, but there
is no skeletal report. 14 vessels were complete enough to be included
in the sample.

Loveden Hill An extensive cemetery has been excavated at Loveden
Hill, firstly by K.R.Fennell, and later by N.Kerr. Both excavations
are unpublished, but those by Fennell are reported in his doctoral
thesis (1964), allowing the urns to be incorporated in the present
study. Fennell records that the cemetery, which is predominantly
cremation, probably exceeded 1000 burials (see also Fennell 1974). By

1962 over 400 cremations had been excavated, and 251 of these are included in the present sample. Kerr is reported to have excavated a further 2000 urns, but these are currently unavailable for study. Fennell's thesis includes a full catalogue, complete with grave-good listings. Drawings of the individual vessels are available in Myres (1977a). In addition, Fennell made available a typescript report by Wells. This described the human and animal skeletal remains from 65 vessels. Fennell dates the cemetery from the early-fifth to the mid-seventh centuries.

Markshall The 7 urns from Markshall are the only complete vessels surviving from fragments of over 100 urns recovered during 1948-9. They were published in the Caistor report (Myres and Green 1973) and the same comments apply as to Caistor (see above), with the addition that Wells was able to produce a full report on the human remains.

Mucking Complete excavation during 1967-77 of Cemetery Two at Mucking produced a medium-sized mixed cemetery, including 468 cremations. The excavators suggest a date of early fifth to mid to late-seventh century for the cemetery (Jones 1980). The excavation is unpublished, but Jones and Jones allowed access to the excavation archive and pottery. Only 77 vessels were usable because of the fragmentary nature of the material. Pre-publication drawings, grave-good catalogue, and a skeletal report including details of age, but not sex, were also available.

Newark Excavations at Newark were conducted from 1957-78, from which a sequence of vessels numbered 1-404 survives. It is likely that more urns remain in situ (Gavin Kinsley, paper presented to Early Anglo-Saxon Pottery Group, 13/3/82). The material has been prepared for publication by G.Kinsley, who collaborated in supplying descriptions of the urns and their surviving contents. It is recognised that some vessels may have become disassociated from their contents and the grave-good catalogue may be incomplete. Kinsley also made available a animal and human bone report by M.Harman. 142 vessels were complete enough to be included in the study.

Sancton The presence of a considerable cremation cemetery at Sancton has been known since at least 1854. Many vessels were recovered in the 1880's and 1890's, and extensive excavations took place between 1954-8, yielding 240 urns. These vessels are published in Myres and Southern (1973). More recently, N.Reynolds has conducted further excavations on the site, and established that the site extends over some 30 acres (Nicholas Reynolds, paper presented to Early Anglo-Saxon Pottery Group, 21/5/83). The published examples must therefore represent a small fraction of the total cemetery. 243 vessels are incorporated in the sample. Details were derived from Myres and Southern (ibid), although the pottery drawings were checked in Myres (1977a), and some minor differences became apparent. Reynolds provided some additional information on grave-good contents and pottery descriptions, and K.Manchester allowed access to his comprehensive report on the human skeletal remains. Animals are simply recorded as being present and are not identified.

Snape West and Owles (1974) report on the excavation of 8 cremation burials at Snape, of which 5 were in complete or nearly complete vessels. Their account includes details of grave-goods, and a report on the skeletal material by Wells. 14 vessels excavated from the same area at earlier dates, and catalogued in Myres (1977a), could not be included in the sample because of the lack of information about their contents.

South Elkington From 1946-7 remains of over 200 cremations were excavated at South Elkington, although the published plan (Webster 1951) appears to indicate that the original cemetery was much larger. The report provides illustrations of each vessel, and a list of objects recovered from them, but there is no bone report. 91 vessels were complete enough to include in the present study.

Spong Hill The sample of 675 urns from the predominantly cremation cemetery at Spong Hill represents the largest number of urns from a single site included in the study. With the exception of a few vessels from earlier excavations, these urns were excavated between 1968-77 under modern excavation conditions, and published as volumes I and II of the Spong Hill Report (Hills 1977b, Hills and Penn 1981; see also Myres 1947, Hills 1980, Hills, Penn and Rickett 1984). Further excavations have revealed the full extent of a cemetery of over 2000 urns, but it is likely that the sample is representative of the total site. The sample consists of the northern half of the site. Since the cemetery is thought to have developed outwards from a central point (Hills pers comm), the sample should therefore contain a range of vessels representing all phases of the cemetery's usage. The published reports provided full urn drawings, descriptions, and grave-good catalogue. In addition each urn was physically examined to provide extra information. With the exception of a few published examples (Putnam 1980, 1981a) the skeletal report was not available at the time of the research.

Worthy Park Myres (1977a) includes 31 vessels from Worthy Park. These comprise burials being prepared for publication by S.Hawkes, who kindly supplied a typescript report and catalogue, including skeletal report by J.Bayley. The excavation revealed a mixed cemetery, including 46 cremations. 22 vessels could be used in the present study.

York - Heworth Myres (1977a) describes and illustrates 44 vessels from Heworth, and also provides some information on grave-goods. 42 were complete enough to include, although the grave-good list may be incomplete, and there is no skeletal information.

York - The Mount Stead (1958) reports on the cremation vessels which had been found on the Mount, York, in 1859-60. He includes illustrations and a list of contents, allowing a further 8 vessels to be included in the study. No skeletal information was available.

In conclusion, there are considerable differences in the size of the individual assemblages included in the sample, and in the quality of the information. Nevertheless, the recording system applied in the research imposes a degree of uniformity on the material, and allows comparisons to be made between sites.

All the vessels used were relatively complete, and had to have a fully reconstructible profile to be included. This should mean that (with the exceptions noted above where they had not been recorded) the record of the grave-goods and skeletal remains should also be relatively complete. If a vessel retains a full profile then there is unlikely to have been a high loss of urn contents through plough damage and other disturbance.

A problem of comparing site assemblages does arise from the fact that some cemeteries are represented by more urns than others. In fact 77% of the sample comes from just 33% of the sites. Clearly, cemeteries represented by very few urns cannot provide a statistical sample for comparison, and so can only be included as part of the total sample. Only ten sites are represented by more than fifty urns, namely Caistor, Elsham, Illington, Lackford, Loveden Hill, Mucking, Newark, Sancton, South Elkington, and Spong Hill. It was thought that each of these was large enough to allow it to be validly compared against the others.

2.21 Phase One

The aim in Phase One was to record as many attributes as possible for each urn, irrespective of pre-conceived notions of decorative styles. Therefore a classification scheme was designed which attempted to identify the smallest possible units of decoration making up the overall scheme. Ideally, these units should correspond to individual decisions taken by the potter during the course of manufacture (section 1.32). The classification system was based upon a general survey of published Anglo-Saxon pottery, but was inevitably modified in the course of use. The final system is discussed below and is listed in full in Appendix C. A fully worked specimen urn is given in Appendix D.

It will be seen that the classification system rests upon a hierarchical model. The justification for this rests upon ethnographic studies of potters in non-industrial societies (section 1.32). At each stage in the production of a vessel the potter has a number of alternative choices (fig.7). One of the first decisions, for instance, is whether or not a pot should be decorated. Having decided that it should be decorated the potter must then choose the type of decoration. If the potter decides to apply incised decoration then the choice is now between the various classes, such as chevrons or arches. Having decided to use chevrons the potter must then choose how many lines each chevron should be made up of, and so on. Whilst it is unnecessary for the potter to have a "mental template" of the completed urn from the start, it can be seen that at each stage he or she is constrained by the decision taken at the last stage. Whether the decisions are conscious or unconscious actions does not alter the process, as they will still be culturally determined. Following from this, each level of the classification system must consist of attribute states which are alternatives to each other.

Figure 7 Schematic representation of the production of an Early
Anglo-Saxon cremation urn

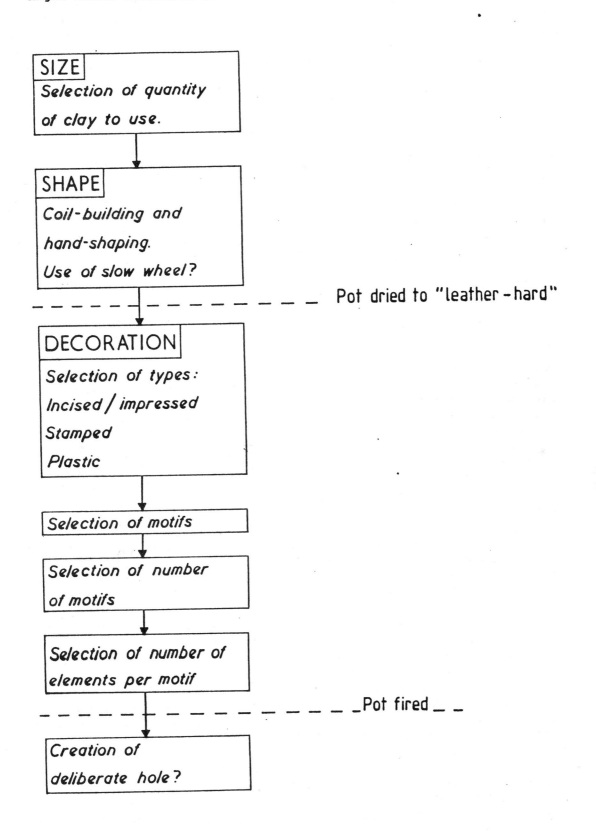

At the completion of the research this approach to classifying the urn decoration still appears to be valid in terms of the research objectives. That correlations between the pottery attributes and the urn occupants were recognised suggests that the classification was, at least to some extent, describing the urns in a manner which would have been meaningful to the Anglo-Saxons, and that a real typology had been discovered. Nevertheless, a number of shortcomings may be identified. As Shorter (1971, 48) wrote for historians:

> if his codebook doesn't seem inadequate by the end of the project he (the recorder) probably hasn't learnt anything.

In particular, with the benefit of hindsight, the classification system now appears to be rather abstract, emphasising the presence or absence of a given motif, and not giving sufficient attention to the position of decorative attributes on a vessel. On the other hand, it is still not apparent how this problem might be surmounted. Since each urn has a different form there are no absolute criteria by which the position of motifs might be classified. For example, to say that a motif is placed above or below the maximum diameter has different implications according to how high up the maximum diameter is.

2.211 Data capture

In order to measure all the variables required in Phase One it was necessary to physically inspect each urn. This was also beneficial in ensuring familiarity with the material and the problems involved in working with it at an early stage of the research. Clear definitions of each attribute state were developed, and during recording these definitions were regularly referred to in order to avoid interpretative drifts in the class boundaries. For grave-goods, the excavator's classifications were accepted and followed throughout.

Each urn was recorded on a pre-printed pro-forma (see Appendix E). This information was then transferred to floppy disc on a Research Machines Ltd 380Z micro-computer. As an aid to recording, a special purpose data capture program called POTCLASS was designed, running in RML BASIC. The program prompted the user to enter each item of data at the keyboard, storing the responses on disc. POTCLASS followed the hierarchical model implicit in the classification system, considerably speeding data capture. Once it had been established, for example, that a particular urn was plain, then the program would skip all questions relating to decoration, and would move on to urn contents.

To economise disc storage space the data was stored in compressed format, in variable length records. A series of flags embedded in the data file was employed to indicate the attribute held in each field (see Richards and Ryan 1985, chapter 5). Further subroutines in the POTCLASS suite allowed the user to amend and retrieve records.

When sufficient numbers of urns had been recorded in this way they were transferred to an ICL 2900 series mainframe computer. Here further programs were used to convert specific aspects of each variable length record (such as those attributes relating to incised

decoration) into fixed length records as required, padding out empty
fields with zeros. The data was then in a form that could be
submitted to standard statistical packages for analysis. As these
expanded data sets frequently occupied several megabytes of computer
storage it was important to have this facility to expand aspects of
the data bank when needed, retaining only the compressed version
permanently on the machine.

2.212 Incised and impressed decoration

The first major class of decoration comprises designs which have been
incised or impressed onto the surface of the vessel. This includes
most linear decoration, whether the lines were scratched into the
surface with a piece of wood or bone, or whether they are wider
grooves which may have been impressed with a rounded object, such as a
finger or thumb. Whilst examples at opposite extremes are obviously
different there is no easy way of distinguishing between them as there
is a continuum from the very narrow to the very wide, sometimes with
considerable variation on a single vessel. At the wider end the class
begins to merge into the classes of plastic decoration which are
defined as channelling and fluting (section 2.213). Here a
distinction was made between those grooves that were wider than the
end of a thumb, i.e. more than 2cm, which were classed as channels,
and those which were narrower, which were included in the incised
decoration category. The majority of this class, however, consists of
much narrower lines, frequently 0.5cm or less.

Slashes and impressed dots were also included in this category, but
all stamped decoration was excluded as comprising a special class of
decoration. Where a round impression had straight sides it was taken
to have been made with a specially prepared tool, rather than a handy
stick, and was classed as stamped.

Twelve broad classes of incised decoration were identified:

        Horizontal continuous linear grooves
        Horizontal discontinuous linear grooves
        Vertical linear grooves
        Diagonal linear grooves
        Curvilinear grooves
        Slashes
        Dots
        Swastikas
        Crosses
        Stars
        Runes
        Animals

Representative examples of the most common types are shown in fig.8.
Most of these groups were then further sub-divided. For example,
diagonal linear grooves were split into the following classes:

        Continuous chevron pattern

Figure 8 Representative examples of principal classes of incised and impressed decoration

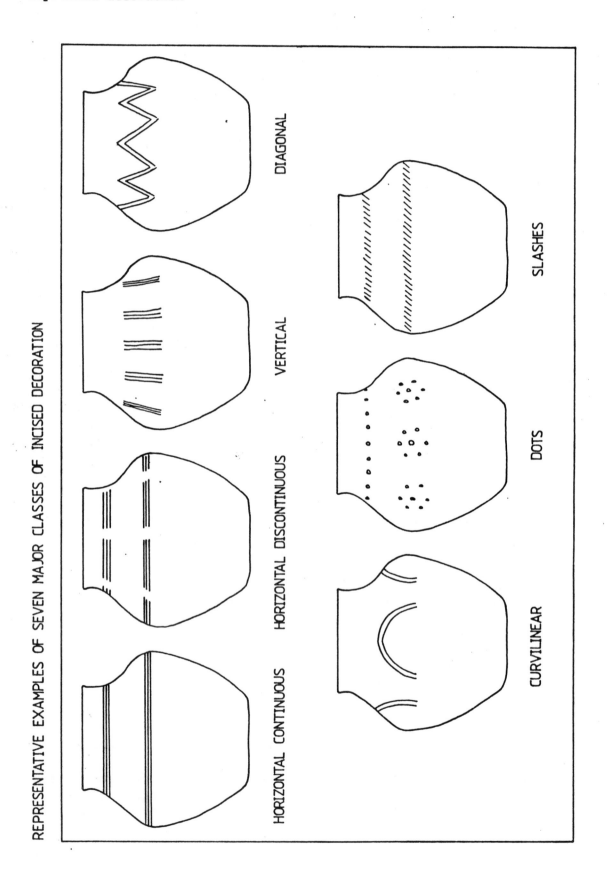

REPRESENTATIVE EXAMPLES OF SEVEN MAJOR CLASSES OF INCISED DECORATION

DIAGONAL

SLASHES

VERTICAL

DOTS

HORIZONTAL DISCONTINUOUS

CURVILINEAR

HORIZONTAL CONTINUOUS

        Broken chevron pattern
        Single upright chevron
        Single inverted chevron
        Single groups of diagonal lines sloping down to the
        left
        Single groups of diagonal lines sloping down to the
        right

Similarly, curvilinear grooves were classed according to:

        Continuous waves
        Discontinuous waves
        Single arch
        Single inverted arch
        Complex pattern of inverted and interlocking arches

        and waves
        Circular/ sub-rectangular grooves

   For each class of decoration the number of bands or fields where it
occurred was recorded, as well as the number of lines making up each
field. A "field" is taken to be an area of decoration, such as a band
of chevrons, or a band of horizontal lines. For certain categories of
incised decoration, such as vertical lines, it was noted if these were
"imposed" on "plastic" decoration, as when vertical grooves are
incised on a boss. The positioning of dotted and slashed decoration
was also recorded.

2.213 Plastic decoration

The second major class of decorated urns are those vessels where extra
clay has been added or the existing body moulded so as to produce
plastic decoration. Eight main categories were distinguished:

        Bosses
        Lugs
        Handles
        Cordons
        Fluting
        Negative bosses
        Facets
        Channels

Several of these groups were then further sub-divided into individual
types. In all cases the number of examples of each was recorded.
Bosses, for example, were categorised according to five classes:

        Vertical
        Diagonal
        Horizontal
        Rounded
        Horned

Applied or solid bosses were not distinguished from those pushed out from inside the vessel, because of the difficulty of drawing a sharp distinction. In many cases bosses appear to be produced by the use of both techniques in conjunction. However, since the end result is the same, this would not appear to be a problem.

Only bosses which had been pierced for suspension qualified as lugs. Where single impressions had been pushed into the vessel sides these were classified as negative bosses. Where such impressions ran continuously around a vessel then the urn was described as fluted. Continuous bands of rounded impressions, rather than vertical ones, usually on the carination, were classified as facetting. Linear ornament, where the grooves were too deep and wide to be described as incised, was classed as channelling.

2.214 Stamped decoration

The main aim in classifying the stamped decoration was to produce a system which would place all stamps with a similar design in the same class, irrespective of whether the same die had been used. The aim of the research was to examine any possible significance in the design itself, not to identify potter's "workshops" using the same tool to produce a design. The system proposed by Briscoe (1981; 1983) was not found to be a suitable means of comparing stamps by computer, so for the purposes of this study another method was devised. The full system is presented in Appendix F, and is discussed below.

The variety of Anglo-Saxon potters' stamps is too complex to allow a classification by either external shape or internal design alone. For example, whilst it may be significant whether or not an impression is square, oval, or triangular, there is also a set of internal designs, such as grid or cross, which may also be significant, and which cut across stamp groupings classified by die shape alone. For instance grid designs may be found on round, oval, rectangular, triangular, and diamond-shaped impressions.

Therefore, the classification system described Anglo-Saxon potters' stamps by two parameters:

(1) SHAPE. The first parameter is the actual outline shape of the die, as inferred from the impression, and irrespective of any internal motif. There are seventeen groups, designated by the prefix letter A - Q.

(2) DESIGN. The second parameter is the form and logic of the internal design of the impression, irrespective of its external shape. There are twenty-four groups, denoted by the numbers 1 - 24. Where there is an overlap between two classes, as in an impression combining radiate and cruciform aspects, then it is described according to the dominant motif.

Therefore, any stamp impression can be described by two characters, A5 for instance, where A is the shape prefix denoting a circular stamp, and 5 the design group, indicating a design consisting of multiple figures. All circular impressions can be retrieved by finding all classes prefixed by the letter A. If one were interested in a figure which may be used both as a die shape and an internal motif then it is necessary to search both shape and design groups. For example, if one were interested in all stamps bearing a cross figure then shape group J and design groups 11-15 should be included. Similarly, for all swastika stamps, shape group M and design group 20 should be included.

Theoretically, there are 408 (17 x 24) possible stamp descriptions, although in practice the execution of many of these on a die less than 2cm in diameter would be impossible for technical reasons, and other combinations are ruled out by logic. In practice there are about one hundred commonly executed classes. The system was found to be very convenient when new stamp types were encountered, as these could be described within the existing system without adding new classes, as other systems require.

The number and relative position of fields of stamped decoration on a vessel was recorded, as well as the number of individual stamp impressions in each field. Where the excavator had indicated other vessels where the same die had been employed this was also noted.

2.215 Form

The form of a vessel, comprising its size and shape, may conveniently be regarded as a separate set of variables from its decorative aspects. This does not mean that form is seen as more "functional" than decoration. The distinction is simply on the grounds that it repesents an independent set of decisions for the potter during manufacture. Although particular decorative styles would appear to be regarded as more suitable for particular shapes of vessels (see section 3.32), there is considerable overlap. Certain straight-sided vessels are usually plain, for instance, but other forms are just as frequently decorated as not. Similarly, most decorative motifs can be found on all forms of decorated vessels.

Form is a difficult variable to categorise. Unlike most mass-produced wheel-thrown wares, Anglo-Saxon cremation urns apparently exhibit a continuous gradation of size and shape and do not fall readily into discrete morphological classes. In attempting to organise this material, researchers have previously applied ill-defined categories derived from Myres (see section 1.4). Unfortunately, the boundaries of these classes have never been defined and so no two researchers have applied the terms in the same manner. Nor does it appear that any individual researcher has used the terms consistently over time.

Manual entry of major dimensions

The first approach adopted during Phase One was to record the major dimensions of each vessel, entering the measurements at the micro-computer keyboard in the course of the data capture program. Height, maximum diameter, height of maximum diameter, rim diameter, and base diameter were recorded to the nearest half-centimetre. This was the finest that the eye could measure on the one-to-three scale drawings used.

A BASIC program then sorted the measurements and the micro-computer's graphics capability was used to display histograms of dimensions and ratios of dimensions for visual inspection. A problem resulted from the fact that the continuous ratio-level measurements had been split into discrete groupings because of the limits of the recorder's perception. This led to a slightly false grouping of urns and gave the histograms a jagged appearance. For example, it might be that there were no urns with a height of 20.0 - 20.5cm, although there may have been several with heights of 19.99cm and 25.51cm included in the neighbouring groups. In addition, studying the frequency distribution for base diameter (fig.9), it was apparent that there were alternate large and small groups, with the larger groups placed on the whole centimetre divisions, i.e. 10cm, 11cm, 12cm, etc. However, rather than reflecting some hitherto undiscovered Anglo-Saxon unit of measurement, this was an unfortunate side-effect of the recorder's perception. Base diameters of Anglo-Saxon pottery are frequently indeterminate as the base is often rounded and ill-defined. It appears that there had been a tendency to record base diameters in whole centimetres, although this was totally unconscious at the time.

In order to remove these problems the micro-computer was used to calculate two-centimetre moving averages for each distribution. This had a smoothing effect and made the distributions more easily interpretable (fig.10).

However, whilst providing distributions and various descriptive statistics, such as means and standard deviations as "fingerprints" of distributions, the recording of major dimensions proved to be of limited value in identifying the significant variability between vessels. Firstly, for the five measurements taken from each urn there are ten possible simple ratios and an almost infinite number of more complex ones. There is no single ratio which is intuitively better than another at accounting for form variability. Secondly, for a data set such as Anglo-Saxon pottery, where there is limited variability between artefacts and no obviously distinct types, the value of the traditional use of pottery classification ratios is limited. Hardy-Smith (1974) plots height against width for post-medieval pottery to distinguish plates, bowls, cups, jugs, and so forth. However, if the same procedure is followed for Anglo-Saxon pottery all urns fall within one tightly clustered group corresponding to Hardy-Smith's bowl form. Lastly, by selecting certain dimensions to represent the variability between artefacts one is assuming that the artefact makers and users must have understood the variability in the same way. One is ignoring the variability that may exist in the rest of the artefact profile.

Automatic capture of complete vessel profile

The next stage in Phase One was to try to identify a limited number of variables expressing most variation in urn form, and to identify how the makers and users of Anglo-Saxon cremation urns regarded urn form. These variables could then be used as an economical basis for

Figure 9 Frequency distribution: Spong Hill base diameter

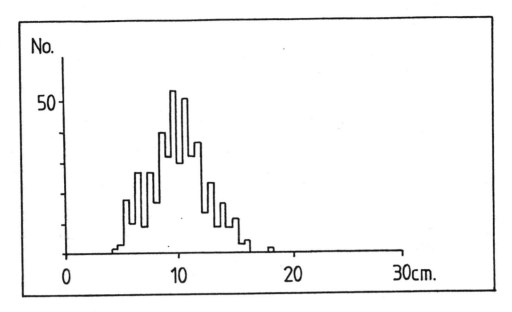

Figure 10 Frequency distribution: Spong Hill 2cm   moving   average   of
base diameter

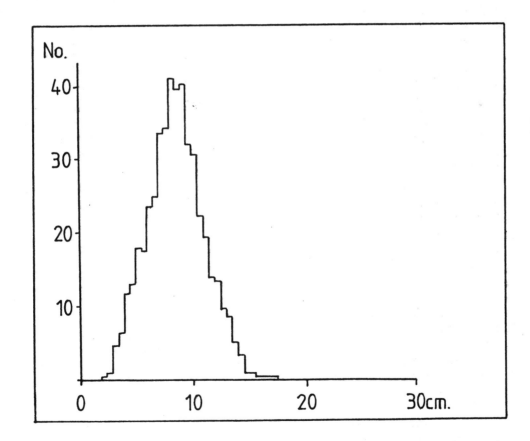

recording all urns in Phase Two. In order to do this it was necessary to record the complete profiles of a number of vessels.

The profiles of a random sample of 100 urns from Spong Hill and 68 from Mucking were fully recorded using a Summagraphics BITPAD ONE digitising tablet linked to a RML 380Z micro-computer.   Suitable drawings of the Elsham urns were not then available for the experiment to be conducted for that site, although given the close correspondence in the size and shape range for Elsham and Spong Hill (see section 3.111) the results could be expected to be very similar.   Profile drawings of the urns were placed on the tablet and the digitising stylus used to follow the outline, recording it as a series of coordinates. The data files were transferred to the ICL mainframe for storage and manipulation by a suite of Pascal programs.

Since the urns were hand-made and are frequently asymmetrical, the drawn profile used was normally a "typical" or idealised one. As an "average" profile was required this was not seen as a major drawback. By rotating each urn in front of a television camera or using digital calipers fully averaged three-dimensional profiles could have been produced.   However, as there is generally more variation between urns than within a single urn a two-dimensional average was considered adequate in this case.   To determine the central axis of the two-dimensional urn profiles the least squares method was used.   If necessary the profiles were then rotated in the two-dimensional plain to align them on the vertical axis. Left and right radii were then averaged to produce the mean radii.

It was decided to consider shape as an independent variable from size, as urns of different size can still have the same shape. Therefore each urn was normalised to a standard height and the radii multiplied by the same scaling factor. The final form of the data was 101 averaged radii spaced at even intervals along the urn profile. These radii were treated as multi-variate data in a similar mannner to the "sliced" method of Wilcock (see Shennan and Wilcock 1975 and Morris and Scarre 1982). The more sophisticated method of comparing profiles by curve fitting (see Main 1981; 1982) was felt to be inappropriate, as the aim was to understand variability in shape, not just to classify the profiles.

Principal Components Analysis

In order to understand the variability between urns Principal Components Analysis, henceforth PCA, (cf. Mather 1976) was employed. The technique takes a large number of correlated variables and extracts a smaller number of composite variables, or components, in such a way that as little as possible of the original variability is lost.   The first component accounts for the most variability, the second the next most, and so on.

The cumulative proportion of the total variance accounted for by the principal components is shown in fig.11. For the 100 Spong Hill urns the first three components accounted for over 93% of the variability between all urns. The first component alone was responsible for 79% of this variability. Examination of the loadings matrix revealed that

Figure 11

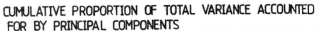

CUMULATIVE PROPORTION OF TOTAL VARIANCE ACCOUNTED
FOR BY PRINCIPAL COMPONENTS

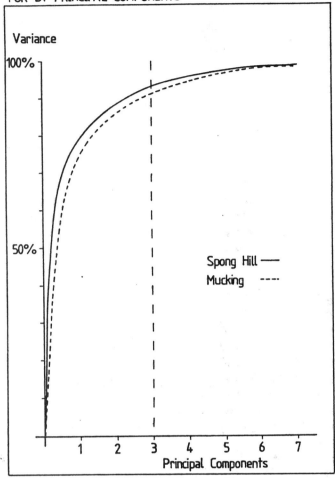

all the variables were more or less equally weighted. Vessels at
opposite ends of the component suggested that it represented the
ratio:

<u>maximum diameter</u>
height

A plot of the principal component scores against the ratio values for
each of the 100 urns confirmed this. Fig.12 shows the almost straight
line which resulted.

The second component accounted for 9% of the variability. It was
increasingly positively loaded towards the middle of the upper half of
each profile, and negatively weighted towards the middle of the lower
half. The best interpretation from examining the scores for
individual urns was that it represented how shouldered the urn was:

<u>height of maximum diameter</u>
height

Figure 12 Plot of 1st PC scores against max.diam./height ratio

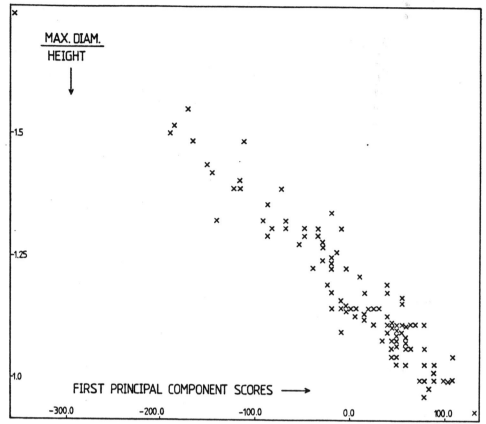

Figure 13 Plot of 2nd PC scores against height of max.diam./height ratio

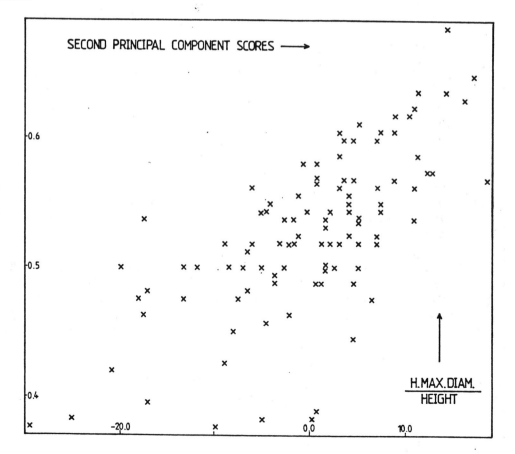

Figure 14 Plot of 3rd PC scores against 'neck' ratio

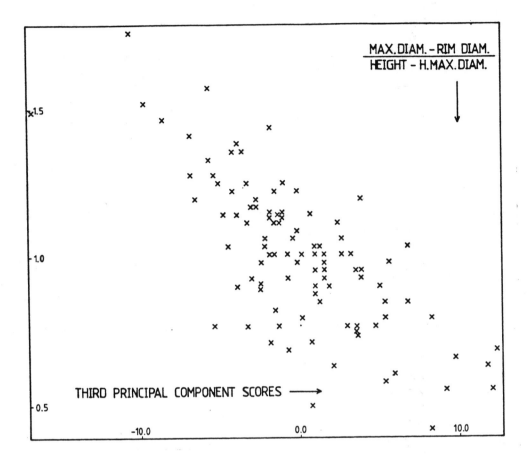

Figure 15 Procedure for removal of vessel width from PC analysis

(1) Calculate mean radius (m)

(2) Calculate difference from
    mean radius for each of
    100 radii (m-r)

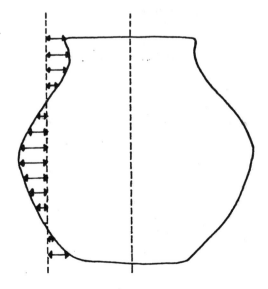

The ratio/principal component score plot (fig.13) again confirmed a linear relationship, although this was not as close as for the first component.

The third component was responsible for 5% of the variability. It was positively weighted for the rim and neck; then negative for most of the rest of the profile. It appeared to correspond to how enclosed the neck was. Several possible ratios were tried, but the best fit to the principal component scores (fig.14) was provided by:

$$\frac{\text{(maximum diameter - rim diameter)}}{\text{(height - height of maximum diameter)}}$$

The remaining 97 components each accounted for significantly less of the variation and were uninterpretable.

In case the large scores for the first component were distorting the subsequent smaller components it was decided to re-run the analyses with width removed. This was achieved by calculating the mean radius for each vessel, and using the difference from the mean for each radius, rather than the raw value (fig.15). However, the nature and relative proportions of the remaining components were the same as before, confirming the original results. An analysis was also conducted using only one variable in five, i.e. twenty radii in all. This also produced identical results.

A separate analysis was performed for the Mucking sample. This contained several urns of apparently different forms. However, the results were remarkably similar (fig.11). The first three components, accounting for 74%, 11% and 5% of the variability respectively, correspond to the same three ratios. This suggests that the results apply to early Anglo-Saxon cremation vessels in general.

Independent support was provided by two intuitively-based studies which had looked at Anglo-Saxon pot shapes. Hills (1976) used:

$$\frac{\text{height of maximum diameter}}{\text{height}}$$

to distinguish between "shouldered", "normal", and "baggy" pots. Fennell (1964), using material from Loveden Hill, had also arrived at the first two ratios and had used a similar value for his third criterion:

$$\frac{\text{rim diameter}}{\text{maximum diameter}}$$

Volume

The volume of Anglo-Saxon urns can rarely be measured by physical means because of the fragile or fragmentary nature of the vessels. However, complete recording of the profiles of 168 urns with a digitising tablet meant that for these urns at least a mathematical estimate of volume could be produced. Each profile was split into a large number of horizontal discs, each with a height of 0.1mm. These discs could then be regarded as cylinders and their volumes were calculated and summed. Of course the digitised profiles were external profiles and so the results had to be adjusted to give the internal capacity. The adjustment factor was calculated by digitising the internal profiles of 15 vessels (a 10% random sample) and noting the difference between internal and external volume. This was found to be a fairly standard error which could be compensated for. Further inaccuracies arose from the asymmetrical nature of the vessels, and the varying thickness of body wall. In order to measure the degree of accuracy of the calculated volumes the real volume of 15 complete and sturdy urns was measured physically using several pounds of wheat grains. The estimated volume was found to differ from the measured volume by an average error of 4.34% of real volume for these 15 vessels. The largest error recorded was 9.88%, for a very asymmetrical vessel, and the smallest was 0.1%.

Other aspects of urn form

Four qualitative attributes of urn form were also recorded. These were the presence or absence of a lid, a pedestal base, and a deliberate hole or holes, and whether the measured urn profile was actual or reconstructed. This latter variable was recorded as a measure of the reliability of the data describing urn form.

The category of urns with deliberate holes included all classes of holed urns, whether or not the hole had later been plugged with lead or a fragment of window glass, as it was felt that these actions each reflected a similar ritual. Where there was simply a hole then it was often difficult to establish whether this was made deliberately at burial, or occurred at a later date. Generally only those holes which had been made from the inside, and so were likely to be deliberate, were included. Sometimes there are two or three deliberate holes in the side and base, and occasionally clusters of holes, as with Newark 12 (Myres Corpus 3278). It has been suggested that at Sancton there is evidence that the urns were damaged and the lead plugs inserted in the ground, as part of some grave-side ritual (Nicholas Reynolds, paper presented to Early Anglo-Saxon Pottery Group, 21/5/83).

A number of speculative interpretations for holed urns have been advanced, including that the purpose was to allow free passage for the spirit of the dead person, or that it was to "kill" the pot, in a similar manner to the deliberate breakage of grave-goods, preventing the urn from being used in an ordinary manner and so dedicating it to the dead[1]. Neither explanation is completely satisfactory as neither explains why the process was only carried out for a minority of urns rather than for all of them.

2.216 Grave-goods

Over half of Anglo-Saxon cremations are accompanied by "grave-goods". These include burnt items, presumably placed with the deceased on the pyre, and unburnt objects, deliberately deposited in the urn. The items recovered may obviously be a small and distorted sample of those originally deposited. Organic material, including textiles, leather, wood, and foodstuffs usually disappear in the burial environment, and in the case of those objects placed on the pyre one must add the extra action of the combustion process. It is sometimes possible to reconstruct what form artefacts may have originally taken on the basis of analogy with the inhumation burials, although caution should be exercised here as cremation is obviously a different rite in at least one important respect, and the requisite grave-goods may also have differed.

Furthermore, there are added difficulties in positively associating grave-goods with individuals for cremation burials. Firstly there is the question of multiple burials, and the problem that in a few cases the ashes and grave-goods of two if not three individuals appear to have been placed in one urn, (see section 1.541). Secondly there is the possibility that where several individuals may have been cremated at one time, or where the site of an inadequately cleared pyre was re-used, then the grave-goods belonging to several rites may become mixed. Myres (1977a, 32) has noted that a Lackford urn (Corpus 853) contained the remains of two brooches, one of which he dates a generation later than the other. Owen (1981, 88), following Myres (1977a, xx), takes this as evidence for the careless gathering of remains by people other than kinsfolk of the deceased. However, it might equally well be the case that one, if not both, of the brooches was an "heirloom". Indeed this seems far more likely than to suppose that a brooch fragment might remain undisturbed on the surface of a pyre for at least thirty years.

It is argued then, that mixing of grave-goods will have occurred on a small enough scale, and in such a random fashion, so as not to have any major effect on correlations between grave-goods and individuals, or grave-goods and urns. With a sufficiently large sample individual mis-associations should cancel each other out. This is supported by the fact that correlations do indeed persist. Therefore the problems of mixing would appear to be more crucial where individual associations are being used for dating purposes, than where whole

NOTE

<1> The use of lead plugs does not tally with the idea that the purpose of the hole was to create an opening, although it does fit in with the explanation that it was to "kill" the pot, as the lead would melt if heating of the vessel was attempted in cooking. The purpose of cremation in many societies is seen as allowing the "spirit" to leave the body, and ascend to the "after-life" on the pall of smoke (James 1928).

cemeteries are being used to study grave-good patterning.

The presence or absence of a series of 45 possible grave-good types was recorded. The categories were largely derived from those used in Hills (1977b) and Hills and Penn (1981), with the addition of a few extra groups not found at Spong Hill. Unusual items found in only one or two urns, such as bells, were not noted as they could not be compared across sites. In Phase Two, frequently occurring items, such as tweezers or shears, were also sub-divided according to whether they were made of bronze or iron. The categorisation and possible significance of each of the grave-good types is discussed below. However, it is dangerous to sex grave-goods conclusively by analogy with inhumation burials. It has already been noted that the two rites are very different, and thus the grave-goods may have been used differently. Even if some overlap could be assumed major problems remain. Very often it transpires that the sex attributed to graves in inhumation reports is based on intuitive assumptions about grave-goods and that there are no skeletal remains. Where skeletal evidence survives associations sometimes appear to run counter-intuitively, such as spears occurring in female graves, and beads and spindlewhorls in male ones. Therefore it is clear that more research must be conducted on inhumation material before it can be used to illuminate the cremation ritual.

Brooches Brooches are most frequently found as burnt bronze fragments, although occasionally complete unburnt specimens are recovered. Only where form or decorative motif makes it clear that a bronze fragment originally came from a brooch has it been classed as such; hence many brooches may have been included in the bronze fragment category. Similarly iron pins and other iron fragments may be the remains of brooches.

Some cremations appear to have contained more than one brooch, but these were not a large enough group to be distinguished as a separate category. Nor was it possible to sub-divide the brooches according to brooch type. Cruciform, penannular, annular, applied, disc, saucer, equal-armed and small-long variants may all be represented in this category.

The difficulty of positively identifying burnt bronze as a brooch may account for the relative rarity of brooches from cremation cemeteries, compared with inhumation burials. In inhumation cemeteries brooches are frequently found in female graves as part of the dress of the deceased. It is generally assumed that those from cremations were also items of dress burnt with the corpse on the funeral pyre.

Toilet sets These consist of tweezers, shears, razors, and occasionally earscoops. They are frequently, but not invariably, found together, sometimes suspended from a ring. Single iron blades, some of which may be broken shears, are also sometimes associated. Most are miniatures, often so small that they can have served no utilitarian purpose, but full-sized examples are also known. Tweezers and earscoops may be of bronze or iron. Shears are usually iron, but bronze miniature replicas are also known. Razors and blades are invariably iron.

Toilet sets are normally unburnt and must have been deliberately placed in an urn with the skeletal remains. Whilst they are amongst the most common grave-goods from cremation cemeteries they are comparatively rare from inhumations, where they appear equally at the belts of men and women. Myres and Green (1973, 111) suggest that they may be taken to indicate male burials. However this appears to be mainly on the basis that they are rarely found with beads which they take to be female. Myres and Green (1973, 110) also note that, at Caistor, toilet sets are associated with urns which they characterise as Anglian. Meaney (1981, 149) argues that whilst some toilet implements may have had a practical function as manicure sets, others must be regarded as amulets. Certainly many are non-utilitarian items. Lethbridge (1951, 12) believes that toilet items were originally placed in an urn to prevent others from using them, because of their magical properties. As the custom grew weaker small dummy or token copies were interred as symbols of the real thing, the original purpose having been forgotten. Shears are later found inscribed on medieval tombstones, where they have been variously interpreted as representing female graves, and burials of clothiers or flock-masters (Butler 1964).

Scrap bronze Fragments of bronze are a common find in Anglo-Saxon cremations, and may be burnt or unburnt. Small unidentifiable globules have been mentioned above as possibly belonging to fused brooches, or other items of bronze jewellery. However, there is also a second category consisting of fragments of sheet bronze, some of which appear to have been broken from or chipped out of a larger piece. Some may come from bronze bowls or cauldrons; others may be remains of binding from wooden buckets, both types being known from inhumation burials. Myres and Green (1973,112) suggest that scrap bronze might possibly have served as a token currency at this period.

A third group of bronze fragments may be identified as fittings, possibly from work boxes or drinking horns.

Other bronze objects A variety of other bronze artefacts are occasionally found in cremations. These include wristclasps, buckles, needles, pins, and girdle hangers. Bronze rings are also known, and while some are toilet set suspension rings, others may be finger rings. The presence of silver rings may also be noted as a separate category.

Other iron objects Various iron objects are found in cremations, although it is more difficult to establish if they have been burnt on the pyre. They include needles, pins, buckles, rings, and fittings, perhaps from belts. Iron nails and rivets are a common find, but most are probably from combs. In addition full size knives and shears, and also arrowheads and spearheads and ferrules are occasionally present. Nevertheless, the range of iron accoutrements accompanying male inhumations is not found in the cremation material. Certainly the main reason for this must simply be that very large blades and shield bosses would not conveniently fit in a cremation urn. However, it is perfectly possible to deposit spear ferrules in an urn, and weapons are sometimes folded and placed on top of urns in continental cemeteries. One would expect to find more in England if the same rite was followed for cremation as inhumation.

Honestones Occasionally honestones are found in cremations, normally of the small variety that might hang from a belt. Simpson (1979) has discussed the connexion between whetstones and Thor, with particular reference to the elaborately decorated whetstone among the ceremonial regalia at Sutton Hoo. Reynolds (1980) has noted the association of a miniature whetstone with an urn from Sancton (A1242) inscribed with a swastika.

Worked flint The occurrence of flints in Anglo-Saxon urns is normally assumed to represent residual prehistoric flints which have fallen in from the surrounding topsoil (Hills 1977b, 27). However it is likely that the properties of flint for use as strike-a-lights (Brown 1977) and even cutting tools was appreciated in the Anglo-Saxon period, and so at least some may be intentional grave-goods (for which some confirmation is given in section 3.32).

Crystal Large facetted crystal beads are found in some cremations. These were probably suspended on necklaces along with glass beads, but Meaney suggests (1981, 78) that they may have been fashioned as spindlewhorls. Nevertheless we know from inhumation burials that some women wore them as necklaces. Crystal is also known from inhumations mounted as curious crystal balls. Meaney (1981, 82) argues that it may have been endowed with magical properties by Anglo-Saxons, although her case rests solely upon its rarity, careful workmanship, and a few contemporary analogies.

Stone spindlewhorls are also found, but these will be discussed with other whorls under bone objects.

Glass Glass is found more often than any other class of grave-good. However, it is nearly always burnt, sometimes making it impossible to distinguish whether it was from beads or a vessel. Therefore three categories are required: unidentifiable glass, glass beads, and glass vessels.

It is frequently impossible to identify how many beads are represented, but there generally appear to be fewer than one finds in an inhumation, perhaps reflecting incomplete collection from the pyre, and the burial of token examples. Occasionally large beads are found, comparable in size to the facetted crystal examples. These are distinguished as a separate category.

Glass which may be positively identified as coming from cone or claw beakers is less common, but many translucent lumps of green or brown glass could be the remains of vessels. In at least two cases, Loveden Hill 1291 and Caistor E19, a complete vessel was buried in an urn.

Combs The most common bone artefacts are combs. A few show clear signs of burning, but most appear unburnt. Most are incomplete and in many cases only a few fragments survive (Hills 1977b, 28). Lethbridge states that all the Lackford combs had been deliberately broken. He

argues that through its association with the hair of a dead person a
comb might be used for sympathetic magic:

> Their inclusion in the urn was clearly magical. They were
> objects so closely associated with the personality of the dead
> individual that no one must be allowed to use them again (1951,
> 12).

Therefore Lethbridge argues that the comb had to be deliberately
"killed". Leach's survey (1958) of the magical nature of hair in many
societies lends this hypothesis some support, although combs also have
other symbolic properties. For example, combs engraved on medieval
tombstones may indicate that the deceased was associated with weaving
and the wool-trade (Butler pers comm).

Many different types of comb are subsumed under this category,
including triangular, semi-circular, double-sided, barred, and also
some miniature examples. Putnam (1981a) notes that at Spong Hill the
barred zoomorphic variety appear to be buried as children's
grave-goods or as female attributes. The association with child
graves appears valid, but the link with females may simply be a
by-product of this, children sometimes being buried with adult
females. In Norwegian contexts of a similar period, combs are found
in graves of all ages and sexes (Sjovold 1974, 179).

Combs are apparently much less common from inhumation cemeteries,
and this cannot simply be ascribed to loss through the action of
acidic soil, as they are still not found where other bone survives.

Playing pieces Small plano-convex counters are sometimes found in
urns, and have been interpreted as gaming pieces. They are usually
burnt, and some have one or more holes bored half way through. Other
gaming pieces may include astragali found in graves. With all types
it was apparently the custom to include either a very few pieces, or a
substantial set in the grave. Playing pieces are also known from
inhumations (Ozanne 1962-3, 37).

Bone beads Where plano-convex bone objects are pierced then they have
been classed as beads. The category also includes pierced round or
rectangular pieces of bone.

Bone fittings Occasionally decorated bone strips are found which
appear to be the remains of casket fittings, rather than ornamented
combs.

Spindlewhorls Spindlewhorls of bone, antler or ivory are a common find
from cremations and inhumations, although some may have served as
beads. Examples of pottery, sandstone, chalk, and even lead are also
known, and have been included in this general category.

Ivory rings Fragments of ivory from larger circular rings appear to
form a distinct category of cremation grave-good. Such rings have
been interpreted as bag handles by Myres and Green (1973, 100-3).

Other objects Four other classes of grave-good were distinguished.

The first are cowrie shells, which are known from cremation and inhumation burials. The second class, namely fragments of what is thought to be coral, has only been identified at Elsham so far, but may have been present on many more sites. Thirdly, potsherds are quite a common find from cremations. These may frequently be residual sherds which have entered the urn whilst it was in the ground, but some may be functionally equivalent to inhumation accessory vessels, and in at least two cases (Spong Hill 2022 and Worthy Park) a complete vessel was placed inside a cremation urn. Alternatively, some sherds, especially of fine Roman wares, may possibly have been included as talismans. The fourth category of find, Roman coins, may have played a similar role, and they are frequently pierced for suspension from a necklace (Meaney 1981, 213-22).

2.217 Skeletal groupings

For some of the more recently excavated cemeteries a certain amount of skeletal information was available about the burials, but few skeletal remains of the Phase One sample had been studied at the time of research. Nevertheless, the coding system which was devised will be discussed here, although it was used more extensively in Phase Two.

The difficulties of analysing cremated bone have been discussed by Wells (1960) and Wilkinson (1980). Wilkinson reports deliberate fragmentation of cremated remains, as well as the effects of combustion and prolonged burial. He notes that because of the tendency of indeterminate fragments to be small there is a danger that they are counted as female traits, which might explain the apparent bias towards females at some cemeteries, such as Sancton and Spong Hill.

Wells (1960, 32) wrote that it is unlikely that more than 30% of cremations may be readily sexed. It is apparent that where sexing is given it must be treated as a probable rather than a positive identification. Nevertheless, in a study of 27 individuals from Loveden Hill sexed by skeletal material, Wilkinson found that in 23 cases the sexing concurred with the analysis based on grave-goods. Wells (1960, 31) also reports that:

> anatomical sexing agrees tolerably well with sexing based on the nature of the grave goods.

There are similar difficulties with age determination, and here there may be a tendency for children and infants to be over-represented, because of the comparative ease with which they can be picked out.

Nevertheless the recording of as much skeletal data as possible was essential for the present study, both as a check on the grave-goods, and as a means of interpreting what grave-good correlations meant.

The number of individuals per urn was recorded, and where possible the sex and age of each was noted. Seven age groupings were used, principally following Wells (1960):

Neonate			Young adult	18-25 years
Infant	1-2	years	Mature adult	26-35 years
Child	3-11	years	Old adult	36+ years
Adolescent	12-17	years		

A general category of "Adult" was also used where closer determination had not been possible. The code used indicated whether the identification was highly likely (90% probability), likely (75%+ probability), or just possible (50%+ probability).

Unfortunately further problems were presented because no two workers who had aged bones had used the same groupings. For example, whereas at Elsham, Harman had distinguished between infants, children, adolescents, young adults, and middle-aged individuals; Manchester, working on material from Sancton, had only identified children (aged up to 15) at the younger end of the age scale, but had distinguished between young, mature, and old adults at the top end. In order to enable comparisons to be made between sites a table of equivalent categories had to be drawn up (table 2), and this indicates how each classification was coded. However one should be aware that these may really be sliding scales, and one suspects, for example, that Harman's "adolescent" may well be equivalent to Manchester's "young adult".

The presence of a variety of animal bones, which had been deposited in the cremations, was also noted. Such remains are likely to represent deliberate burial offerings.

Table 2 Concordance list for classification of skeletal remains

CEMETERIES AND BONE SPECIALISTS

AGE	CODING	Caistor Markshall (C.Wells)	Illington Loveden Hill (C.Wells)	Elsham Newark (M.Harman)	Mucking	Sancton Baston (K.Manchester)	Spong Hill (G.Putnam)
	NEONATE		Neonate (Loveden)				Neonate
1-2	INFANT	Infant	Infant	Infant	Infant I Infant II	Infant (Baston)	Infant I Infant II
2-11	CHILD	Child	Child	Child	Child	Child (up to 15)	Child
12-17	ADOLESCENT		Adolescent	Adolescent	Juvenile		Adolescent
18-25	YOUNG ADULT		Young adult	Young adult		Young adult (20-30)	
26-35	MATURE ADULT		Full adult (Illington)	Aging/ middle-aged		Mature adult (30-50)	
36+	OLD ADULT		Middle-aged			Old adult (50+)	
	ADULT	Adult	Adult	Adult	Adult	Adult	Adult

2.22 Phase Two

In Phase Two a smaller number of variables was recorded for a larger number of sites, enabling the use of published reports rather than primary material. The variables recorded were those which had been identified in Phase One as being significant, in terms of exhibiting correlations with the skeletal material and grave-goods. In most cases these corresponded to the presence or absence of individual motifs, rather than the number of motifs, or the number of lines making up a motif. In addition a few variables which had not displayed any significant correlations but which were easily measured were also recorded, in case these might exhibit correlations with the larger Phase Two sample.

The variables which were recorded are listed in full in Appendix G, and are discussed in sections 2.222 - 2.225. Firstly the method of data capture will be described.

2.221 Data capture

The most convenient means of recording the Phase Two data was found to be writing it directly onto standard 80-character coding sheets. Each record, or individual cremation, occupied four lines on a coding sheet. The sheets were then punched and verified by professional data processing staff and the data fed into an ICL 2966 mainframe computer. Existing Phase One records were converted into Phase Two format using the data management facilities of SPSS. The complete Phase Two data bank, consisting of 2440 records, occupied approximately 1 Mb of storage.

2.222 Decoration

The decorative motifs recorded in Phase Two were:

    Incised decoration
    Number of horizontal fields
    Number of lines in each horizontal field
    Vertical
    Continuous chevron
    Discontinuous chevron
    Upright chevron
    Reversed chevron
    Diagonals sloping to left
    Diagonals sloping to right
    Continuous curvilinear
    Hanging arch
    Standing arch
    Circle
    Slashes
    Dots
    Swastikas
    Crosses
    Cross on base

      Plastic decoration
      Number of vertical bosses
      Number of round bosses
      Cordons
      Number of different stamp dies

Having identified the stamp dies which might be encountered in Phase One it was now possible to record stamp types in terms of the presence or absence of 96 possible stamp dies. The full list is given in Appendix G.

2.223 Form

The PCA conducted in Phase One had identified three ratios which described most variation in urn shape. These ratios required four measurements:

      Height
      Maximum diameter
      Height of maximum diameter
      Rim diameter

Additionally, whether the urn profile was reconstructed, and whether it had a lid, or a deliberate hole, was recorded.

2.224 Grave-goods

The same set of forty-five possible grave-goods as had been recorded in Phase One was retained in Phase Two.

In addition, in order to maximise the information provided by the grave-good data, it was decided to combine co-occurring grave-goods into clusters, which may be termed "social identity" groupings. This reduced the number of variables, and meant that where an individual grave-good was missing, perhaps due to preservation or recovery factors, the urn would nevertheless be counted if the other requisite grave-goods were present, hopefully increasing the strength of any correlations. It seemed intuitively reasonable to combine grave-goods in this way as it is unlikely that each of the possible 45 grave-goods represented separately defined social classes. Rather it is probable that several grave-goods were used to indicate a particular identity group. There is frequently a certain amount of redundant signification in mortuary ritual (see section 1.54). Several facets of the ritual each reflect the same dimension of the social persona of the deceased. Similarly several grave-goods may be used to express the same aspects of the identity of the deceased. Many may also have been substitutes for each other. Others may simply have been chance inclusions and may not have indicated anything.

In these circumstances the most appropriate statistical technique again appeared to be Principal Components Analysis (see section 2.215). Applying PCA to the grave-good data produced components consisting of grave-goods which commonly occur together in urns. PCA is particularly appropriate to the analysis of social dimensions of mortuary practices (cf. Van de Velde 1979). Society is essentially multi-dimensional. An individual may fulfil several roles at once. Among the dimensions of the social identity which may be recognised in mortuary practices are age, sex, rank, and group affiliation (cf. Binford 1971). Various attributes of the burial may be used to represent different dimensions.

It has already been noted that some urns may contain multiple burials. The grave-good lists for any single urn may therefore include objects associated with several individuals. However this should not invalidate the use of PCA. Assuming that the same sets of items would be included for an individual placed in a multiple burial and an individual buried alone, then PCA permits the grave-goods belonging to each individual to be separated. Suppose, for instance, that a particular group of females were regularly buried with beads and brooches, and a particular group of children with miniatures. As long as they occurred frequently enough on their own then these would be identified as independent components. Where they occur together in a burial of female and child, then that urn would be scored on both components.

PCA was applied to the correlation matrix for presence/absence (P/A) data for all those urns from the Phase Two sample with grave-goods, comprising 1170 urns in total. Applying the analysis to P/A data had the disadvantage that each variable was treated as of equal importance. For example, the absence of a grave-good that occurred in only ten urns would be given the same weight as the absence of one that occurred in one hundred. However, if the variables were weighted according to how common they were it was found that the most common grave-goods (such as the 337 urns containing glass beads) swamped all the other variation. Instead, the rare grave-goods were therefore excluded and the analysis conducted on P/A data for items that occurred in at least ten urns.

The loadings matrix for the first three components, with the proportion of total variance accounted for, is given in table 3. The three components account for 15% of the total variance, which is rather low, but is a consequence of using P/A data and including several uncommon grave-goods. The choice of three components is arbitrary, corresponding to a cut-off point of an eigenvalue of about 1.4, but beyond this the components apparently become uninterpretable. The interpretation of the components rests upon their "loadings", or how much of each original variable they are made up of. For each component, those grave-goods which form a significant part of it (with a loading greater than 0.3) have been taken into account. It should be noted that positive and negative loadings should be given equal significance. The component may be regarded as an axis, or a balance arm, on which various grave-goods are positioned. The loading indicates the place of each grave-good. Some are positively loaded and are on one side of the central pivot; others are negative and so are on the opposite side. The greater the loading the nearer to the ends of the balance the grave-goods are placed. Some may be clustered at one end, indicating a group of urns in which they regularly co-occur, but these may be balanced by another grouping of grave-goods

Table 3 Grave-goods Principal Components Analysis
         Phase Two sample - the 1170 urns containing grave-goods

	1	2	3
Eigenvalue	2.3248	1.4282	1.3925
Cumulative proportion of total variance	0.0681	0.1104	0.1513
Bone bead	-0.0749	0.0848	0.0210
Bone fitting	0.0428	-0.1968	-0.2627
Bone ring	0.0786	-0.1914	-0.1213
Bronze fitting	-0.0055	0.0205	0.1187
Bronze fragment	0.2131	-0.4042	-0.1317
Bronze ring	-0.0012	0.0671	0.0542
Bronze sheet	0.0624	0.0736	-0.0054
Brooch	0.1856	-0.1161	0.2621
Buckle	-0.0101	0.1877	-0.1910
Comb	-0.1040	-0.0252	-0.0025
Crystal	0.1829	-0.3605	0.0267
Glass	0.1060	-0.3337	-0.5788
Glass bead	0.3567	-0.0919	0.5660
Glass vessel	0.0366	0.3054	0.1501
Iron fitting	-0.0210	0.0201	0.1424
Iron fragment	-0.1039	-0.0097	0.0192
Iron knife	-0.0858	0.0984	-0.2732
Iron nail	-0.0246	0.1302	-0.2438
Iron ring	-0.1994	-0.2149	0.2502
Iron rivet	-0.1193	0.2178	0.0698
Ivory	0.2997	-0.3233	0.1401
Large bead	0.0025	-0.0272	-0.0911
Miniature bronze tweezers	-0.1554	0.1993	-0.3033
Miniature iron blade	-0.6697	-0.2510	0.1375
Miniature iron shears	-0.8143	-0.1937	0.0595
Miniature iron tweezers	-0.7252	-0.2004	0.1567
Needle	0.0174	-0.1885	0.1595
Pin	0.1228	-0.2521	0.0007
Playing piece	-0.0771	0.2556	0.0472
Potsherd	0.1185	0.0772	0.2328
Razor	-0.3815	-0.0776	-0.0621
Spindlewhorl	0.1677	-0.4052	-0.0617
Worked flint	-0.0554	0.1798	-0.0012
Wristclasp	0.0805	-0.0081	0.1072

on the other end of the arm which rarely occur in conjunction with them. The first component, for example, defines one group of urns containing glass beads and ivory and marked by the absence of miniature shears, tweezers, blades or razors. Further principal components may also be identified. These are orthogonal, that is, variation due to prior components has been removed. PC2 appears to distinguish urns with glass vessels and without iron, bronze, crystal, spindlewhorls or pins. PC3 defines urns with glass beads (other than in PC1), brooches and iron rings, and without other iron, bone, and unidentified glass.

Individual PCA were conducted for each of the six sites where sample size and level of grave-good recording were sufficient to warrant it, namely Caistor-by-Norwich, Elsham, Loveden Hill, Newark, Sancton, and Spong Hill. With the exceptions noted below, the first component was identical to that for the Phase Two sample as a whole, with toilet sets loaded at above 0.3 in one direction, and glass beads and ivory in the opposite direction. At Elsham glass beads were not significantly loaded on the first component, although the "unidentified glass" variable was highly loaded, reflecting the cautious identification of beads at that site. Iron tweezers were not loaded as strongly as elsewhere, but were still above 0.25. Similarly, at Caistor, ivory was only loaded at above the 0.25 level, and was not significant at all in making up the first component at Sancton, where it was a comparatively rare grave-good, found in only four urns in the sample. Otherwise all the sites exhibited a remarkable conformity in the co-occurrence of the grave-goods identified by the first component (table 4).

For the subsequent components, however, no other groupings were found which were common to all sites, or even to more than two sites of the six analysed. This may be partially explained by regional variation in the grave-goods deposited, but must also be attributed to discrepancies in the recognition and categorisation of grave-goods between sites. The PCA method was unfortunately sensitive to this because of the importance given to infrequently occurring grave-goods. One way to proceed would have been to produce individual groupings for each site, and indeed this was done for Elsham and Spong Hill (Richards 1984). However, it was felt that this was too cumbersome to undertake for every Phase Two site and would render intra-site comparison impossible. On the other hand it would have been inappropriate to use those groupings produced by analysis of the combined Phase Two sample as variables in the examination of individual sites where they might have no meaning. Therefore it was ultimately decided to use only those artefacts, defined by the first component, which were common to all sites. The first identity grouping, therefore, is defined by the presence of one or more of the following items: miniature iron tweezers, miniature iron shears, miniature iron blade(s), razor, miniature bronze tweezers, miniature bronze shears. It is henceforth known as GROUP ONE, and consists of 252 urns from the Phase Two sample. The second group is defined by the presence of either glass beads or ivory, and is termed GROUP TWO. It incorporates 404 urns of the Phase Two sample. In addition 1270 of the Phase Two urns did not contain any grave-goods. Under the model followed here, these urns may represent a social group or groups whom

Table 4   Grave-goods Principal Components Analysis
          Loadings matrix for first three components for six sites

```
+ Positive loading > 0.25      C  Caistor         N  Newark
- Negative loading > 0.25      E  Elsham          S  Sancton
                               L  Loveden Hill    SH Spong Hill
```

	First component						Second component						Third component					
	C	E	L	N	S	SH	C	E	L	N	S	SH	C	E	L	N	S	SH
Bone fitting				+				−		+	−						−	+
Bone ring								+	+					−				
Bronze fitting																+		
Bronze fragment		−	+				+		+				+				+	
Bronze ring											+							+
Bronze sheet		−					−		−	−		+	−		+			
Brooch	+				+		+	−	+			+	+				−	
Buckle									−	+						+		
Comb			+				−				+	+	+					
Crystal	−							+										
Glass	−	−								−	−				+		+	
Glass bead	+	+	−	−	+		+	+					+		−	−	−	
Glass vessel		+									−							+
Iron fitting							+											
Iron fragment				−	−								+	−	+	−	−	
Iron knife			+					+			+	+	−		+	+		
Iron nail													−					
Iron ring							+		+			+						
Iron rivet							−		−				+		+	−	−	
Ivory	+	−	+	−		+	+	+										
Large bead																		−
Miniature bronze tweezers		+	+	+					+							−		
Miniature iron blade	−	+	−	+	+	−	+			−			+			−	−	
Miniature iron shears	−	+	−	+	−		+						+			−		
Miniature iron tweezers	−	+	−	+	−											+		
Needle											+							
Pin		+					+										+	
Playing piece																		+
Potsherd							−											
Razor			−															
Spindlewhorl	−								+	−	+					+		
Worked flint							−								−			−
Wristclasp																	−	

it was considered should not be, or could not be, buried with personal items or accessories. Although several classes of person may have fulfilled this role, as there is no way of distinguishing between them on the basis of grave-goods, all these urns were treated as a further identity grouping, henceforth termed GROUP ZERO.

The correlations with urn form, decoration, and skeletal attributes exhibited by each of these identity groupings will be discussed in Chapter 3. Meanwhile it might be asked why the skeletal data was not incorporated in the PCA in order that co-occurring grave-goods might be linked with skeletal attributes. In fact such analyses were conducted, but did not yield significant results since the number of urns with skeletal identifications was invariably too small.

CHAPTER 3

RESULTS

In order to provide a coherent account of the results of the research,
each aspect will be considered in a logical order, rather than in the
order of discovery. Hence the results from Phase One and Phase Two
are conflated in this section. The total research sample will be
discussed in section 3.1, and comparisons will be made between sites.
The significance of particular aspects of the cremations will then be
analysed in subsequent sections. Grave-goods will be examined in
section 3.2, pottery form in section 3.3, and finally, pottery
decoration in section 3.4.

3.1 Inter-site comparison

Ten sites, each with more than 50 urns, were identified in section
2.2. These samples were considered to be large enough to allow valid
inter-site comparisons to be made, for pottery, grave-goods, and
skeletal remains.

3.11 Comparison of pottery assemblages

The characteristics of the total pottery sample are summarised in
table 5. This reveals that almost 80% of Anglo-Saxon cremation urns
are decorated, 75% have some form of incised decoration, 40% have
stamped decoration, and 30% have plastic decoration. It is clear,
therefore, that the majority of cremation vessels are decorated, in
contrast to the settlement pottery (cf. 2.112). If anything, the
figure of 80% may be an underestimate. Since the study demanded
completely reconstructible vessels, the proportion of decorated
vessels may be slightly underestimated. It is more difficult to
deduce what the original vessel was like for urns with complicated
decoration than it is for plain urns. Therefore more fragmentary
decorated than plain vessels had to be excluded from the sample.

3.111 Vessel form

The average height of vessels at each site is compared in table 6.
The standard deviation represents the spread about the mean. It is
immediately clear that all the averages are very tightly clustered

Table 5 Characteristics of sample

	No	%
Lid	33	1.4
Deliberate hole	112	4.6
Decoration	1886	77.3
Incised decoration	1805	74.0
Horizontal	1781	73.0
Vertical	761	31.2
Continuous chevron	571	23.4
Discontinuous chevron	41	1.7
Upright chevron	121	5.0
Reversed chevron	117	4.8
Diagonals sloping to the left	164	6.7
Diagonals sloping to the right	125	5.1
Continuous curvilinear	32	1.3
Hanging arch	133	5.5
Standing arch	164	6.7
Circle	22	0.9
Slashes	246	10.1
Dots	316	13.0
Swastikas	28	1.2
Crosses	71	2.9
Cross on base	8	0.3
Plastic decoration	741	30.4
Vertical bosses	573	23.5
Round bosses	142	5.8
Cordons	137	5.6
Stamped decoration	930	38.1
Grave-goods	1170	48.0

Table 6 Mean urn heights

Site name	Mean height (cm)	Standard deviation
Abingdon	18.67	4.48
Baston	21.0	4.38
Caistor-by-Norwich	19.09	3.88
Elsham	19.87	3.82
Illington	18.71	3.91
Lackford	19.17	4.18
Longthorpe	17.71	3.43
Loveden Hill	20.02	4.2
Markshall	18.86	3.97
Mucking	18.44	3.89
Newark	19.93	4.6
Sancton	20.12	4.19
Snape	19.7	3.07
South Elkington	21.13	4.11
Spong Hill	19.57	3.98
Worthy Park	15.02	3.29
York - Heworth	19.94	4.5
York - The Mount	18.38	4.02
TOTAL	19.56	4.12

Table 7 Mean values for shape ratios

	Width Mean	S.D.	Shoulder Mean	S.D.	Neck Mean	S.D.
Caistor	1.202	1.69	1.068	1.37	0.915	3.28
Elsham	1.132	1.51	1.031	1.38	0.946	3.81
Illington	1.131	1.51	1.070	1.49	0.829	3.02
Lackford	1.147	1.51	1.012	1.43	0.895	3.22
Lovedon Hill	1.125	1.41	1.001	1.42	0.886	3.24
Mucking	1.101	1.50	1.121	1.92	0.792	3.98
Newark	1.177	1.65	1.014	1.36	1.054	2.96
Sancton	1.144	1.44	1.035	1.26	0.911	2.87
S.Elkington	1.141	1.56	1.022	1.12	0.946	2.64
Spong Hill	1.188	1.53	1.054	1.13	0.979	3.32

Figure 16 Relationship of height and diameter for sites with more than thirty vessels

1	Abingdon	7	Loveden
2	Caistor	8	Mucking
3	Elsham	9	Newark
4	Heworth	10	Sancton
5	Illington	11	South Elkington
6	Lackford	12	Spong Hill

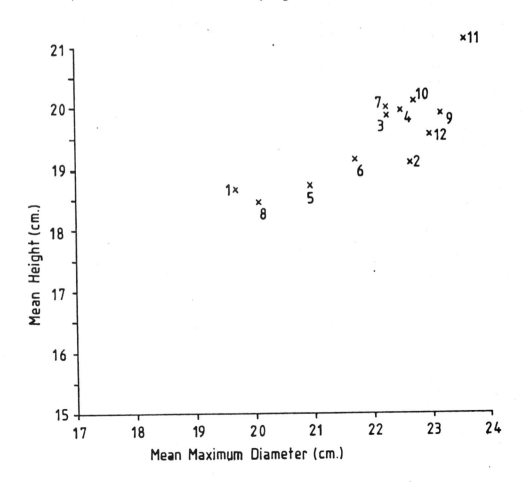

about 19.5cm. For sites with more than fifty urns, there is only a 2.7cm difference between the largest and smallest mean. This represents a rather high level of consistency in the production of urns. There are no functional reasons why funerary urns should be made to this height. Instances are known of cremation vessels as short as 8cm high, or as tall as 28cm. Therefore we must conclude that Anglo-Saxon potters were generally working to an ideal mental template or cultural type, and that this type was recognised throughout Anglo-Saxon England, emphasising the common derivation of all Anglo-Saxon pottery. Of the eighteen sites, only Abingdon, Mucking, and Worthy Park are in what is traditionally regarded as a Saxon rather than Anglian area of settlement (see Myres 1970). As these only amount to a total of 135 urns, it is not really valid to compare "Anglian" against "Saxon" pottery. However, it may be significant that at each of these sites the mean height for the site is lower than the mean for the total sample. Perhaps this may indicate a difference developing between Saxon and Anglian potter's templates, with the Saxon potters favouring shorter vessels. Interestingly, Illington is also low (fig.16), maybe indicating links with the Saxon rather than the Anglian area.

Table 7 gives mean figures for those ratios which the PCA identified as describing the vessel shape most completely (see section 2.215), for the ten sites with more than fifty vessels. It is again clear that there is generally a tight correspondence between each site. However, the one "Saxon" site included, Mucking, is again different, having the lowest mean width ratio, and highest mean shoulder and neck ratios. The values for the standard deviations indicate how much variation there is within urns from the individual sites. They show that there is more variation in the degree to which the neck is restricted than there is in other features. It is also interesting to compare standard deviations for specific sites. At Spong Hill and Elsham, for example, there is little variation in the height of the maximum diameter (as shown in the shoulder ratio), whereas at Mucking there is the greatest variation.

In addition to measuring basic dimensions, it was possible to calculate a fairly accurate volume for the 100 vessels from Spong Hill and 68 from Mucking which had been digitised. The bar charts in fig.17 demonstrate the range of volumes of vessels at these two sites. At Spong Hill the mean volume was found to be 4430cc; at Mucking it was 2557cc. The figure for Spong Hill is likely to be more typical of Anglo-Saxon pottery in general.

Table 8 compares other aspects of urn form, including the proportion of vessels at each site which had been deliberately holed, and the proportion of vessels with lids.

The number of deliberately holed vessels is consistently low at each site, and is generally below 5% of the total, except at Elsham and Spong Hill, where almost 10% of vessels were holed. Since these latter two sites are the most recently excavated and the urns were carefully scrutinised to detect any intentional holes, this suggests that the number of deliberate holes at the other sites might also be increased if the vessels were given similar attention. Nevertheless,

Table 8 Percentage of aspects of urn form

	Caistr	Elsham	Illgtn	Lckfrd	Lovedn	Muckng	Newark	Sanctn	S.Elkn	Spong
Deliberate holes	4.0	7.3	2.1	1.7	1.2	1.3	1.4	1.2	1.1	10.1
Lids	0.4	0.5	-	0.7	-	-	1.4	-	-	3.7

Table 9 Percentage of classes of incised decoration

	Caistr	Elsham	Illgtn	Lckfrd	Lovedn	Muckng	Newark	Sanctn	S.Elkn	Spong
Decoration	78.9	86.3	73.4	82.9	77.3	37.7	81.0	78.2	81.3	77.9
Incised decoration	73.6	82.9	71.3	78.0	72.9	28.6	78.2	77.0	79.1	76.0
Horizontal	72.7	82.0	71.3	76.2	71.7	28.6	77.5	76.1	79.1	74.5
Vertical	43.2	35.1	7.4	31.8	35.9	14.3	38.0	26.7	36.3	30.1
Continuous chevron	18.1	26.0	21.3	25.5	24.3	9.1	27.5	27.6	23.1	22.5
Broken chevron	0.9	1.5	-	3.1	-	1.3	1.4	4.1	3.3	1.2
Upright chevron	5.3	4.4	3.2	7.7	5.2	-	1.4	4.9	11.0	4.3
Reversed chevron	3.1	3.9	1.1	3.1	6.4	1.3	4.2	7.8	8.8	5.3
Diagonals sloping to left	9.3	8.8	2.1	3.8	8.4	1.3	3.5	9.1	15.4	5.6
Diagonals sloping to right	7.9	3.9	2.1	1.0	6.4	-	3.5	6.2	12.1	4.7
Continuous curvilinear	1.3	2.4	1.1	1.0	-	1.3	2.1	2.9	1.1	1.0
Hanging arch	3.1	2.9	18.1	7.3	2.0	-	4.9	6.6	4.4	7.1
Standing arch	6.2	7.8	1.1	4.5	6.4	3.9	6.3	4.9	12.1	8.3
Circle	0.4	1.0	-	1.4	1.6	2.6	0.7	0.4	1.1	0.6
Slashes	11.0	11.2	6.4	13.3	8.8	7.8	8.5	9.5	11.0	10.1
Dots	15.0	9.8	2.1	12.6	9.6	10.4	12.0	9.9	20.9	16.7
Swastikas	1.3	2.9	1.1	0.7	0.4	1.3	-	4.1	-	0.4
Crosses	5.3	5.9	1.1	1.0	2.0	1.3	3.5	2.5	2.2	3.4
Cross on base	-	-	2.1	-	0.8	-	1.4	0.4	-	-

Figure 17 Mucking and Spong Hill: comparison of urn volumes

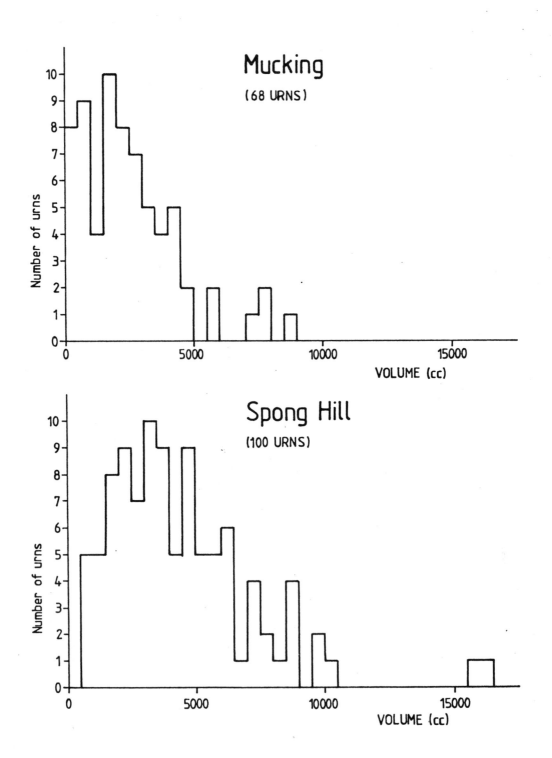

the number of vessels receiving this special treatment is still a small proportion of the total population. Whatever the interpretation of this ritual, the fact that it was only carried out for a minority of vessels must indicate that it was only considered appropriate for a minority of the population.

The number of vessels with lids is similarly low, although it should be remembered that all urns probably had lids originally, but most were of leather or textile and decayed in the ground. The differential survival of pottery lids between sites may well be a function of the amount of disturbance, particularly plough damage.

3.112 Incised and impressed decoration

Table 9 compares proportions of various classes of incised decoration for each of the 10 major sites. The most remarkable feature is the high level of consistency in the classes used at each site, indicating tightly defined cultural ideas of pottery style.

With the exception of Mucking (where the proportion of vessels with all classes of incised decoration simply reflects the low number of vessels with any type of decoration) all sites have c.75% of urns with incised or impressed decoration.

The percentage of vessels with horizontal incised lines is virtually the same, indicating that where incised decoration is used then it is normal to include a band of horizontal lines, usually around the neck[1].

There is more variation in the percentage of urns with vertical incised lines, and Illington stands out with relatively few examples. Since the use of vertical lines is generally seen as developing as

NOTE

[1] When the actual number of lines used at each site was compared, then a few significant differences were found. The number of bands of lines at each site was compared with the distribution for the total sample, and the Kolmogrov-Smirnov test was used to test the significance of any differences. At Caistor, it was found that there was a tendency for urns to have less than two bands, (significant at 0.01), whilst at Illington and Lackford there was a tendency for vessels to have more than two bands (significant at 0.01 and 0.05 respectively). It is likely that this reflects the preferred style of the Illington-Lackford potter (for alternate bands of lines and stamps) and therefore the large number of vessels of this style in the Illington and Lackford samples. The variation between sites appears to be related to potters' style, not to ethnic or regional variation.

part of an Anglian style of decoration, this supports the case for a strong Saxon element at Illington, as suggested above. This does not explain why Sancton should also have a relatively low small proportion of vessels with vertical incised decoration.

The percentage of vessels with a continuous chevron design is relatively constant at all sites, ranging between 18.1% at Caistor, and 27.6% at Sancton. In the case of individual upright and reversed chevrons, South Elkington stands out with a higher proportion of each than any other site. Caistor, Elsham, Illington, Lackford and South Elkington have more upright than reversed chevrons. At Loveden Hill, Mucking, Newark, Sancton and Spong Hill, the picture is reversed.

Similarly, for the proportion of vessels with single groups of lines sloping to left and right, South Elkington is well above the other sites. All the sites, except for Illington and Newark where the proportions are the same, have more groups of lines sloping downwards to the left than sloping to the right. When one considers the action of incising such lines, this may be taken as evidence of a preponderance of right-handedness amongst potters, it being easier to work from top right to bottom left than top left to bottom right with a tool held in the right hand.

There is wider variation in the numbers of hanging arches, and of standing arches. Again Illington and South Elkington are unusual, with far more hanging arches at Illington, and more standing arches at South Elkington. The other sites have relatively similar proportions, averaging 5%.

Illington also stands out when percentages of vessels with slashes, and those with dots, are compared. It has the lowest proportion of each, whereas South Elkington has the highest proportion of dots. The other sites average c.10% of each class, although it should be noted that relative to the number of pots decorated Mucking scores the highest of all sites for slashes and dots.

In conclusion, whilst the individual differences between sites are of interest, the overall impression is one of a high degree of conformity between sites.

3.113 Plastic decoration

This impression is confirmed when we compare proportions of vessels with plastic decoration (table 10). There is a spread of percentages ranging from Illington with only 12.8% of vessels with plastic decoration, to Newark with 43%, but most sites have c.30% vessels with plastic decoration. Despite the low number of pots with any decoration, Mucking is not the lowest, indicating the relative popularity of plastic decoration at this site. Vertical bosses, as the most common form of plastic decoration, follow a similar distribution, but round bosses and cordons are more evenly represented on each site. Relative to its amount of plastic decoration Mucking has by far the greatest number of vessels with round bosses.

Table 10   Percentage of classes of plastic decoration at 10 main sites

	Caistr	Elsham	Illgtn	Lckfrd	Lovedn	Muckng	Newark	Sanctn	S.Elkn	Spong
Plastic decoration	31.3	26.8	12.8	34.3	35.1	20.8	43.0	25.5	28.6	31.3
Vertical bosses	23.3	19.5	8.5	29.0	29.1	14.3	37.3	21.4	19.8	23.0
Round bosses	4.4	3.9	2.1	7.3	3.6	6.5	5.6	6.6	4.4	7.0
Cordons	5.7	4.4	4.3	6.3	5.6	2.6	4.2	2.9	6.6	7.3

Table 11   Proportion of vessels with odd or even number of bosses

	ODD		EVEN	
	No	%	No	%
Caistor	18	30.5	41	69.5
Elsham	14	32.6	29	67.4
Illington	4	40.0	6	60.0
Lackford	39	44.8	48	55.2
Loveden Hill	16	21.6	58	78.4
Mucking	8	61.5	5	38.5
Newark	18	32.7	37	67.3
Sancton	14	25.5	41	74.5
South Elkington	9	52.9	8	47.1
Spong Hill	71	41.5	100	58.5
TOTAL	219	35.7	395	64.3

Table 12   Percentages of stamped decoration at 10 major sites

	Caistr	Elsham	Illgtn	Lckfrd	Lovedn	Muckng	Newark	Sanctn	S.Elkn	Spong
Stamped decoration	26.0	41.0	59.6	49.0	41.0	11.7	41.5	32.5	34.1	39.1

The number of bosses per urn at each site should also be compared. The average number of each type of boss per vessel at each site was compared against the average number of each type of boss per vessel for the total Phase Two sample. With the exception of Caistor and Sancton, it was found that there was no significant difference between sites. At Caistor and Sancton the proportions of round and vertical bosses were both different to the total sample at the 0.01 level.

Finally, table 11 compares the proportion of vessels which have an even number of bosses with the proportion which have an odd number, for the ten major sites in the sample. With the exception of Mucking, which has about two-thirds of vessels with an odd number of bosses to one third with an even number, and Elkington which has about half of each, every site has significantly more vessels with an even number of bosses. This, surely, must be a reflection of the mind of the Anglo-Saxon potter, and a preference for evenness and symmetry?

3.114 Stamped decoration

When we examine the percentage of vessels at each site with stamped decoration (table 12) we do not observe such a regular distribution as for incised and plastic decoration. The range is from Mucking, with only 11.7% of vessels with stamped decoration, to Illington, with nearly 60%. Clearly, the unpopularity of incised and plastic decoration at Illington is made up for by the increased use of stamping, and Illington can be clearly distinguished from Mucking on these grounds. Although most of the other sites cluster around the 40% level, Caistor is also unusual with only 26% stamped decoration. One obvious conclusion from this wide variation is that the use of stamping is not so narrowly dictated within Anglo-Saxon culture as a whole, and that there is greater potential for using it to mark regional differentiation. The fact that stamping only becomes widely used on pots in Anglo-Saxon England would support this interpretation as cultural controls would be less well developed than for traditional styles of decoration for which there are closer continental parallels.

Within those vessels with stamped decoration there is also considerable variation in the degree to which different dies may be used on the same pot. Vessels range from those where a single stamp is used, to those where six or more different designs are used in combination to produce an elaborate stamped effect. Fig.18 presents a cumulative frequency curve for the number of different stamp dies used on one urn for all stamped vessels in the total sample. It can be seen that there is a steady fall-off, with most vessels with just one die, the next most with two dies, and so on. Table 13 compares the distributions for each of the major sites with that for the total sample. The Kolmogorov-Smirnov test was used to test if individual distributions were significantly different. It revealed that Elsham was significantly different at the 0.15 level (with a higher proportion of vessels with just one stamp die), and Illington was significantly different at the 0.05 level (with more vessels with more than one stamp die). These results imply that stamping at Elsham was less elaborate than at other sites, whilst at Illington it was more elaborate. This is in line with the high level of use of stamping at

Figure 18 Cumulative frequency distribution for number of different stamp dies per urn, for all stamped vessels in Phase Two sample.

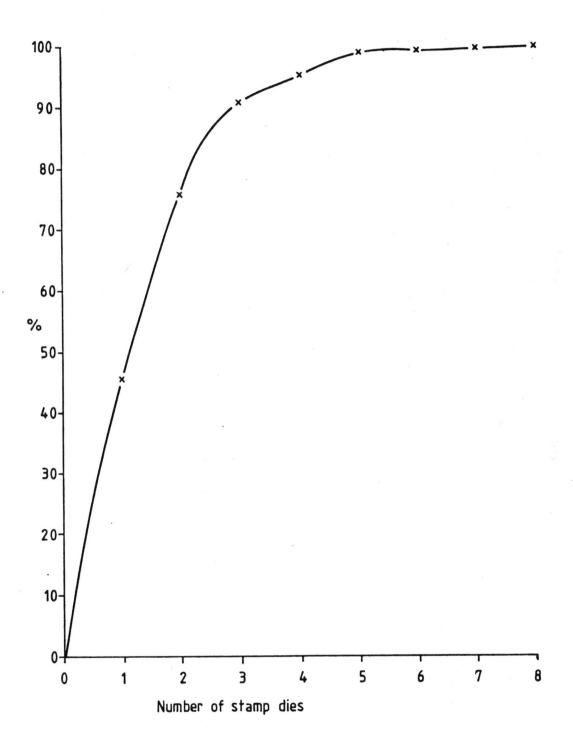

Number of stamp dies

Table 13   Number of stamp dies per vessel at 10 major sites

| | NUMBER OF STAMP DIES | | | | | | | | | SIG. LEVEL |
	1	2	3	4	5	6	7	8	9	(Kolmogorov-Smirnov test)
Total sample	424	281	139	41	28	7	6	3	1	
Caistor-by-Norwich	21	20	9	2	5	1			1	
Elsham	50	20	11	2		1				0.15
Illington	15	17	21		1	1		1		0.05
Lackford	63	38	21	8	6		3	1		
Loveden Hill	48	38	12	4		1				
Mucking	6	1	1			1				
Newark	29	12	10	5	3					
Sancton	37	26	11	2	3					
South Elkington	16	10	3	2						
Spong Hill	112	87	37	12	10	2	3	1		

Table 14   Number of stamp types in total sample

DESIGN	FORM A	B	C	D	E	F	G	H	I	J	K	L	M	O	P	Q	Totals DESIGNS
1	24	–	5	17	1	–	4	1	5	17	50	3	8	–	3	32	170
2	107	14	–	15	–	–	2	8	5	46	50	–	1	3	–	16	267
3	2	–	–	13	–	–	–	2	–	–	10	–	–	–	–	–	27
4	22	–	–	–	–	–	–	14	–	–	1	–	–	–	–	6	43
5	136	–	–	33	1	4	5	9	41	–	11	–	–	–	–	–	240
6	3	–	13	18	21	–	2	7	–	8	11	8	–	–	–	–	91
7	72	–	16	–	101	–	66	25	–	–	–	–	–	–	–	2	282
8	–	–	–	–	5	1	5	4	–	–	–	–	–	–	–	–	15
9	24	–	–	4	–	–	–	–	–	1	1	–	–	–	–	–	30
10	24	–	–	8	–	–	–	–	1	–	1	–	–	–	–	–	34
11	166	–	–	–	31	2	9	–	–	–	–	–	–	–	–	–	208
12	30	–	–	–	8	–	–	–	–	14	–	–	–	–	–	–	52
13	41	–	–	–	2	–	9	–	–	–	–	–	–	–	–	–	52
14	12	–	–	–	–	6	–	–	–	–	–	–	–	–	–	–	18
15	10	–	–	–	–	–	–	–	–	–	–	–	–	–	–	–	10
16	132	–	–	–	11	–	–	–	–	–	–	–	–	–	–	–	143
17	10	–	–	–	–	–	–	–	–	–	–	–	–	–	–	–	10
18	26	–	–	–	–	–	–	–	–	–	–	–	–	–	–	–	26
19	–	–	–	–	–	–	–	–	–	–	–	–	–	–	–	–	–
20	3	–	–	–	12	–	–	–	–	–	–	–	–	–	–	–	15
21	–	–	–	–	2	–	–	–	–	–	–	–	–	–	–	–	2
22	–	–	–	–	1	–	–	–	–	–	–	–	–	–	–	–	1
23	–	–	1	–	–	–	–	–	–	–	–	–	–	–	–	–	1
24	2	–	–	–	9	2	–	–	–	–	4	–	–	–	–	5	22

| Totals | 846 | | 35 | | 205 | | 102 | | 52 | | 139 | | 9 | | 3 | | |
| for FORMS | | 14 | | 108 | | 15 | | 70 | | 86 | | 11 | | 3 | | 61 |

Illington, but suggests that Illington is not only distinguished by a higher proportion of stamped vessels, but that these tend to have more types of stamps as well.

We can also compare the proportion of different types of stamps at each site. The classification scheme described in 2.214 categorised stamped designs according to two parameters: one expressing the external form (coded by letter), and another describing the internal design (coded by number). The numbers of each possible stamp type for the total sample are shown in table 14. These show that A (circular) is the most popular form, followed by E (rectangular) and K ('wyrm'). The most popular types of design are 5 (multiple repeated designs), 2 (outline figures), 7 (gridded figures), and 11 (simple crosses). The most popular individual types are A11, A5, A16, A2 and E7, each with more than 100 examples.

Table 15 compares the proportions of stamp forms at each of the ten major sites. These reveal a familiar consistency between sites, with between 40% and 60% of form A (except at Mucking), and similar proportions of each of the less popular forms. Illington is once again unusual having the least of form A and form E (the two most popular forms), and more of form C, H, and J than any other site. This underlines the way in which the use of a variety of stamps is more highly developed at Illington.

The same pattern is repeated when the proportion of different stamp designs at each of the ten major sites is compared in table 16. Most sites tend to favour the same designs, but at Illington type 2 and type 13 are more popular than at any other sites. Mucking also stands out as being different from the norm. As with other types of decoration it appears that the relative proportions of stamp types can be used as a 'fingerprint' to identify each assemblage.

For the Elsham and Spong Hill pilot sample the actual number of impressions of each die per vessel was recorded. These can range from 1 to 290, although the average is around 60. Fig.19 shows the frequency distribution for the number of stamp impressions per die for Elsham and Spong Hill. These are evidently different, and the Kolmogorov-Smirnov test indicates that this is significant at the 0.01 level. Even though Elsham and Spong Hill have a relatively similar proportion of stamped vessels it appears that the way stamps are used can vary between sites.

3.12 Comparison of grave-goods

Grave-goods were recovered from 48% of the vessels in the total sample. This should be regarded as a minimum figure, subject to post-depositional and recovery distortions. It would appear, therefore, that grave-goods were included for more than half of the deceased in the Anglo-Saxon world. Furthermore, one should be aware of the distinction between deliberate grave-goods and "accidental" inclusion of objects associated with the body during cremation (section 2.215).

Table 15 Percentage of stamp form types at 10 major sites

	Caistr	Elsham	Illgtn	Lckfrd	Lovedn	Muckng	Newark	Sanctn	S.Elkn	Spong
Total no.	130	132	130	282	220	17	112	137	50	505
A	50.8	45.5	40.8	44.0	56.4	70.6	51.8	43.1	56.0	50.5
B	2.3	-	-	0.4	0.5	-	-	0.7	-	0.6
C	1.5	0.8	6.9	1.4	1.8	5.9	0.9	1.5	-	1.8
D	10.8	9.1	4.6	2.1	4.1	5.9	7.1	5.8	4.0	6.3
E	7.7	7.6	4.6	13.1	10.0	-	6.3	24.1	20.0	11.3
F	2.3	-	-	0.7	0.5	-	-	0.7	-	1.4
G	3.9	13.6	5.4	4.6	4.1	11.8	9.8	6.6	-	4.0
H	4.6	5.3	11.5	4.6	2.7	-	0.9	5.8	4.0	3.2
I	5.4	2.3	2.3	1.4	3.2	-	3.6	0.7	4.0	4.6
J	3.1	1.5	11.5	8.2	2.3	-	3.6	2.2	-	5.4
K	3.1	11.4	10.0	8.2	10.5	5.9	9.8	5.8	4.0	7.3
L	-	-	-	-	0.9	-	-	-	4.0	1.8
M	0.8	-	-	-	0.5	-	1.8	0.7	-	0.8
O	-	-	-	0.7	-	-	0.9	-	-	-
P	-	-	-	-	-	-	-	-	-	0.6
Q	3.9	3.0	2.3	6.4	2.7	-	3.6	2.2	4.0	2.6

Table 16 Percentage of stamp design types at 10 major sites

	Caistr	Elsham	Illgtn	Lckfrd	Lovedn	Muckng	Newark	Sanctn	S.Elkn	Spong
1	10.8	12.1	5.4	9.9	14.1	5.9	15.2	4.4	8.0	7.5
2	10.0	18.2	21.5	19.2	11.8	5.9	17.0	13.9	14.0	13.3
3	3.8	-	2.3	-	2.7	-	5.4	-	-	1.2
4	1.5	0.8	1.5	1.4	2.7	-	3.6	4.4	-	2.8
5	16.2	13.1	8.5	13.5	9.1	5.9	10.7	13.1	12.0	17.6
6	4.6	6.2	3.9	4.3	2.7	5.9	2.7	9.5	4.0	6.1
7	10.8	21.5	22.3	13.8	11.4	11.8	16.1	24.1	24.0	13.3
8	-	0.8	-	0.4	0.9	-	0.9	0.7	2.0	1.2
9	-	0.8	1.5	1.1	1.8	17.7	1.8	2.2	-	2.2
10	2.3	1.5	1.5	2.5	3.6	-	3.6	1.5	-	0.8
11	13.9	12.1	10.8	7.5	14.6	17.7	10.7	16.1	20.0	10.9
12	6.2	-	3.1	3.9	-	5.9	0.9	0.7	4.0	4.4
13	0.8	4.6	12.3	1.8	-	5.9	0.9	0.7	-	4.0
14	1.5	0.8	-	1.4	0.9	-	0.9	-	2.0	1.4
15	-	-	-	-	-	-	-	-	-	2.0
16	13.9	7.6	3.8	11.4	3.2	11.8	7.1	8.0	10.0	6.9
17	-	-	-	0.4	0.5	-	-	-	-	1.6
18	0.8	1.5	-	2.1	1.4	5.9	1.8	1.5	4.0	1.0
19	-	-	-	-	-	-	-	-	-	-
20	1.5	-	-	1.1	0.5	-	-	-	-	1.8
21	-	-	-	-	-	-	-	-	-	0.4
22	-	-	-	-	-	-	-	-	-	0.2
23	-	-	-	-	-	-	-	-	-	0.2
24	1.5	-	0.8	2.8	-	-	0.9	1.5	-	1.4

Figure 19 Elsham and Spong Hill: frequency distributions of number of
stamp impressions per urn

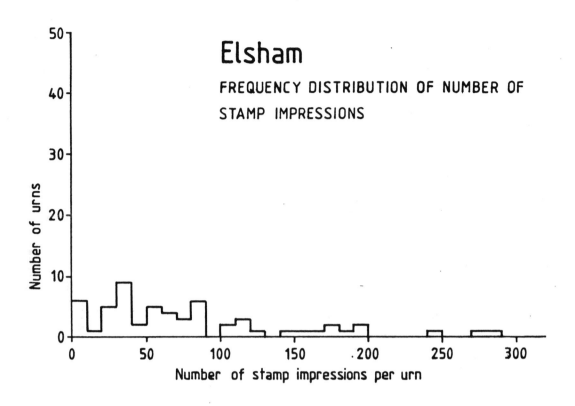

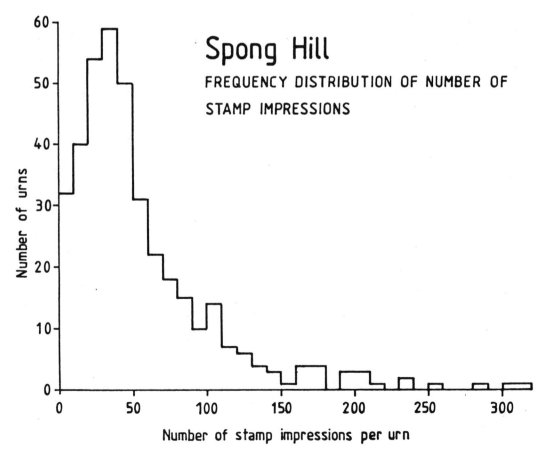

The proportion of urns with grave-goods at each of the 10 major sites is compared in table 17. Clearly there is considerable variation in the proportion of vessels with grave-goods at each site, ranging from about two-thirds at Elsham and Spong Hill, to Lackford and South Elkington with less than a quarter. One should be cautious, however, of simplistic interpretations that explain the number of grave-goods as representing the relative wealth of the sites, and a "wealth-score" analysis has not been performed. Some of the differences may be a product of differential survival and recording, and this is certainly the reason for the low figure at Lackford. Other differences may be real, but may represent regional variations in the preference for including grave-goods, rather than the wealth of a site.

Table 17 Percentage of vessels with grave-goods

	Caistr	Elsham	Illgtn	Lckfrd	Lovedn	Muckng	Newark	Sanctn	S.Elkn	Spong
Vessels with grave-goods	46.3	64.9	34.0	21.3	37.8	31.2	59.9	56.0	22.0	63.7
1 object	21.6	17.1	20.2	13.6	12.8	11.7	22.5	20.2	14.3	25.3
2 objects	13.2	17.1	5.3	4.2	10.4	11.7	11.3	18.1	5.5	16.4
3 objects	6.2	13.7	4.3	1.8	9.2	6.5	13.4	11.5	1.1	9.3
4 objects	4.0	7.3	-	0.7	3.6	1.3	7.0	3.3	-	8.2
5 objects	0.4	4.9	4.3	0.7	1.6	-	3.5	1.7	1.1	2.4
6 or more objects	0.9	4.4	-	0.4	0.4	-	2.1	1.2	-	2.1

It is also interesting to compare the relative proportions of numbers of grave-goods per vessel in table 17. All the sites exhibit a gradual fall-off, with most vessels containing only one object, and fewer vessels containing respectively greater numbers of objects. There are differences, however, in the rate of fall-off at each site. At Elsham, Loveden Hill, Mucking and Sancton, for example, almost as many vessels contain two objects as contain one. At Caistor, Illington, Lackford, Newark, South Elkington and Spong Hill, on the other hand, about twice as many vessels contain one object as contain two objects. These distinctions are independent of the actual proportion of vessels with grave-goods, and it may be tempting to relate them to the relative numbers of people thought to be worthy of a number of objects, rather than just one "token" gesture.

The Kolmogorov-Smirnov test was used to provide a rigorous means of comparison of sites. The cumulative proportion of grave-goods for each site was compared against the cumulative proportion of grave-goods per urn for the total sample of 2440 vessels. At the 0.01 level Elsham, Lackford, Loveden Hill, South Elkington and Spong Hill were each significantly different from the total sample. Elsham and Spong Hill were identified as significant because of a greater number of grave-goods, whilst Lackford, Loveden Hill and South Elkington had a significantly smaller number of grave-goods.

Table 18 presents the percentage occurrence of each class of grave-good for each of the ten major sites. The objects fall into two major groups: those that are unusual, and only occur in small numbers on one or two sites; and those that appear to be standard equipment in

Table 18 Percentage of types of grave-goods at 10 major sites

	Caistr	Elsham	Illgtn	Lckfrd	Lovedn	Muckng	Newark	Sanctn	S.Elkn	Spong
Arrow head	-	-	-	-	-	-	-	-	-	0.1
Bone bead	-	0.5	-	-	0.8	-	-	0.4	1.1	2.8
Bronze shears	-	-	-	-	0.4	-	1.4	1.2	-	0.1
Coin	0.4	-	-	1.0	-	-	-	-	-	0.3
Coral	-	3.4	-	-	-	-	-	-	-	-
Cowrie shell	-	2.4	-	-	-	-	0.7	-	-	-
Earscoop	-	-	-	-	-	-	0.7	-	-	1.2
Girdle hanger	-	-	-	-	0.4	-	-	0.8	-	-
Honestone	-	0.5	-	-	-	-	-	-	-	0.9
Iron nail	3.1	-	-	-	0.4	-	2.8	0.8	-	-
Iron ring (non toilet set)	1.3	0.5	-	-	0.8	-	-	-	-	0.7
Iron rivet (non-comb)	-	0.5	-	-	0.8	-	-	1.6	-	2.8
Large bead	0.4	-	-	-	1.2	-	0.7	-	-	0.6
Razor	-	1.0	-	-	-	-	-	-	-	3.0
Silver ring	0.4	1.0	-	0.7	-	-	-	-	-	-
Spear	-	-	-	-	-	1.3	-	0.4	-	-
Bone fitting	0.4	4.9	1.1	-	-	-	2.1	4.9	1.1	0.3
Bone ring	-	1.5	2.1	-	1.2	-	4.9	0.4	-	1.3
Bronze fitting	0.4	1.5	1.1	0.7	0.4	-	2.1	0.8	1.1	1.5
Bronze fragment	2.2	21.0	6.4	1.4	10.0	14.3	15.5	14.8	4.4	8.1
Bronze ring	0.4	0.5	-	0.3	0.8	-	0.7	1.2	-	1.2
Bronze sheet	6.2	5.4	4.3	1.0	1.6	3.9	4.9	1.2	2.2	8.1
Bronze tweezers	2.6	4.9	1.1	3.5	2.4	-	5.6	4.9	-	3.6
Brooch	3.0	2.0	4.3	3.2	3.2	1.3	3.5	4.9	1.1	7.0
Buckle	0.4	-	1.1	-	1.2	3.9	0.7	2.9	-	0.4
Comb	9.7	25.4	13.8	9.1	9.6	-	23.9	14.0	-	13.0
Crystal	-	5.9	1.1	0.3	0.8	1.3	1.4	0.8	-	1.5
Glass	0.9	17.6	3.2	-	2.4	-	18.3	12.8	1.1	3.7
Glass beads	9.3	16.1	9.6	-	11.6	11.7	9.9	18.5	7.7	23.0
Glass vessel	1.8	2.4	1.1	-	1.2	2.6	0.7	0.4	-	4.3
Iron fitting	0.4	1.5	-	-	0.8	1.3	1.4	-	-	0.9
Iron fragment	2.6	2.9	-	0.7	2.0	2.6	6.3	2.1	5.5	3.6
Iron knife	1.8	0.5	-	0.3	2.4	-	0.7	2.5	2.2	1.2
Iron rivet	2.6	1.0	-	0.7	1.2	-	-	4.1	-	5.0
Iron shears	0.9	0.5	-	0.3	-	-	-	0.4	1.1	0.3
Ivory	1.8	13.7	5.3	2.8	2.8	-	11.3	1.6	-	6.1
Miniature iron blade	9.3	2.9	1.1	0.7	2.0	-	2.8	1.6	-	5.2
Miniature iron shears	11.0	3.9	2.1	0.3	3.6	-	4.9	0.8	-	8.7
Miniature iron tweezers	11.5	1.5	1.1	1.0	6.4	2.6	2.8	0.8	1.1	8.0
Pin	-	1.5	1.1	0.3	1.6	-	1.4	2.9	2.2	0.1
Playing piece	0.9	2.9	2.1	1.0	6.0	1.3	1.4	0.8	2.2	2.4
Potsherd	1.3	2.0	-	-	-	5.2	-	-	-	9.0
Spindlewhorl	-	9.3	1.1	1.0	0.8	-	2.8	2.9	-	2.1
Worked flint	-	1.5	1.1	-	-	3.9	2.8	0.8	-	3.6
Wristclasp	-	1.0	-	2.1	0.8	-	2.1	1.2	-	0.4

cremation burials, and turn up regularly on most sites. Into the
first category fall: arrow heads, bone beads, bronze shears, coins,
coral, cowrie shells, earscoops, girdle hangers, honestones, iron
nails, iron rings (not from miniature toilet sets), iron rivets (not
from combs), large beads, razors, silver rings, and spear heads. All
the other items fall into the second category of objects which are
present on several sites. Since the first group are defined by their
rarity few points of comparison can be made and we can only note their
presence. For the second group it may be worth noting the relative
frequency of individual classes, and discussing possible explanations.

At Caistor, there is a very high proportion of vessels with
miniature toilet implements. Over 10% contain iron shears and
tweezers, closely followed by iron blades. By contrast, glass, glass
beads and glass vessels are relatively infrequent. Combs, ivory and
bronze fragments are also comparatively scarce, although the low
proportion of bronze fragments may be partially explained by their
identification as bronze sheet.

At Elsham there is almost the reverse pattern. Miniatures are
poorly represented, whilst over 35% of vessels have some form of glass
object. A very high proportion of urns (over 25%) contain combs,
nearly 15% contain ivory, and over 20% have bronze fragments. Amongst
the other grave-goods, crystal and spindlewhorls are particularly well
represented. Elsham also has two examples of exotic items, namely
coral and cowrie shells, indicating, perhaps, the relative wealth of
the cemetery.

Illington provides yet another situation. Miniatures are even more
unusual than at Elsham, but glass is not particularly common either.
Illington does have reasonable proportions of combs and ivory, but in
comparison to Elsham it appears relatively poor.

The figures for Lackford must be treated with caution (section 3.1).
In particular, the absence of any glass objects is to be mistrusted,
as are the low figures for the miniatures and many other items. In
general, the site appears to fit into the Illington pattern.

Loveden Hill is also similar to Illington, although miniatures are
more frequent, and combs and ivory less so. Loveden also has average
proportions of glass objects.

As we have already noted, grave-goods are altogether less common at
Mucking. Nevertheless, it has relatively large numbers of glass
objects and bronze fragments whilst ivory, combs, and miniature toilet
implements are virtually absent, confirming the view that the latter
are Anglian traits.

When we examine Newark, we find a site which fits much more into the
Elsham pattern. Over 10% of vessels contain ivory, and nearly 25%
contain combs, whereas miniatures are infrequent. Bronze fragments
and glass objects are also well represented, and amongst other
objects, full size bronze tweezers, iron fragments and spindlewhorls
are more common than average. Newark is also the only site, apart
from Elsham, to produce a cowrie shell.

Sancton also bears some similarities to Elsham, with over 30% of vessels with glass objects, nearly 15% with bronze fragments, 15% with combs, and bronze tweezers and spindlewhorls well represented. On the other hand, miniatures are very rare, and ivory is also found in very few of the urns.

South Elkington appears to fall within the same class as Mucking, which is interesting considering its geographical location. All grave-goods are scarce, and ivory, combs, and miniatures are virtually absent. Glass beads, iron fragments and bronze fragments are the only relatively common objects.

Finally, nearly all classes of grave-good are represented at Spong Hill, as would be expected, this being the largest site included in the study. However, when one considers the proportions of the common grave-goods various factors emerge. In terms of miniature toilet implements, Spong is similar to Caistor, with c.8% of tweezers and shears, and over 5% iron blades. On the other hand it is closer to Elsham, Newark, and Sancton in the number of glass beads, with nearly 25%. If the number of bone fragments and bronze sheet fragments are combined Spong Hill also shares a relatively high number of bronze objects. Ivory and bronze tweezers are also relatively frequent. Yet, like Sancton, it has fewer combs than either Elsham or Newark; although still higher than most other sites.

In conclusion, it is possible to make the following generalisations about proportions of grave-goods at each of the ten sites.

(i) Firstly, we should not allow these minor differences to allow us to lose sight of the fact that the overall impression is of a high level of consistency between sites. We may conclude that Anglo-Saxons at each site were practising a broadly similar burial rite. They buried the same range of grave-goods and presumably these objects were used to mark the same features of social identity. Differences between sites must reflect regional variation in the use of grave-goods or regional differences in the proportions of social identity groupings represented in the cemeteries.

(ii) Secondly, and following on from the first conclusion, there are some grave-goods which appear regularly in the same proportions at each site, whilst there are others where the proportion varies between sites much more. Brooches are a particularly good example of the first type of object. They never occur in less than 1% of vessels, and never in more than 7%. Thus their use as identity makers seems highly consistent throughout the cremating areas of Anglo-Saxon England. In contrast, items such as combs may appear in 25% of vessels at some sites (Elsham, Newark) and be entirely absent at others (Mucking, S. Elkington). There is tremendous regional variation in the use of these objects as identity markers.

(iii) Thirdly, using those objects which are used in different proportions at different sites, it may be possible to distinguish between groups of sites which share the same traditions. At first sight, it may seem that there is simply random variation between sites, with continuous gradations in the proportions of grave-goods used. One should be cautious of arbitrarily creating groups of similar sites. Nevertheless, as has been indicated above, it does appear possible to isolate certain reasonably distinctive groups. A hierarchical clustering procedure was applied to the information about proportions of commonly occurring grave-goods contained in table 18, namely bronze fragments and bronze sheets, bronze tweezers, brooches, combs, glass fragments and glass beads, iron fragments, ivory, miniature iron blades, shears and tweezers[1]. The hierarchical clustering model is appropriate as the groups are not especially discrete, and are each part of a larger group of similar sites at a higher level. The results are presented in the distance coefficient matrix in table 19 and the dendrogram and minimum spanning tree in fig.20.

Illington and Loveden clearly fit into one group of sites with relatively low proportions of combs, ivory, bronze fragments and glass beads, and very low numbers of miniatures. Caistor joins this group at a higher level because of the greater number of miniatures present. Mucking and South Elkington form another category of sites with few grave-goods, and where combs, ivory and miniatures are extremely scarce. However, all these sites are clearly distinguished from the remaining four by the clustering procedure. Elsham and Newark each have a high proportion of ivory, combs, glass beads, bronze fragments and relatively infrequent miniatures. Spong Hill, and perhaps Sancton, may also belong with them, especially when the number of small rivets is added to the number of combs.

3.13 Comparison of skeletal remains

Analyses of the burnt human skeletal remains recovered from cremations should, in theory, provide an excellent data set from which to study Anglo-Saxon demography. In practice there are a number of difficulties inherent in this approach. Firstly, the analysis of cremated bone has generally only been carried out for cemeteries excavated relatively recently. Secondly, there is differential preservation of bone from cremations within cemeteries, meaning that only in a minority of cases is survival adequate for identifications to be made. Thirdly, the technique is in its infancy with a high probability of mis-identifications. Following from this, fourthly, there is the problem of the lack of agreed criteria for identification with different experts using different age groupings.

Nevertheless, it was considered that as several skeletal analyses

NOTE

[1] Lackford was excluded because of the incomplete grave-good data. The values for glass and glass beads were combined as were those for bronze fragments and bronze sheets. Iron rivets were added to the figures for combs, as they probably represented the only surviving fragments of additional combs.

Table 19   Distance coefficient matrix

	Caistr	Elsham	Illgtn	Lovedn	Muckng	Newark	Sanctn	S.Elkn	Spong
Caistr	0.00								
Elsham	11.83	0.00							
Illgtn	5.39	9.73	0.00						
Lovedn	4.00	10.01	2.36	0.00					
Muckng	7.36	12.19	5.48	4.63	0.00				
Newark	9.28	3.09	7.37	7.53	10.28	0.00			
Sanctn	9.04	5.92	6.51	6.50	8.73	4.46	0.00		
S.Elkn	7.04	13.97	5.46	4.94	3.92	11.57	9.89	0.00	
Spong	6.56	6.16	6.13	5.50	8.77	3.91	4.21	9.88	0.00

Figure 20 Dendrogram and minimum spanning tree for hierarchical clustering of 9 sites by grave-goods

```
Distance              10            20            30            40

    Caistr ------------¦-------------------¦
    Illgtn ----¦--------¦                  ¦-----------------------------------------¦
    Lovedn ----¦                           ¦                                         ¦
    Muckng -------¦-------------------------¦                                         ¦-----
    S.Elkn --------¦                                                                  ¦
    Elsham ------¦----------------¦                                                   ¦
    Newark ------¦                ¦----------------------------------------------------¦
    Sanctn --------¦---------------¦
    Spong  --------¦
```

Cophrenetic correlation coefficient = 0.47327

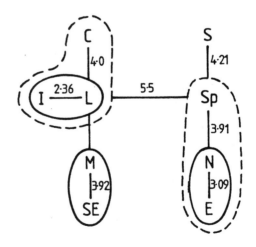

had been brought together for the present study, some attempt at comparison was required. Analyses of the human skeletal remains were available for eight sites: Caistor, Elsham, Illington, Loveden, Mucking, Newark, Sancton and Worthy Park. Sexing of the adult material had been attempted for five of these sites: Elsham, Illington, Loveden, Mucking and Sancton. The classification system outlined in section 2.217 was imposed on the various skeletal analyses in an attempt to render them comparable. The actual numbers of each age and sex grouping are given in table 20 to indicate the size of samples involved at each site. The relative proportions of age and sexes for each site are presented in the pie charts in figs.21-28. In the diagrams, certain identifications are scored as 1.0, probable identifications as 0.75 and possible identifications as 0.5. This appeared the best technique to maximise the potential of the available data. Where identifications were only "possible", generally another alternative would be given, which would also be scored as 0.5. Therefore the overall comparability of population statistics was maintained.

The percentage figures are percentages out of the number of urns for which a skeletal identification had been performed. They do not represent a percentage of the total number of urns from the site.

3.131 Sex ratio

The relative proportions of male and female burials are not what one would expect. Only two sites, Elsham and Illington, have equal numbers of each sex. At Loveden males outnumber females by almost 2 to 1, whilst at Mucking the ratio is nearer 5 to 1. At Sancton, females outnumber males by a factor of 2 to 1. At Loveden and Mucking it is possible that the numbers involved are small enough to make this a sampling problem. At Sancton, however, the numbers involved are large enough to force us to conclude that, at least wthin the urns examined for sex of occupant, this is a real difference.

That leaves the following possibilities:-

i) It is easier to sex the remains of one gender than the other.

ii) There was a large difference in the life expectancy of the respective genders in Anglo-Saxon society.

iii) The sexed urn contents represent a biased sample of the total cemetery population, males being concentrated in one area and females in another.

iv) The cemeteries examined do not represent a representative section of the Sub-Roman population, with a higher proportion of one sex being given different mortuary treatment, such as being buried in an alternative cemetery which has not been recovered.

The first two hypotheses are both unlikely because the bias is not always in one direction; sometimes there are more males than females,

Table 20 Number of human skeletal remains present

	Caistr	Elsham	Illgtn	Lovedn	Muckng	Newark	Sanctn	Worthy
Neonate	–	–	–	1	–	–	–	–
Infant	8	5	3	2	5	6	4	1
Child	23	40	9	4	3	13	41	5
Adolescent	–	8	9	9	1	19	5	8
Young adult	–	40	14	10	–	1	65	–
Mature adult	–	34	10	–	–	17	43	–
Old adult	–	–	8	11	–	–	13	–
Adult	17	107	6	19	52	52	15	9
Male	NA	25	10	21	14	NA	39	NA
Female	NA	28	10	12	3	NA	84	NA

Table 21 Number of cremated animals present

	Elsham	Illgtn	Lovedn	Newark	Sanctn
Animal bones present	57	10	7	26	38
Sheep	31	4	4	11	NA
Cow / Ox	13	1	1	5	NA
Pig	11	1	–	8	NA
Horse	13	1	–	3	NA
Deer	–	–	–	1	NA
Bird	2	–	4	1	NA
Dog	–	1	–	–	NA

Remains identified as "possible" or "probable" counted as positive
identifications

NA: Information not available

Figure 21 Skeletal remains - relative proportions - Caistor

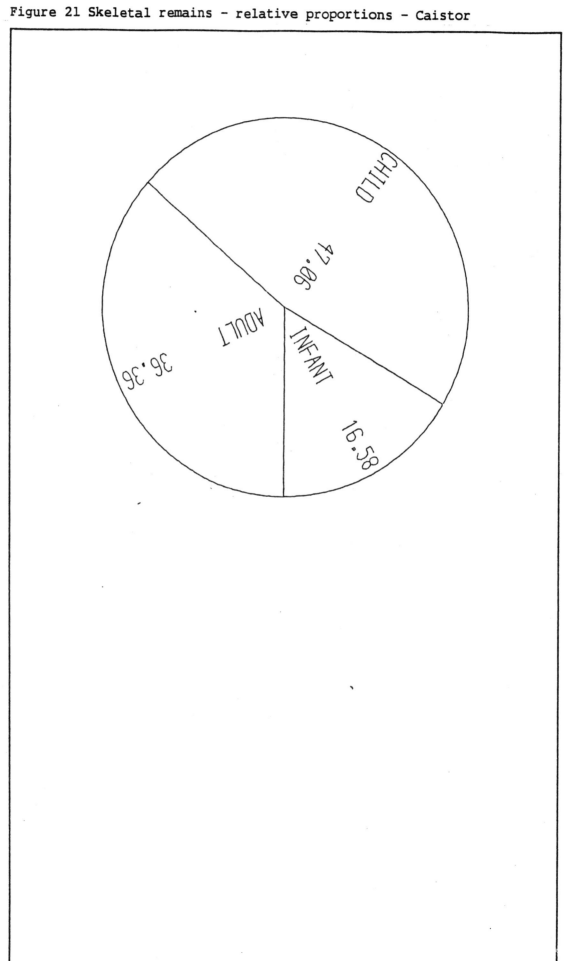

Figure 22 Skeletal remains - relative proportions - Elsham

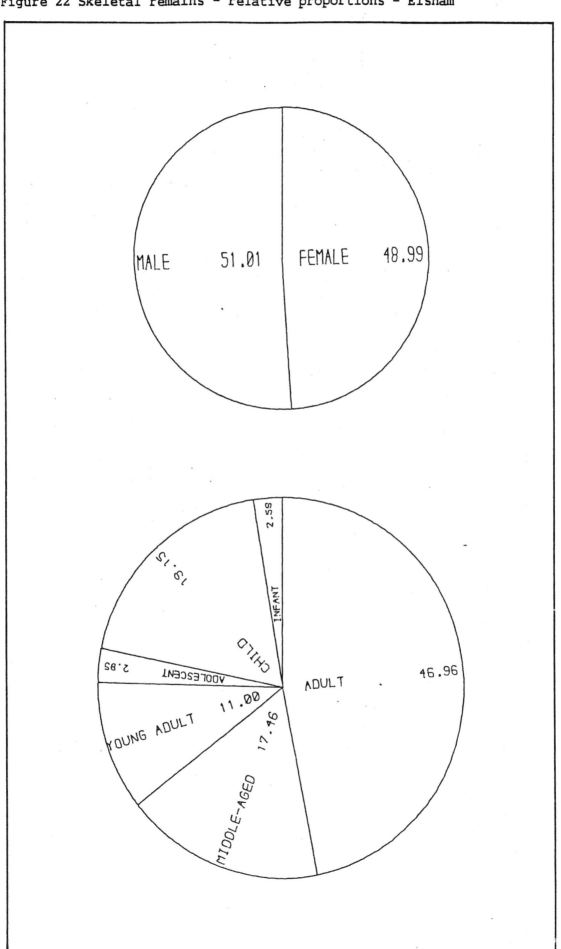

Figure 23 Skeletal remains - relative proportions - Illington

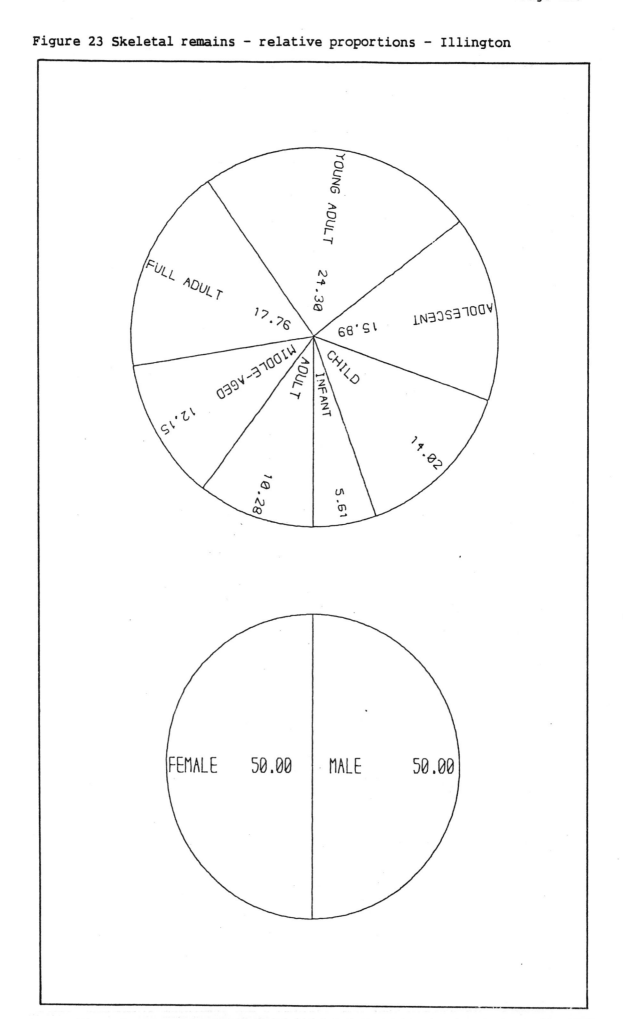

Figure 24 Skeletal remains - relative proportions - Loveden Hill

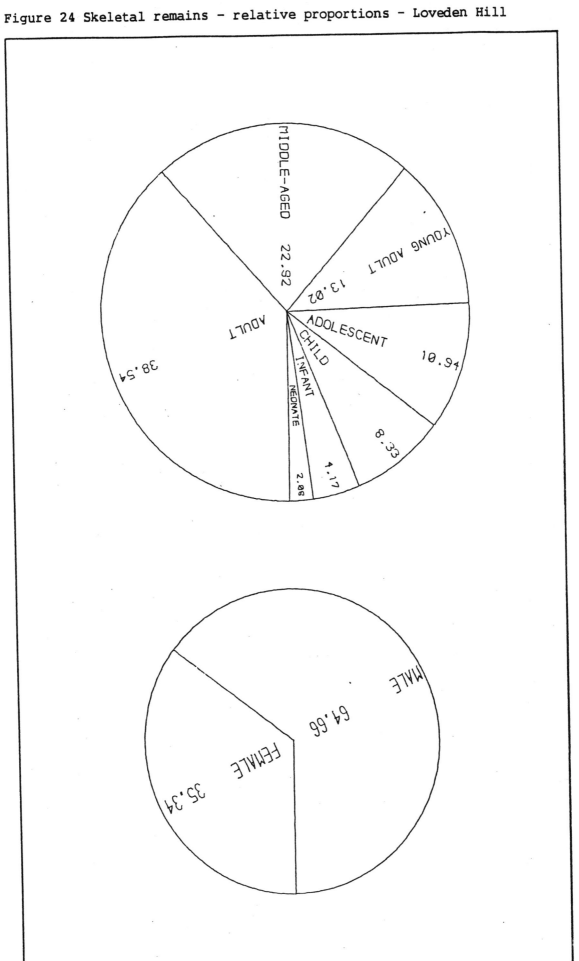

Figure 25 Skeletal remains - relative proportions - Newark

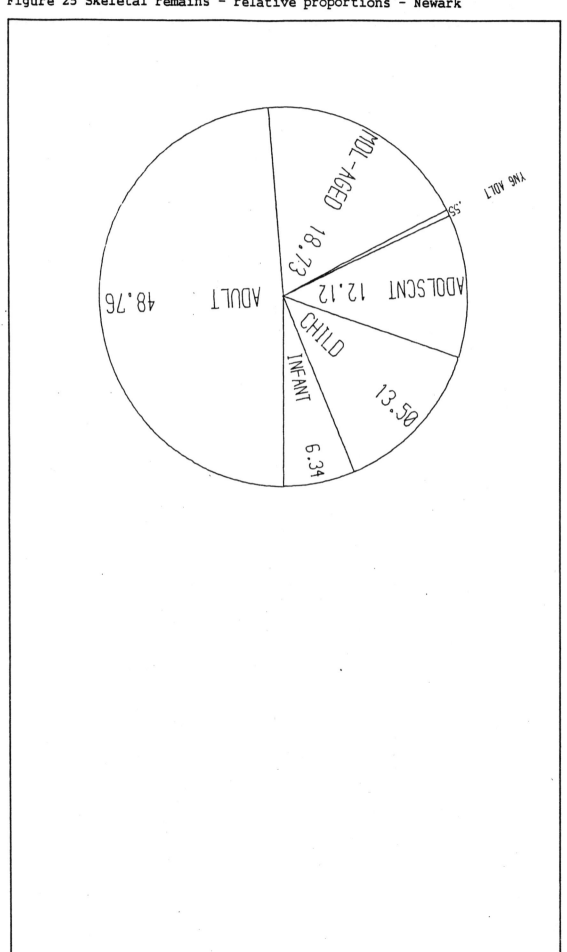

Figure 26 Skeletal remains - relative proportions - Mucking

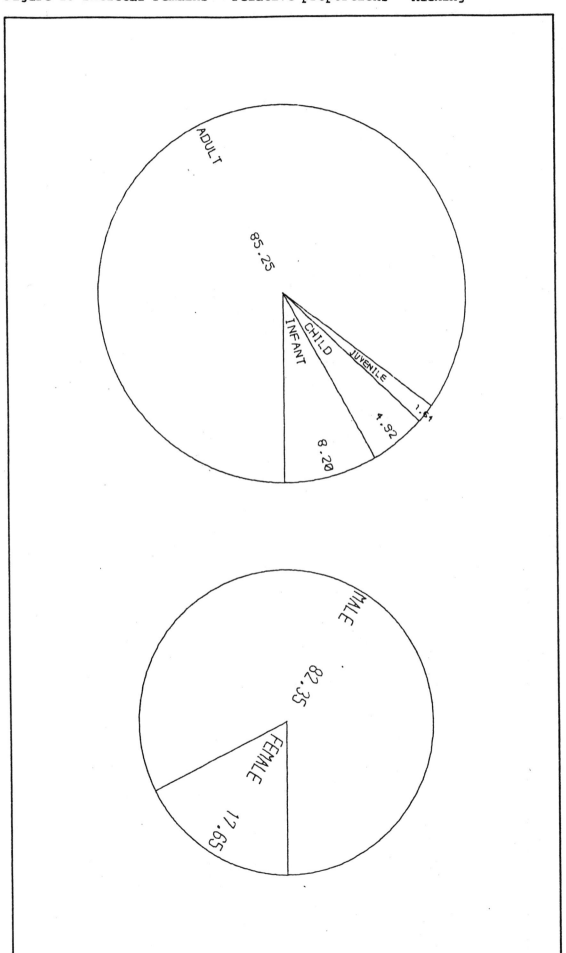

Figure 27 Skeletal remains - relative proportions - Sancton

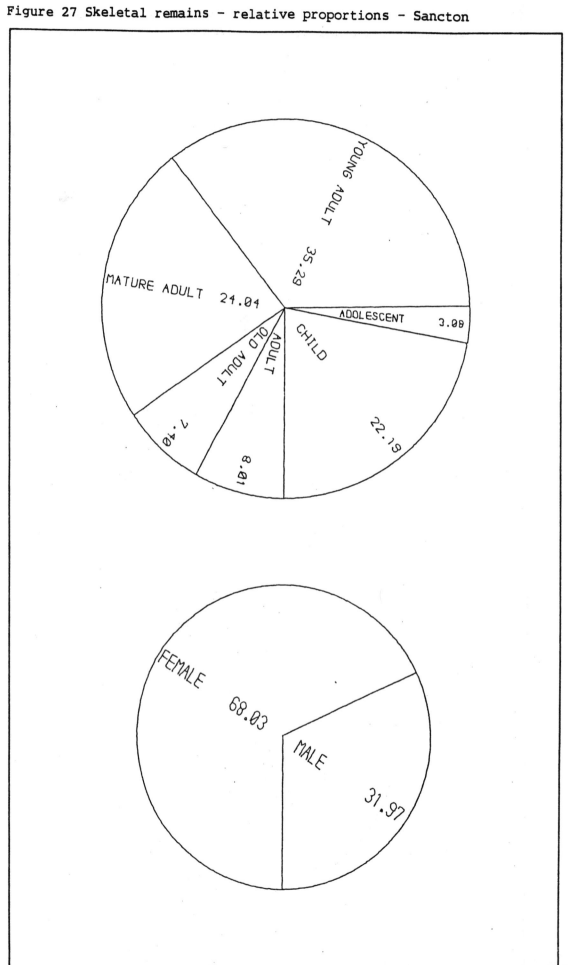

Figure 28 Skeletal remains - relative proportions - Worthy Park

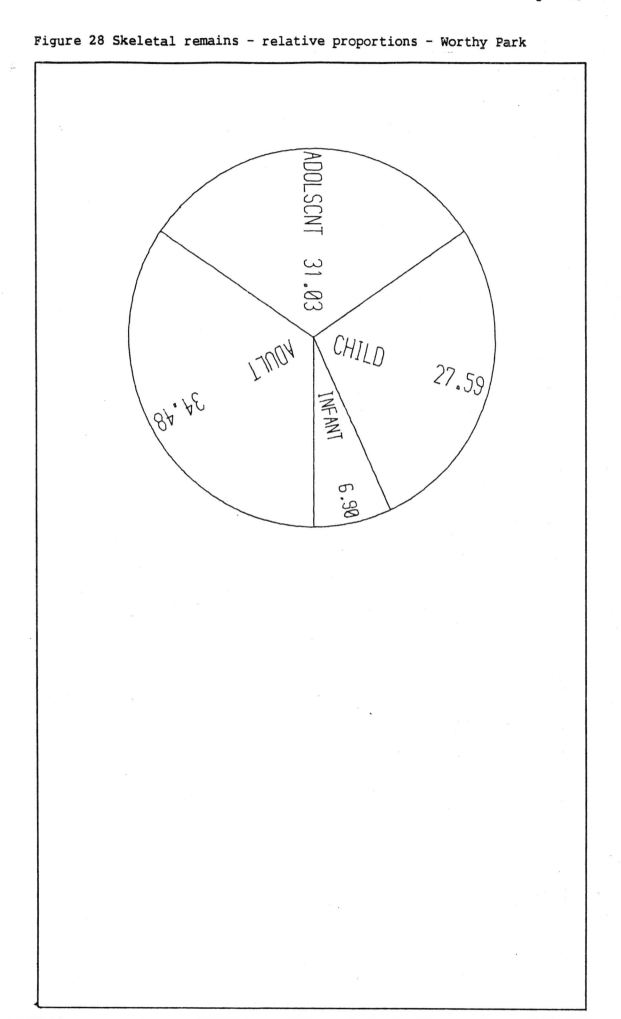

sometimes vice versa. Nevertheless, we should not rule out the possibility that some palaeo-pathologists are identifying more bones as females and fewer as male than other analysts, or vice versa.

The third hypothesis is also unlikely given that these samples are thought to be representative of the cemeteries as a whole (see section 3.1).

That leaves the fourth hypothesis that the different sexes are being treated differently with "specialised" male and female cemeteries. In the absence of any other information (in particular a detailed regional study) we are not in a position to test this model. The fact that we do have equal proportions at two sites does, however, tend to argue against this theory.

We can only conclude that at some sites there appears to be differential representation of the sexes but that the reasons for this remain unclear.

3.132 Age ratio

Problems of preservation and identification must also prevent us from drawing from conclusions over the age structure of the Anglo-Saxon population. At Caistor deliberate selection of bones from small vessels by Mann must have lead to over-representation of infant and child burials. At Worthy Park the overall sample size is too small to allow valid comparison. For the remaining sites it should nevertheless be possible to make some observations.

In general the age structure is what one would expect of peasant agricultural communities with a low level of medical care. Where they are distinguished, for instance at Sancton, it can be seen that a relatively small proportion of the population survived to enjoy old age. Again at Sancton the fact that 60% of the population were dead before the age of 30 compares closely with figures for the Roman cemetery at Lankhills and more recent figures from India (Molleson 1981, 20).

A large number of these fatalities had occured before the age of 12. Excluding Caistor and Worthy Park the proportion of infant and child mortalities is fairly consistently between 15-20%. However, this figure is actually rather low in comparison with Lankhills (35%) and modern India (50%). Indeed, at Lankhills Molleson (ibid) suggests that the number of infant and child burials may be under-represented. In Roman cemeteries, as in many anthropologically documented societies (e.g. Goody 1962) infants may not have been considered to be real people (as a means of coping with the trauma of a high infant mortality rate) and may have been specially treated elsewhere. In Anglo-Saxon cemeteries, on the other hand, it generally seems that children, at least, were treated as "small adults", and were generally given the same range of grave-goods as adults. We are therefore led to the conclusion that, unless some children - but not all - were disposed of elsewhere, there was a surprisingly low level of infant and child mortality in Anglo-Saxon England.

For Roman Lankhills and modern India the mortality rate falls once adolescence is reached, to around 5% of the population dying between the ages of 12 and 18. At Elsham, Mucking and Sancton the mortality rate was actually lower than that, but at Illington, Loveden Hill and Newark it is surprisingly high, between 10-16%. Such a high level of juvenile mortality is surprising, as having made it through childhood more people would be expected to survive, at least (for women) until child-bearing age.

3.133 Animal cremations

Details of the burnt animals included in the cremation deposit were available for five sites: Elsham, Illington, Loveden, Newark, Sancton. The results are presented in table 21. The proportion of vessels including animal remains ranged from Loveden with c.15% to Elsham and Newark with c.30%. It is probably significant that these two sites were also grouped together in terms of proportions of grave-goods. For Elsham, Illington, Newark and Loveden, details were available of the actual animals cremated. At each site, sheep were the most popular, followed by roughly equal numbers of each of cow, pig and horse. Various birds, dogs and deer were occasionally present in smaller numbers. At Sutton Hoo, Bruce-Mitford (1975, 714) has interpreted the charred bone from the Anastasius dish as representing animal remains gathered up from a burial feast or grilled joints provided for the dead. More recently, an anomalous sand-shape observed at the feet of the occupant of one of the Sutton Hoo flat-graves has been interpreted as an animal bone derived from a joint of meat (Carver 1986, 146), and animal bones have been found at the feet of each of the group of Anglian burials recently discovered at Garton Station (Current Archaeology 1987, 103, 234-7).

It appears likely more likely, however, that the animal bones recovered from cremation urns represent deliberate sacrifices of beasts to accompany their masters/mistresses, rather than simply the remains of funeral feasting, although we cannot be certain that they were not used for this purpose as well. Particular animals often accompany certain social groupings and must have been linked with these groups. At Sancton some urns apparently contained only cremated animal bones (Nicholas Reynolds pers comm). Furthermore, at Elsham there is evidence that all the horse bones were carefully selected and included in the cremations, (Chris Knowles, paper presented to Early Anglo-Saxon Pottery Group, 19/3/83). According to Bede (Colgrave and Mynors III.14) the possession of a good horse was regarded as a status symbol amongst the Angles of the seventh century.

The high number of sheep no doubt reflects their relative importance in the Anglo-Saxon economy. It is supported by their equal importance in the faunal collections on settlement sites and by the evidence for weaving. The significance of all the animals may become clearer when we consider which other attributes of the cremation they are correlated with in the following sections. Certainly, the killing of such large numbers of animals indicates the relative importance attached to the treatment of the dead.

3.2 The significance of grave-goods

We have observed that a wide variety of grave-goods may be included in Anglo-Saxon cremations, but that most of these fall into a number of regularly occurring classes. If the choice of grave-goods is meaningful then we must now try to identify the criteria which determine the selection of particular classes. It is generally assumed that classes of grave-good are age- or sex-linked (section 2.216). The collection of skeletal and grave-good data for a large number of vessels presents us with the opportunity to test this assumption in a rigorous fashion.

Those vessels which contained grave-goods, and for which skeletal data was available, were isolated from the total sample. They comprised a total of 442 vessels. In order to examine links between age/sex groupings and grave-good classes each skeletal attribute was cross-tabulated with specific classes of commonly occurring grave-good[1]. Most of the other grave-goods were too rare to overcome minimum cell frequency problems for the chi-square test. It was assumed that those grave-goods used to mark particular age and sex groupings should be correlated with those groupings at a higher level than would be expected under a random distribution of grave-goods amongst all age and sex groups. The chi-square test was applied to identify significant associations. As well as the objects included in the cremation burials, a number of vessels also contained burnt animal remains. It has been proposed (3.133) that these represent deliberately chosen offerings rather than the remains of funeral feasts. If this is so then they should be treated as grave-goods, and may also exhibit links with particular human skeletal groups.

3.21 Sex links

The most startling result was that very few grave-goods appear to be sex-linked. The significant links are all highlighted in table 22. Ivory is more frequently included in female rather than male burials, supporting the view that it is derived from bag handles, and that these were items of female equipment (see 2.216). Miniature iron shears and tweezers more frequently accompany males rather than females, although the numbers involved are very small. Surprisingly, single miniature iron blades do not show any sex-link. Since bronze tweezers are also equally common in male and female burials, one may conclude that the material, as well as the type of object, may be significant in indicating gender.

NOTE

[1] Not all grave-goods are found in sufficient numbers to provide valid results. Nineteen items occur in 30 or more cremations in the total sample. Throughout chapter 3 the analyses described will, therefore, be restricted to results for these 19 items.

Table 22 Associations of grave-good classes with sex of individual

	Total No	SKELETAL GROUPING: Male		Female		Signif. level
		No	Row%	No	Row%	
Total	188	73	38.8	115	61.5	

GRAVE-GOOD PRESENT:

	Total No	Male No	Row%	Female No	Row%	Signif. level
Bone fitting	12	4	33.3	8	66.7	0.92
Bronze fragment	47	13	27.7	34	72.3	0.11
Bronze sheet	13	6	46.2	7	53.8	0.79
Bronze tweezers	14	5	35.7	9	64.3	1.0
Brooch	10	2	20.0	8	80.0	0.37
Comb	63	24	38.1	39	61.9	1.0
Crystal	6	1	16.7	5	83.3	0.48
Glass	38	10	26.3	28	73.7	0.11
Glass beads	57	19	33.3	38	66.7	0.39
Glass vessel	5	3	60.0	2	40.0	0.6
Iron fragment	7	2	28.6	5	71.4	0.86
Iron rivet	13	4	30.8	9	69.2	0.75
Ivory	21	4	19.0	17	81.0	0.08
Miniature iron blade	7	3	42.9	4	57.1	1.0
Miniature iron shears	12	8	66.7	4	33.3	0.08
Miniature iron tweezers	11	8	72.7	3	27.3	0.04
Playing piece	12	7	58.3	5	41.7	0.26
Spindlewhorl	14	5	35.7	9	64.3	1.0
Worked flint	5	1	20.0	4	80.0	0.68

Table 23 Associations of identity groupings with sex of individual

	Total No	IDENTITY GROUPING: GROUP 0			GROUP 1			GROUP 2		
		No	Row%	Sig	No	Row%	Sig	No	%	Sig
Total	706	264	37.4		76	10.8		151	21.4	
SEX:										
Male	119	40	33.6	0.41	19	16.0	0.07	23	19.3	0.63
Female	153	42	27.5	0.01	15	9.8	0.78	47	30.7	0.002

NOTE

In tables of cross-tabulations presented throughout Part 3, correlations significant at the 0.1 level or above are underlined. Where 25% of the valid cells have an expected cell frequency less than 5.0 the result is also marked with an asterisk. In these cases low numbers must lead to some doubt about the meaning of high significance levels.

Other objects show tendencies to be associated with either males or females, but none are significant at the 0.1 level. No items are exclusively male or female and even allowing for multiple burials and misidentifications, it would appear that the grave-goods are not generally used simply as representing gender.

Contrary to general assumption, therefore, items such as brooches and spindlewhorls should not be seen as sex-specific, and may equally well mark male or female burials. Even glass beads, whilst found more frequently with females, occur in 19 male burials. As the number of beads present was not distinguished, it is possible that these 19 cases might all be examples of single beads attached to sword pommels, and known as "sword beads". In late Iron Age graves in Norway, the presence of a few glass beads in male graves has often been observed (Sjovold 1974, 176-7, 226ff; Petersen 1919, 169-70).

Combs are found in almost equal proportions in male and female burials, and we may safely conclude that they were not seen as sex-specific. This also follows the pattern observed in the Scandinavian Iron Age (Sjovold 1974, 179-80).

Nevertheless, it may be that the results have been confused by multiple burials and misidentifications, as well as suffering from small sample size. A possible means of overcoming these difficulties may depend on using groups of grave-goods rather than specific items. The isolation of 3 identity groupings, using PCA, was described in section 2.224. These groups were also cross-tabulated with the skeletal groupings, as a check for any sex-specific groups of objects (table 23).

In fact, each grouping was found in both male and female burials, although each has a significant preference. Firstly GROUP ZERO, which was defined by the absence of any grave-goods, is associated less frequently with female burials than would be expected by chance. Apparently there was a higher proportion of Anglo-Saxon women than men for whom it was considered appropriate to provide grave-goods.

Secondly, GROUP ONE, which was identified by the presence of toilet implements, is more frequently associated with male burials, than would be expected by chance.

Finally, GROUP TWO, consisting of those urns containing glass beads or ivory, is significantly linked with female burials, but not with males.

In conclusion, none of the identity groupings is exclusively associated with male or female burials, but each exhibits a significant link with one or the other. This may lead us to interpret the identity groupings as not simply representing sex roles. Rather, they may represent social groups which cross sexual divisions, but draw their membership from one sex more than the other.

When one considers animal bones there is a clear sex link between the inclusion of animal bones and male cremations (table 24). Apparently it was considered more appropriate that males should be accompanied by animals than females. On the other hand, the choice of animal appears to be less important and none of the four main species are significantly represented in male rather than female burials. However, it seems that horses are the animals most associated with males and sheep those least associated with female identifications.

Table 25 presents the associations between identity groupings and the inclusion of animal bones. Each of the species identified, and the presence of any animal bone has a negative relationship with GROUP ZERO.   In other words, urns without artefactual grave-goods are also unlikely to contain animal offerings.   None of the animals are significantly linked with GROUP ONE, but pigs stand out as possibly being positively linked with GROUP TWO although the numbers involved are small.

Table 24 Associations of animal groupings with sex groupings

ANIMAL GROUPING:

	Total No	Animal bones No Row% Sig	Sheep No Row% Sig	Cow / Ox No Row% Sig	Pig No Row% Sig	Horse No Row% Sig
Total	706	144 20.4	50 7.1	20 2.8	21 3.0	18 2.5
SEX:						
Male	119	38 31.9 0.001	9 7.6 0.98	6 5.0 0.2	2 1.7 0.54	6 5.0 0.12
Female	153	29 19.0 0.7	6 3.9 0.12	4 2.6 1.0	2 1.3 0.27	2 1.3 0.42

Table 25 Associations of identity groupings with skeletal groupings

IDENTITY GROUPING:

	Total No	GROUP 0 No Row% Sig	GROUP 1 No Row% Sig	GROUP 2 No Row% Sig
Total	706	264 37.4	76 10.8	151 21.4
Animal present:	144	36 25.0 0.001	17 11.8 0.76	36 25.0 0.28
Sheep	50	12 24.0 0.06	5 10.0 1.0	13 26.0 0.52
Cow / Ox	20	4 20.0 0.16	1 5.0 0.63	4 20.0 1.0
Pig	21	3 14.3 0.05	4 19.0 0.38	9 42.9 0.03
Horse	18	3 16.7 0.11	2 11.1 1.0	4 22.2 1.0

3.22 Age links

Each of the skeletal age groupings was also cross-tabulated with each of the grave-good classes (table 26). Since infants and children may frequently be placed in "multiple" burials with adults, such multiple burials were deliberately excluded from these tables in order to reduce background noise. Most grave-goods again show little or no correlation with a specific age grouping. In particular, with some minor exceptions, children are simply treated as adults, and receive the same range of grave-goods as their adult counterparts. This is in contrast to other societies where they are given a burial rite peculiar to them. In early Anglo-Saxon England it seems that status was ascribed at birth, and a young child could be granted the same range of grave-goods as an adult[1].

Miniature toilet implements provide the major exceptions. Iron tweezers are positively linked with the general adult category, (although the figures suggest a negative relationship with those identified as young and mature adults). Similarly iron shears are never found with young adults, and are positively associated with child burials. Iron blades are again absent in young adult burials and positively linked with children (although here the cell frequencies are too low to be sure of the significance). Iron fragments (which may represent fragments of other toilet implements) are also negatively linked with young adults.

Of the other grave-goods, bronze sheet fragments and ivory are also positively linked with adults, and bone fittings and the general glass category are positively linked with mature adults. The same glass category also exhibits negative links with children. Bone rings are linked with adolescents, and bronze fragments are linked with children. Combs are rarely associated with infant burials, although they are found with children. Finally, there may be a positive association between playing pieces and the burial of old adults. Perhaps they spent much of their time playing games. There are no other significant links with any other classes of individual grave-goods.

If the skeletal groupings are cross-tabulated with the identity groups described in section 2.224 some additional significant links become apparent (table 27).

GROUP ZERO, without grave-goods, is positively linked with infants and adolescents, but negatively linked with mature adults. This appears to confirm the impression that this social group, for whom

NOTE

[1] It will be observed later, (section 3.31), that whilst the grave-goods for a child may have been identical to those for an adult, a child cremation was normally distinguished from an adult one in other ways.

Table 26 Associations of grave-goods and age of individual

	Total No	SKELETAL GROUPING: Infant No Row% Sig			Child No Row% Sig			Adolescent No Row% Sig		
Total	391	14	3.6		61	15.6		28	7.2	
GRAVE-GOOD PRESENT:										
Bone fitting	21	1	4.8	1.0	2	9.5	0.63	1	4.8	1.0
Bronze fragment	109	2	1.8	0.39	11	10.1	0.09	7	6.4	0.89
Bronze sheet	29	-	-	0.58	3	10.3	0.59	-	-	0.24
Bronze tweezers	27	1	3.7	1.0	3	11.1	0.7	2	7.4	1.0
Brooch	25	-	-	0.66	3	12.0	0.82	4	16.0	0.17
Comb	129	1	0.8	0.07*	21	16.3	0.91	12	9.3	0.35
Crystal	16	-	-	0.92	-	-	0.16	-	-	0.52
Glass	85	1	1.2	0.31	6	7.1	0.02	5	5.9	0.78
Glass beads	99	1	1.0	0.2	16	16.2	0.99	7	7.1	1.0
Glass vessel	9	-	-	1.0	1	11.1	1.0	-	-	0.85
Iron fragment	28	4	14.3	0.01*	4	14.3	1.0	2	7.1	1.0
Iron rivet	15	-	-	0.96	2	13.3	1.0	1	6.7	1.0
Ivory	48	1	2.1	0.86	3	6.2	0.09	5	10.4	0.53
Miniature iron blade	17	2	11.8	0.23	7	41.2	0.01*	2	11.8	0.79
Miniature iron shears	30	-	-	0.56	10	33.3	0.01*	3	10.0	0.80
Miniature iron tweezers	28	1	3.6	1.0	3	10.7	0.64	4	14.3	0.26
Playing piece	15	-	-	0.96	2	13.3	1.0	-	-	0.56
Spindlewhorl	27	-	-	0.62	3	11.1	0.7	-	-	0.27
Worked flint	11	1	9.1	0.86	1	9.1	0.86	-	-	0.73

	Total No	Young Adult No Row% Sig			Mature Adult No Row% Sig			Old Adult No Row% Sig			Adult No Row% Sig		
Total	442	84	19.0		82	18.6		21	4.8		181	41.0	
GRAVE-GOOD PRESENT:													
Bone fitting	25	5	20.0	1.0	9	36.0	0.04*	-	-	0.51	8	32.0	0.47
Bronze fragment	119	26	21.8	0.43	21	17.7	0.87	7	5.9	0.67	56	47.1	0.14
Bronze sheet	32	7	21.9	0.85	4	12.5	0.5	-	-	0.38	19	59.4	0.04
Bronze tweezers	32	8	25.0	0.51	6	18.8	1.0	4	12.5	0.09*	14	43.8	0.88
Brooch	31	8	25.8	0.45	3	9.8	0.28	1	3.2	1.0	13	41.9	1.0
Comb	149	26	17.5	0.64	26	17.5	0.77	7	4.7	1.0	66	44.3	0.36
Crystal	19	6	31.6	0.26	3	15.8	0.98	1	5.3	1.0	11	57.9	0.19
Glass	91	17	18.7	1.0	23	25.3	0.09	1	1.1	0.12	40	44.0	0.59
Glass beads	118	26	22.0	0.4	22	18.6	1.0	6	5.1	1.0	52	44.1	0.49
Glass vessel	10	2	20.0	1.0	1	10.0	0.77	-	-	1.0	7	70.0	0.12
Iron fragment	28	1	3.6	0.06	5	17.9	1.0	1	3.6	1.0	12	42.9	0.99
Iron rivet	19	4	21.1	1.0	4	21.1	1.0	3	15.8	0.08*	7	36.8	0.89
Ivory	56	10	17.9	0.96	9	16.1	0.74	-	-	0.15	32	57.1	0.01
Miniature iron blade	20	-	-	0.05*	4	20.0	1.0	1	5.0	1.0	6	30.0	0.43
Miniature iron shears	31	-	-	0.01	3	9.7	0.28	3	9.7	0.37	13	41.9	1.0
Miniature iron tweezers	29	1	3.4	0.05	1	3.4	0.06	1	3.4	1.0	19	65.5	0.01
Playing piece	16	3	18.8	1.0	3	18.8	1.0	3	18.8	0.04*	6	37.5	0.98
Spindlewhorl	30	6	20.0	1.0	7	23.3	0.65	1	3.3	1.0	15	50.0	0.39
Worked flint	12	3	25.0	0.87	2	16.7	1.0	-	-	0.92	4	33.3	0.81

grave-goods were not considered appropriate, was drawn chiefly from the lower status individuals, including some infants and juveniles. In many societies, infants are not considered to be full human beings, and so are not considered worthy of receiving the full status burial rites. Similarly, mature adults, as perhaps the highest status individuals are more likely to be given grave-goods.

However, the picture is made more complicated by the fact that not all infants and adolescents are in GROUP ZERO; rather infants and adolescents are just more likely to be in GROUP ZERO than in other identity groupings. Other infants must have been born into higher status groups. Furthermore, it is interesting that the intermediate age group, children, are just as likely to be in any of the social groups. Apparently full status was acquired on reaching childhood, although it could be lost again in adolescence. If the presence of grave-goods can indeed be seen as relating to status then the peak of status in Anglo-Saxon society was reached in mature adulthood. Once individuals passed into old age, then they were just as likely to be buried without grave-goods again.

GROUP ONE, on the other hand, exhibits no significant association with any of the skeletal age groupings. Whilst we have already observed that it tended to have a higher proportion of males than expected, the actual age of the individuals appears to have been irrelevant to their membership of this group.

Finally, the membership of GROUP TWO again seems to be irrespective of age, with one exception. Infants were less likely to be members of GROUP TWO, just as they were more likely to be in GROUP ZERO. On the whole, however, membership of GROUPS ONE and TWO appears to have been independent of age, whereas membership of GROUP ZERO is related to age, although not determined by it.

A greater number of significant links emerge when one considers the links between animal bones and human age groupings (table 28). Apparently animal offerings were used more than artefactual material to indicate age. Firstly, infant burials are less likely to contain animal bones than one would expect, whereas mature adults are more likely to. Here there is apparently a direct link between age status and the provision of animals. Turning to the individual animals, each of the four major species represented occurs with each age grouping, but there are clear preferences for certain animals with certain ages. In particular, horse, cow and pig are significantly linked with adults, whereas sheep are not positively linked, and indeed show a negative correlation with young adults. Conversely, cow and horse are never found with children, and pig rarely, although sheep are frequently included.

In conclusion, it appears that the addition of animal bones is used to mark the age and sex of the deceased. Males are more likely to be given animals than females, and adults are given horse and cow especially, whereas sheep are considered as suitable companions for children. Yet age and sex were not seen as criteria which should be reflected in the grave-goods and there are few clear links between specific grave-goods and age and sex groupings. If the deposition of

Table 27   Associations of identity groupings with age of individual

IDENTITY GROUPING:

	Total No	GROUP 0 No Row% Sig	GROUP 1 No Row% Sig	GROUP 2 No Row% Sig
Total	706	264 37.4	76 10.8	151 21.4
AGE:				
Infant	39	21 53.8 0.04	5 12.8 0.87	3 7.7 0.05
Child	149	58 38.9 0.73	15 10.1 0.87	35 23.5 0.55
Adolescent	61	30 49.2 0.06	8 13.1 0.69	13 21.3 1.0
Young adult	134	50 37.3 1.0	10 7.5 0.22	30 22.4 0.84
Mature adult	108	26 24.1 0.003	11 10.2 0.97	28 25.9 0.26
Old adult	33	11 34.4 0.86	5 15.6 0.54	6 18.8 0.88
Adult	286	105 36.7 0.82	35 12.2 0.36	69 24.1 0.17

Table 28   Associations of animals with age of individual

ANIMAL GROUPING:

	Total No	Animal bones No Row% Sig	Sheep No Row% Sig	Cow / Ox No Row% Sig
Total	706	144 20.4	50 7.1	20 2.8
AGE:				
Infant	39	3 7.7 0.07	3 7.7 1.0	- - 0.55
Child	149	24 16.1 0.18	13 8.7 0.48	- - 0.04
Adolescent	61	9 14.8 0.33	5 8.2 0.93	1 1.6 0.85
Young adult	134	28 20.9 0.97	4 3.0 0.06	3 2.2 0.86
Mature adult	108	29 26.9 0.09	9 8.3 0.73	3 2.8 1.0
Old adult	33	5 15.6 0.65	2 6.2 1.0	1 3.1 1.0
Adult	286	67 23.4 0.12	24 8.4 0.33	14 4.9 0.01

	Total No	Pig No Row% Sig	Horse No Row% Sig
Total	706	21 3.0	18 2.5
AGE:			
Infant	39	- - 0.52	- - 0.61
Child	149	2 1.3 0.29	- - 0.05
Adolescent	61	3 4.9 0.59	1 1.6 0.96
Young adult	134	1 0.7 0.16	2 1.5 0.58
Mature adult	108	1 0.9 0.29	4 3.7 0.62
Old adult	33	- - 0.63	- - 0.72
Adult	286	18 6.3 0.001	12 4.2 0.04

grave-goods is a meaningful act, then they must be marking other roles in Anglo-Saxon society; roles which cross-cut simple age and sex bands and are perhaps considered to be more important. It remains to determine what these roles might be.

3.3 The significance of vessel form

The form of Anglo-Saxon cremation urns has been defined (section 2.215) by a number of attributes, including size, three ratios expressing shape, and several qualitative variables, most notably the presence of a deliberate hole. Variation in all but the last of these has traditionally been explained in terms of changes in fashion through time, and changes in style through space. In this section I shall discuss the relationship between these attributes of form and other attributes of the cremation, including decoration, grave-goods and skeletal groupings, in an attempt to explore other interpretations of vessel form.

3.31 Vessel size

We have observed (section 3.111) that there is a high level of similarity in the range of sizes of cremation vessels found at each of the cemeteries in the study sample. Within each cemetery, however, there is considerable variation in the sizes of vessels; often ranging from c.10cm to c.35cm in height. There are no obvious breaks in this range on any of the sites. Rather than discrete sizes, therefore, there is just a continuous gradation of sizes. Each site exhibits a normal distribution, with more vessels of average height, and a gradual decline in numbers towards the two extremes. This variability may simply be the result of "stylistic error" of potters working towards an idealised mental template, in which case the range of sizes represents a random spread of sizes within an accepted range. Alternatively, the size of the cremation vessels may be related to another variable such as the social identity of the individual buried in it. In this case the number of vessels of a particular size will be directly proportional to the number of individuals of the social group represented by that size.

The size of a vessel bears no relation to whether it is decorated or not. Nor does it relate to the type of decoration which may be used. When the different sizes of vessels at Elsham and Spong Hill were cross-tabulated against the main types of decoration, no significant links were found.

However, when the frequency distributions of sizes of vessels belonging to particular identity groupings were compared to the overall distribution (using the Kolmogorov-Smirnov test), then each identity was found to constitute an assemblage of vessels which differed significantly from the total sample (at the 0.01 level). The distributions are shown in table 29. The top line gives the cumulative frequency (as a percentage) of vessels at five divisions of height for the total sample. The main body of the table gives the respective figures for urns in each grouping, and the significance

Table 29 Frequency distribution of vessel height for each identity
grouping

| | VESSEL HEIGHT (CM) | | | | (Cum. freq.%) | SIG. LEVEL |
	15.0	17.5	20.0	22.5	25.0	(Kolmog.- Smir. test)
Total	13.9	28.8	48.9	73.3	90.9	
GROUP ZERO	18.9	35.5	55.7	77.3	92.1	0.01
GROUP ONE	9.9	17.1	33.3	63.1	87.3	0.01
GROUP TWO	6.2	21.8	45.8	72.8	89.9	0.01

Table 30 Frequency distribution of vessel height for each grave-good

| | VESSEL HEIGHT (CM) | | | | (Cum. freq.%) | SIG. LEVEL |
	15.0	17.5	20.0	22.5	25.0	(Kolmog.- Smir. test)
Total	13.9	28.8	48.9	73.3	90.9	
GRAVE-GOOD PRESENT:						
Bone fitting	9.1	12.1	24.2	51.5	78.8	0.01
Bronze fragment	7.8	15.1	35.3	68.8	89.4	0.01
Bronze sheet	3.7	13.0	33.3	63.0	89.8	0.01
Bronze tweezers	5.0	8.7	31.3	60.0	88.7	0.01
Brooch	9.6	25.0	48.1	81.7	96.2	
Comb	8.2	21.5	39.4	68.1	89.3	0.01
Crystal	6.5	9.7	35.5	64.5	87.1	0.2
Glass	6.7	11.2	32.8	66.4	87.3	0.01
Glass beads	6.2	22.6	46.0	71.8	89.6	0.05
Glass vessel	4.2	12.5	25.0	43.8	89.6	0.01
Iron fragment	7.0	18.3	40.8	63.4	81.7	0.2
Iron rivet	12.7	20.6	38.1	73.0	90.5	
Ivory	4.3	13.8	37.9	69.8	88.8	0.05
Miniature iron blade	15.7	25.3	36.1	59.0	85.5	0.01
Miniature iron shears	10.7	23.1	38.0	63.6	83.5	0.05
Miniature iron tweezers	9.1	18.2	32.2	61.2	86.0	0.01
Playing piece	5.5	7.3	14.5	41.8	80.0	0.01
Spindlewhorl	9.3	25.9	40.7	70.4	87.0	
Worked flint	8.1	24.3	48.6	59.5	91.9	

level for the difference between these and the cumulative frequency
for the total sample. The five divisions have been selected to
present any difference as clearly as possible. The Kolmogorov-Smirnov
test, of course, was calculated on the basis of the complete
cumulative frequency distributions, at 1cm intervals. GROUP ZERO
(without grave-goods) was found to be concentrated in vessels of below
average height. This cannot be a simple function of not being able to
fit grave-goods in the smaller vessels, as most objects could easily
fit inside the smallest cremation vessel. Rather, we must conclude
that the Anglo-Saxons often considered that it was appropriate to bury
those individuals without grave-goods in smaller vessels. Conversely,
GROUP TWO, with glass beads and ivory, tend to be buried in larger
vessels, whilst GROUP ONE, with miniatures, are found most frequently
in larger vessels still. If size were crudely related to status then
that would make these the highest status individuals.

When the frequency distributions of sizes of vessels containing
specific grave-goods are compared against the overall distribution
(table 30) then a large number of significant differences are
observed. As well as the miniatures, a high proportion of the other
grave-goods also tend to be concentrated in vessels of above average
height. Bone fittings, bronze fragments and bronze sheets, bronze
tweezers, combs, crystal, glass and glass vessels, iron fragments,
ivory, and playing pieces are all found more frequently in taller
pots.

Glass vessels and playing pieces especially are found most
frequently in the tallest vessels. In addition, glass beads are less
common in very small vessels, but are found in small to average pots.
In fact, the only grave-goods which do not tend to be found more often
in larger vessels are brooches, iron rivets, spindlewhorls and worked
flints. Whilst the height of the cremation vessel appears to be in
direct proportion to the age of the deceased (see below) we have
already observed that few of the grave-goods are age-linked (section
3.22). Therefore the concentration of most grave-goods in larger
vessels does not just reflect that these are adult burials. Rather it
appears that the size of vessel signifies not only age at death, but
it may also mark the inclusion of particular objects. The deposition
of glass vessels or playing pieces in very tall pots may mark these as
burials of the highest status individuals.

The links between size and social identity are reinforced when the
sizes of vessels containing specific skeletal groupings are compared
against the overall distribution (table 31).

Clearly, there is a close correlation between the age and sex of an
individual and the size of vessel that he or she was buried in,
ranging from infants in the shortest, to old adults in the tallest.
In Anglo-Saxon society, age was probably one of the means by which an
individual gained status. In death, this appears to have been marked
in the cremation urn. The relationship between age and height of pot
is so direct that it should be possible to estimate the age of the
deceased within a known range of error simply from the height of the
cremation urn, and with no knowledge of its contents. Both male and
female adults tend to be buried in vessels of above average height,

Table 31 Frequency distribution of vessel height for each skeletal grouping

	VESSEL	HEIGHT	(CM)	(Cum.	freq.%)	SIG. LEVEL
	15.0	17.5	20.0	22.5	25.0	(Kolmog.-Smir. test)
Total	13.9	28.8	48.9	73.3	90.9	
SKELETAL GROUP PRESENT:						
Infant	48.7	64.1	82.1	92.3	97.4	0.01
Child	33.8	58.3	70.2	88.1	98.0	0.01
Adolescent	17.5	38.1	58.7	81.0	95.2	
Young adult	10.4	20.9	41.8	75.4	91.8	
Mature adult	4.6	12.0	32.4	62.0	82.4	0.01
Old adult	-	11.8	26.5	50.0	88.2	0.05
Adult	10.8	24.7	44.9	69.0	90.2	
Male	4.2	8.3	26.7	49.2	84.2	0.01
Female	4.5	17.8	36.3	68.2	91.1	0.05
Animal bones present:	5.6	15.0	35.0	61.2	85.6	0.01
Sheep	9.1	21.8	43.6	65.5	89.1	
Cow/Ox	9.1	13.6	31.8	54.5	86.4	0.1
Pig	-	-	17.4	56.5	87.0	0.05
Horse	5.0	10.0	20.0	35.0	75.0	0.01

but it is clear that this is less marked for the females. If one equates age and status, then since females are not generally buried in the tallest urns, one might conclude that they were regarded as being of proportionally lower status. On the other hand, there is a clear contradiction here with the fact that a higher proportion of females are buried with grave-goods. Apparently simple divisions by gender are misleading and conceal distinct groups of low and high ranking females.

Table 31 also shows that many of the animals included as grave offerings also tend to be in taller vessels. This does not apply to sheep, but cows, and especially pig and horse are found in vessels of above average height. This would make pig and horse the highest status offerings, cow the next most prestigious, and sheep the most lowly accompaniment.

Three other dimensions relating to vessel size were recorded for every urn in the sample, namely maximum diameter, height of maximum diameter, and rim diameter. Maximum diameter and height of maximum diameter have a linear relationship with vessel height, and, as one would expect, the results reinforce those obtained for height.

Table 32 presents the frequency distributions of maximum diameter for urns with each grave-good. Again, all grave-goods, except bronze fragments, brooches, iron rivets, spindlewhorls and worked flints, tend to be deposited more frequently in urns which are wider than the average. Bronze sheet, bronze tweezers, glass vessels, and playing

Table 32 Frequency distribution of vessel maximum diameter for each grave-good

	VESSEL MAX DIAM (CM)			(Cum.freq.%)		SIG. LEVEL
	15.0	20.0	22.5	25.0	30.0	(Kolmogorov-Smirnov test)
Total	5.1	26.7	46.3	70.1	95.7	
GRAVE-GOOD PRESENT:						
Bone fitting	3.0	15.2	24.2	48.5	97.0	0.1
Bronze fragment	0.9	17.4	41.3	67.0	94.0	
Bronze sheet	1.9	9.3	21.3	52.8	93.5	0.01
Bronze tweezers	-	10.0	18.8	52.5	96.2	0.01
Brooch	3.8	20.2	41.3	67.3	96.2	
Comb	1.9	18.9	39.1	66.6	94.3	0.05
Crystal	-	6.5	35.5	74.2	93.5	0.05
Glass	1.5	11.9	30.6	61.9	93.3	0.01
Glass beads	1.8	15.1	41.2	66.8	95.8	0.01
Glass vessel	-	12.5	25.0	45.8	87.5	0.01
Iron fragment	1.4	18.3	35.2	56.3	90.1	0.05
Iron rivet	1.6	14.3	34.9	66.7	96.8	
Ivory	-	9.5	36.2	68.1	96.6	0.01
Miniature iron blade	4.8	20.5	33.7	59.0	91.6	0.05
Miniature iron shears	3.3	21.5	31.4	57.0	88.4	0.01
Miniature iron tweezers	2.5	15.7	30.6	55.4	90.9	0.01
Playing piece	-	7.3	12.7	34.5	85.5	0.01
Spindlewhorl	1.9	18.5	53.7	74.1	92.6	
Worked flint	2.7	21.6	35.1	64.9	97.3	

Table 33 Frequency distribution of vessel maximum diameter for each skeletal grouping

	VESSEL MAX DIAM (CM)			(Cum.freq.%)		SIG. LEVEL
	15.0	20.0	22.5	25.0	30.0	(Kolmogorov-Smirnov test)
Total	5.1	26.7	46.3	70.1	95.7	
SKELETAL GROUP PRESENT:						
Infant	28.2	64.1	84.6	92.3	100.0	0.01
Child	13.9	57.6	72.2	89.4	98.7	0.01
Adolescent	4.8	31.7	58.7	76.2	98.4	
Young adult	3.0	22.4	41.0	76.1	97.8	
Mature adult	1.9	14.8	30.6	57.4	94.4	0.01
Old adult	-	8.8	23.5	52.9	97.1	0.15
Adult	2.1	22.0	43.6	66.6	95.8	
Male	0.8	17.5	33.3	57.5	96.7	0.05
Female	1.9	12.7	32.5	61.8	97.5	0.01
Animal bones present:	1.9	11.9	31.9	62.5	95.0	
Sheep	3.6	16.4	43.6	70.9	96.4	
Cow/Ox	4.5	13.6	31.8	59.1	100.0	
Pig	-	8.7	26.1	56.5	100.0	0.15
Horse	-	15.0	25.0	50.0	90.0	

pieces are found especially in the very wide vessels. Table 33 compares the maximum diameters for each of the skeletal groupings. Again, age is in direct relation to vessel width and both male and female adults also show a prefeence for the wider vessels. Similarly, more animal offerings are buried in wider pots, but this does not apply to sheep, whilst only pig is significantly different from the overall distribution.

The height of the maximum diameter of a cremation vessel is largely determined by the overall vessel height, and so most of the grave-goods tend to be in vessels with an above average height of maximum diameter (table 34). Of course, this dimension does not indicate anything about the shoulderedness of a vessel; to consider this we need to look at shape, which is examined in the next section. Brooches, spindlewhorls, and worked flints again stand out as not bearing any relation to vessel size. Obviously, the aspects of social identity which they represent are not related to age, or to anything else reflected in size. In table 35 the frequency distributions for the skeletal groups are presented. Once more, age is in direct proportion to the height of the maximum diameter; males are concentrated in vessels with a high maximum diameter, and females less so. Animals are also more common in these vessels, pigs and horses significantly so.

Rim diameter is not directly related to vessel size. Whilst a tiny pot cannot have a large rim, there is still considerable freedom of choice for the potter. Large pots can have narrow necks, whilst straight-sided vessels will have a rim diameter almost as large as their maximum diameter. The results for rim diameter (tables 36-37) therefore reflect this, with far fewer significant links. Bronze sheet is found in vessels with a large rim, but since this was one of the strongest links for the other dimensions, this is probably a hangover from the relationship with vessel size. Similarly glass beads and vessels are significant at a lower level than for the other dimensions. Infants and children are significantly clustered in vessels with a small rim diameter, and again echo the size relationship. Turning to the sex of the occupant however, it appears that rim diameter may have some independent significance. Whilst males are not particularly clustered in vessels with large rim diameters, females, whose link with size was not so pronounced, are significantly concentrated in vessels with a rim diameter above the mean. Thus it appears that the size of a vessel's rim can be used to signify if the occupant is female.

Finally, the relationship between size of vessel and the age and sex of the deceased is examined regionally in figs.29-37. These scattergrams plot height against the maximum diameter at each site for each vessel with a skeletal identification. Thus tall wide vessels are plotted towards the upper right, whilst short narrow vessels are in the lower left-hand corner. It can be seen that at each site there is a fairly direct relationship between height and maximum diameter, which will be considered further in section 3.32. However, by examining where particular ages and sexes tend to cluster along this line, some interesting features of individual sites become apparent.

Table 34 Frequency distribution of vessel height of maximum diameter
for each grave-good

| | HEIGHT MAX DIAM (CM) | | | | (Cum.freq.%) | SIG. L. (Kolmog. Smir. test) |
	6.0	8.0	10.0	12.0	14.0	
Total	3.2	15.7	43.0	75.7	93.6	
GRAVE-GOOD PRESENT:						
Bone fitting	3.0	12.1	30.3	66.7	97.0	0.2
Bronze fragment	1.8	9.2	31.7	69.3	93.1	0.01
Bronze sheet	1.9	5.6	24.1	63.0	91.7	0.01
Bronze tweezers	-	7.5	28.7	63.7	95.0	0.1
Brooch	2.9	8.7	34.6	77.9	96.2	
Comb	2.2	10.4	37.2	70.7	92.1	0.1
Crystal	3.2	9.7	25.8	67.7	93.5	
Glass	3.0	6.0	29.9	68.7	96.3	0.05
Glass beads	1.5	9.2	38.3	72.4	92.9	0.1
Glass vessel	-	6.3	22.9	54.2	83.3	0.01
Iron fragment	2.8	12.7	32.4	62.0	85.9	0.05
Iron rivet	6.3	11.1	34.9	73.0	95.2	0.15
Ivory	0.9	10.3	31.9	70.7	96.6	0.1
Miniature iron blade	3.6	19.3	33.7	66.3	89.2	0.05
Miniature iron shears	2.5	15.7	34.7	64.5	90.1	0.05
Miniature iron tweezers	2.5	12.4	28.1	60.3	91.7	0.01
Playing piece	1.8	3.6	25.5	49.1	81.8	0.01
Spindlewhorl	3.7	11.1	29.6	74.1	90.7	
Worked flint	-	10.8	37.8	62.2	100.0	

Table 35 Frequency distribution of vessel height of maximum diameter
for each skeletal grouping

| | HEIGHT MAX DIAM (CM) | | | | (Cum.freq.%) | SIG. L. (Kolmog. Smir. test) |
	6.0	8.0	10.0	12.0	14.0	
Total	3.2	15.7	43.0	75.7	93.6	
SKELETAL GROUP PRESENT:						
Infant	15.4	48.7	74.4	89.7	97.4	0.01
Child	9.3	35.8	66.9	87.4	97.4	0.01
Adolescent	3.2	17.5	49.2	82.5	96.8	
Young adult	3.7	7.5	35.1	72.4	95.5	0.1
Mature adult	0.9	6.5	27.8	67.6	91.7	0.01
Old adult	-	2.9	23.5	55.9	88.2	0.01
Adult	1.0	12.2	38.0	74.2	92.7	
Male	-	5.8	24.2	61.7	90.0	0.01
Female	1.3	5.7	34.4	68.8	96.8	0.01
Animal bones present:	1.2	8.7	30.6	68.8	90.6	0.01
Sheep	1.8	10.9	40.0	67.3	96.4	
Cow/Ox	4.5	13.6	36.4	72.7	95.5	
Pig	-	4.3	17.4	78.3	95.7	0.1
Horse	-	10.0	30.0	55.0	90.0	0.1

Table 36 Frequency distribution of vessel rim diameter for each grave-good

	RIM DIAMETER (CM) (Cum.freq.%)					SIG. LEVEL (Kolmog. Smir. test)
	10.0	12.5	15.0	17.5	20.0	
Total	7.4	40.5	70.5	87.5	95.2	
GRAVE-GOOD PRESENT:						
Bone fitting	6.1	54.5	72.7	78.8	93.9	
Bronze fragment	5.5	39.4	67.0	85.8	94.5	
Bronze sheet	2.8	29.6	57.4	77.8	91.7	0.05
Bronze tweezers	5.0	37.5	73.7	88.7	95.0	
Brooch	5.8	35.6	66.3	84.6	95.2	
Comb	5.7	42.6	73.5	91.2	97.2	
Crystal	3.2	35.5	71.0	93.5	100.0	
Glass	4.5	45.5	71.6	88.1	97.0	
Glass beads	3.0	35.0	65.6	84.9	94.7	0.15
Glass vessel	6.3	31.3	58.3	79.2	87.5	0.2
Iron fragment	2.8	39.4	66.2	84.5	93.0	
Iron rivet	6.3	39.7	69.8	93.7	98.4	
Ivory	2.6	34.5	69.8	85.3	94.0	
Miniature iron blade	9.6	42.2	74.7	91.6	100.0	
Miniature iron shears	8.3	41.3	75.2	91.7	95.9	
Miniature iron tweezers	5.8	38.0	73.6	92.6	100.0	
Playing piece	3.6	36.4	61.8	85.5	96.4	
Spindlewhorl	3.7	48.1	72.2	87.0	96.3	
Worked flint	10.8	37.8	83.8	94.6	100.0	

Table 37 Frequency distribution of vessel rim diameter for each skeletal grouping

	RIM DIAMETER (CM) (Cum.freq.%)					SIG. LEVEL (Kolmog. Smir. test)
	10.0	12.5	15.0	17.5	20.0	
Total	7.4	40.5	70.5	87.5	95.2	
SKELETAL GROUP PRESENT:						
Infant	23.1	64.1	94.9	97.4	100.0	0.01
Child	21.2	64.2	83.4	89.4	98.7	0.01
Adolescent	3.2	39.7	74.6	90.5	98.4	
Young adult	3.0	34.3	67.9	84.3	94.8	
Mature adult	4.6	39.8	65.7	82.4	92.6	
Old adult	8.8	29.4	61.8	76.5	88.2	
Adult	4.9	40.8	67.6	85.4	93.7	
Male	1.7	42.5	71.7	88.3	96.7	
Female	3.2	31.2	63.1	79.6	91.1	0.01
Animal bones present:	1.2	34.4	64.4	85.0	93.1	
Sheep	3.6	30.9	67.3	85.5	94.5	
Cow/Ox	4.5	54.5	81.8	90.9	100.0	
Pig	8.7	43.5	78.3	95.7	95.7	
Horse	5.0	45.0	60.0	70.0	95.0	

Figure 29 Key to figures 30-37

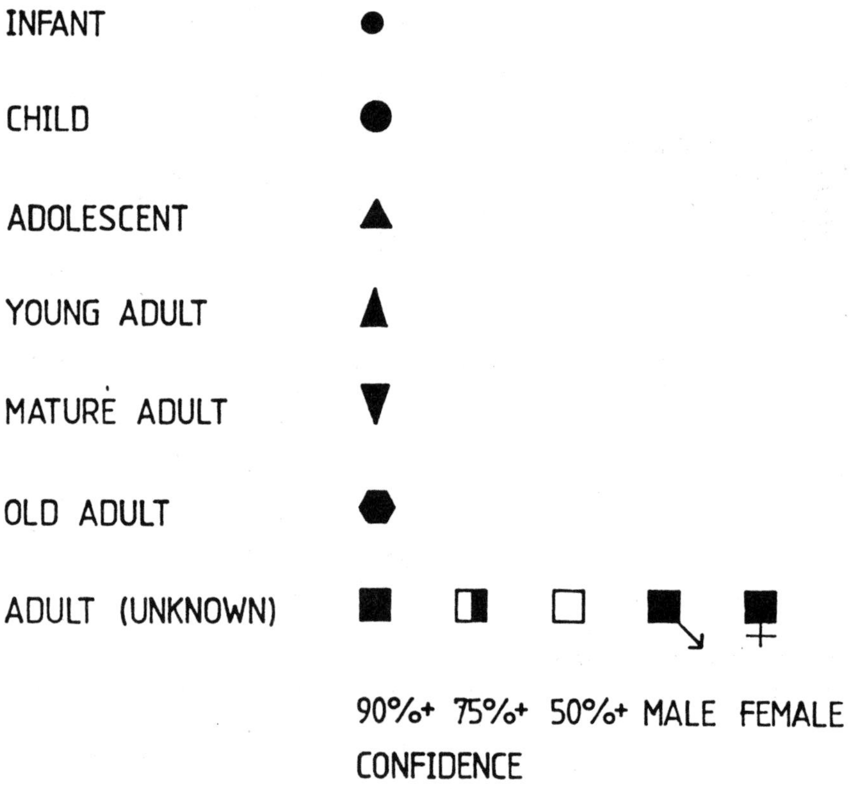

INFANT	●
CHILD	●
ADOLESCENT	▲
YOUNG ADULT	▲
MATURE ADULT	▼
OLD ADULT	⬡
ADULT (UNKNOWN)	■ ◨ □ ◪↘ ■⚲

90%+ 75%+ 50%+ MALE FEMALE
CONFIDENCE

At Caistor (fig.30) there is a clear break between adult and child burials, with infants generally in smaller vessels still. Apart from double burials of adult and child together there are just two cases of children in large vessels. Indeed, one is in the largest vessel in the sample, and must represent an exceptional child. Although the number of sexed individuals is small, it may be of interest that the males are both in larger vessels than the females. At Caistor, one must be somewhat suspicious of the clear child/adult break, because of Mann's selection of child burials for analysis (possibly on the basis of size of vessels). However, this pattern is repeated on other sites, where there was no selection.

At Elsham (fig.31) infants and children are again concentrated in the lower left of the graph. Male adults are found more at the top right, whilst most female adults are clustered around the centre. It is tempting to speculate that those females which are found in larger vessels may have been higher status women.

Figure 30

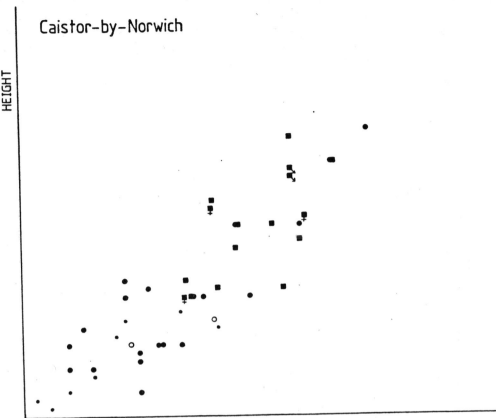

Caistor-by-Norwich

Figure 31

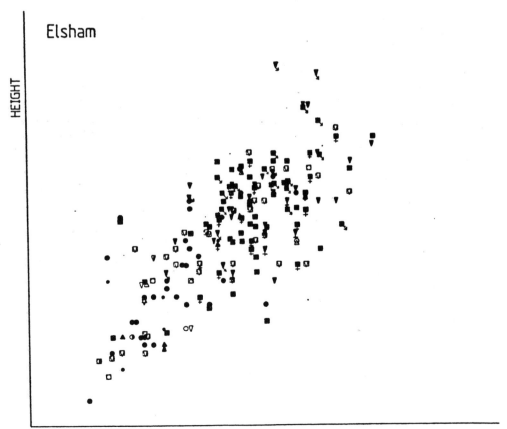

Elsham

At Illington (fig.32), infants are clearly in the smallest vessels, although children are more evenly spread. Adolescent and young adults are in some of the largest vessels, and males and females are also more intermixed. Perhaps the significance of vessel size was not so rigorously applied within this cemetery. Possibly age/sex distinctions were not held to be so important.

Figure 32

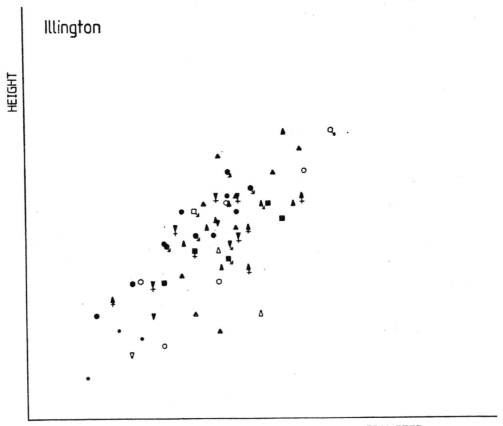

In the Loveden sample (fig.33) there are few chidren, but they are
in the smaller vessels. Adults are in the larger ones, with males,
especially, in the largest. The old adult males are all in vessels of
average sizes, or above.

At Newark (fig.34) the infants are tightly clustered in the smallest
urns.   Most children are also in this group, although some are buried
in vessels of more average size. Too few of the cremations are sexed
to allow us to draw any conclusions about their relative disposal.

At Mucking (fig.35) we can observe a situation similar to that at
Illington.   Infants and children are fairly evenly spread, and are
found in some large vessels.   Male and female adults are equally
intermixed.   If the skeletal evidence can be relied upon then we must
conclude that age-sex distinctions were again not so rigorously
defined in this community.

Figure 33

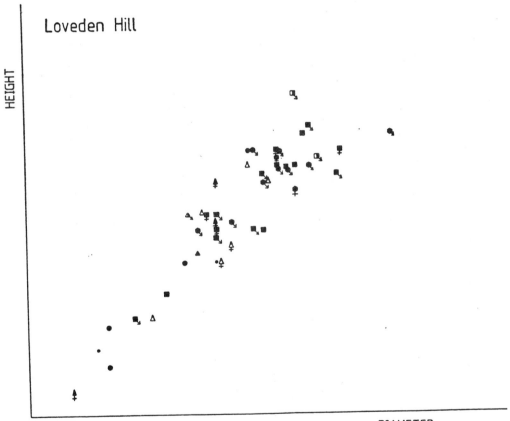

Figure 34

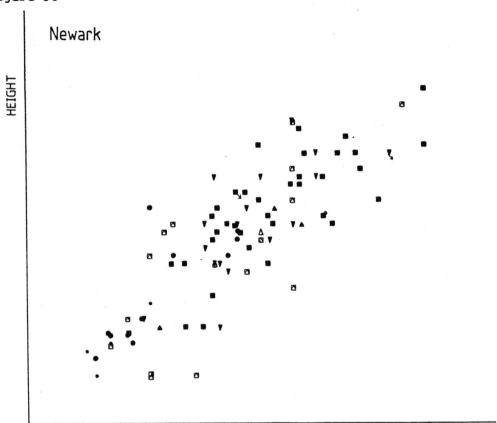

Figure 35

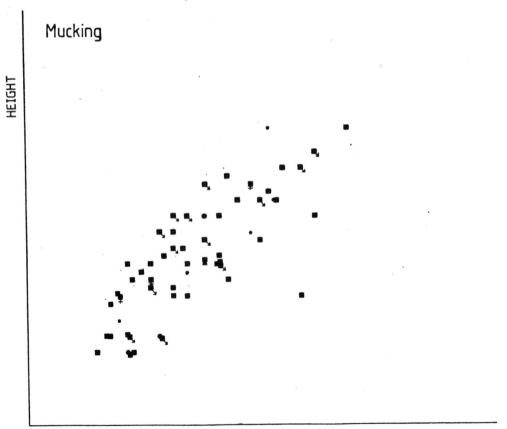

Figure 36

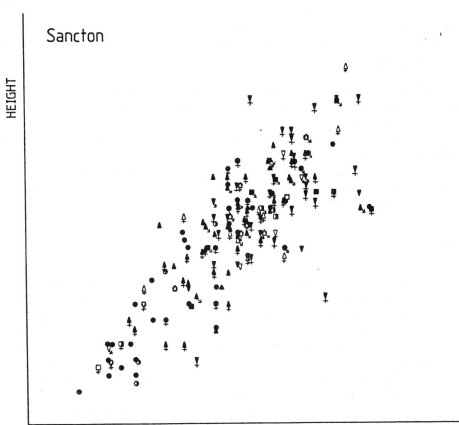

Figure 37

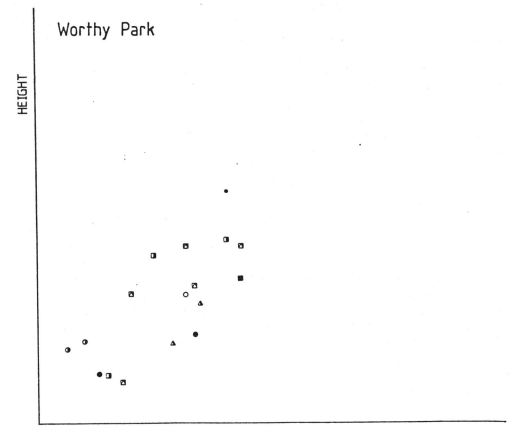

We see a more familiar picture at Sancton (fig.36). With one or two exceptions all the children are in the smaller vessels, and adults in the larger ones. However, there are a number of female burials in large vessels at this site, and the male/female distinction is not as clear as elsewhere.

At Worthy Park (fig.37) the sample size is rather small, but there does not appear to be any clear pattern as the age groupings seem evenly spread, as at Illington and Mucking. We have noted the similarities between these three sites before, and have associated it with traits which have distinguished them as Saxon, rather than Anglian. If this is correct, then it would imply that age and sex distinctions were less well-defined in Saxon society, or at least that they were less marked in death.

3.32 Vessel shape

The shape of Anglo-Saxon cremation urns varies independently of their size, but as with size, no discrete groupings are apparent. It has been demonstrated (section 2.215) that variability of shape can be described by three ratios derived from PCA. It will be argued here, that as well as describing shape efficiently, these ratios also describe shape in a similar manner to that in which it was conceived by the Anglo-Saxon makers and users of the cremation pottery. The contents of the cremation vessels are correlated, to varying degrees, with the three shape ratios. Therefore the Anglo-Saxons must have been aware of variability in these terms, and must have categorised vessels, at least intuitively, according to them. Variability in shape is not random variation about a single norm, or ideal template. Either the cremation pottery was consciously produced in the different forms considered appropriate for each individual, or, even if existing pottery was selected, then it was chosen as being appropriate for the individual. Either way, (and even if variability in form represents types of domestic vessels), the Anglo-Saxons conceived of shape according to these criteria, and used them to signify social identity.

The relationship between shape of vessel and the various classes of decoration at Spong Hill has been examined elsewhere (see Richards 1982). These results revealed that shape was a major influence on the types of decoration considered appropriate to particular vessels. All three ratios appeared to be correlated with decorative classes. For example, vertical and curvilinear incised decoration, and bosses, were seen to be more frequently used on those wider vessels, with a high value for the maximum diameter/height ratio; shouldered urns are less likely to be decorated; vessels with restricted necks have a higher proportion of many types of decoration. It was concluded that most of these correlations cannot have been due to chronological factors of shape and decorative motifs changing together through time. Most decorative classes were widely used thoughout the Early Anglo-Saxon period. It was suggested that the correlations resulted from an Anglo-Saxon conception that particular forms of vessel were suitable for particular motifs.

Table 38 Frequency distribution describing vessel shape for each identity grouping

| | VESSEL WIDTH (Cum.freq%) | | | | SIG. LEVEL (Kolmogorov-Smirnov test) |
	1.0	1.1	1.2	1.3	
Total	24.4	53.1	75.3	89.7	
GROUP ZERO	26.3	54.3	76.0	90.0	
GROUP ONE	19.4	47.2	73.0	92.5	
GROUP TWO	21.0	46.5	72.8	85.9	0.1

| | SHOULDEREDNESS (Cum.freq%) | | |
	0.9	1.0	1.1
Total	22.9	55.8	84.4
GROUP ZERO	24.3	56.1	83.7
GROUP ONE	25.0	58.7	84.1
GROUP TWO	18.3	51.5	82.9

| | NECK RESTRICTION (Cum.freq%) | | | | |
	0.6	0.8	1.0	1.2	
Total	19.2	40.5	65.9	84.4	
GROUP ZERO	24.4	47.5	71.8	88.1	0.01
GROUP ONE	7.5	20.6	46.4	69.0	0.01
GROUP TWO	13.9	35.1	61.1	82.7	

Certain grave-goods were also found to be associated with particular shapes of vessel, implying that both shape, and decoration, were linked to social identity. It was possible to examine these correlations in more detail, and for other sites, in the total research sample.

Table 38 shows the relationship between vessel shape and the three identity groupings[1]. The first ratio, of maximum diameter to height, indicates how wide a vessel is. The larger the value, the

NOTE

[1] As in section 3.31, suitable intervals have been selected for these tables to demonstrate the differences in cumulative frequency distributions. The calculations for the Kolmogorov-Smirnov test, however, were based upon the complete distributions, at intervals of 0.1.

wider the vessel. GROUP ZERO and GROUP ONE are each found just as
frequently in wide and narrow urns. GROUP TWO, however, are
significantly correlated with wider vessels. Thus, whilst individuals
without grave-goods, or those with miniatures, could be buried in
vessels of all widths, there was a tendency to bury those with glass
beads and ivory in wider urns.

The second ratio expresses the "shoulderedness" or "bagginess" of an
urn. "Baggy" urns have low ratio values, whilst shouldered vessels
will have a value greater than 1.0. However, none of the identity
groups appeared to be related to this aspect of shape. Finally, the
third ratio represented the degree to which the neck of a pot was
restricted. Open-mouthed urns are characterised by a low ratio value,
whilst vessels with necks which narrow towards the mouth have
respectively higher values, according to the degree to which the neck
is constricted. Those individuals without grave-goods (GROUP ZERO)
were more likely to be buried in wide-mouthed vessels, whilst those
with miniatures (GROUP ONE) tended to be deposited in vessels with
highly restricted necks. GROUP TWO was not correlated with this
aspect of shape. Wide-mouthed urns are often described as cooking
pots and even if deliberately made for use as cremation vessels, they
may still have borne domestic connotations. Therefore it seems as if
they were regarded as suitable containers for those individuals who
did not deserve grave-goods. GROUP ONE, as a high status group, would
have to be treated so that this status was signified. Therefore it
was considered appropriate that they should be placed in vessels with
narrow necks, in effect marking these as non-functional as domestic
cooking pots.

Tables 39-44 show the relationship between each of the three ratios
and each grave-good and skeletal grouping. Both bronze sheet and
glass beads are significantly linked with wider vessels. The other
grave-goods, however, do not appear to be correlated with vessel
width, altough two skeletal groups are. Old adults are markedly
clustered in narrower vessels. Not only, then, is their age marked by
the height of the vessel, but in many cases the pot will also be
narrower than others. Male adults in general are also linked with
narrower pots. Given the link between glass beads and wider vessels,
this would seem to be a sex and status link, with males in narrower,
and females in wider pots.

Glass beads may also be linked wth vessels with a high shoulder
although, since the unidentified glass category exhibits the opposite
trend, this may just be a freak result. However, brooches certainly
are associated with shouldered urns, whilst all other grave-goods are
found in expected proportions thoughout the range. This is
particularly interesting, for whilst most grave-goods were correlated
with size of vessel, brooches were the chief exception, and turned up
in all sizes of pot. Clearly then, individuals with brooches are not
signified by the size of a pot, but are represented by its shape,
particularly in the relative height of the shoulder. Similarly, no
human skeletal groups are linked with shoulderedness. Cows do show a
slight tendency to congregate in baggy vessels, but the result appears
anomalous since they are the only possible link.

Table 39 Frequency distribution of vessel width for each grave-good

	VESSEL WIDTH		(Cum.freq.%)		SIG. LEVEL (Kolmogorov-Smirnov test)
	1.0	1.1	1.2	1.3	
Total	24.4	53.1	75.3	89.7	
GRAVE-GOOD PRESENT:					
Bone fitting	39.4	66.7	87.9	97.0	
Bronze fragment	28.9	57.8	76.6	89.0	
Bronze sheet	18.5	42.6	63.9	79.6	0.15
Bronze tweezers	23.7	46.2	70.0	93.8	
Brooch	20.2	51.0	70.2	86.5	
Comb	26.5	54.3	76.3	89.0	
Crystal	32.3	58.1	67.7	93.5	
Glass	24.6	57.5	81.3	91.8	
Glass beads	20.8	45.7	71.8	86.1	0.05
Glass vessel	25.0	52.1	72.9	87.5	
Iron fragment	26.8	49.3	74.6	88.7	
Iron rivet	15.9	44.4	73.0	84.1	
Ivory	25.0	51.7	77.6	87.9	
Miniature iron blade	22.9	48.2	69.9	89.2	
Miniature iron shears	19.0	47.9	71.1	91.7	
Miniature iron tweezers	18.2	48.8	75.2	92.6	
Playing piece	16.4	47.3	81.8	96.4	
Spindlewhorl	33.3	51.9	77.8	90.7	
Worked flint	21.6	54.1	86.5	91.9	

Table 40 Frequency distribution of vessel width for each skeletal grouping

	VESSEL WIDTH		(Cum.freq%)		SIG. LEVEL (Kolmogorov-Smirnov test)
	1.0	1.1	1.2	1.3	
Total	24.4	53.1	75.3	89.7	
SKELETAL GROUP PRESENT:					
Infant	20.5	51.3	74.4	94.9	
Child	23.8	50.3	70.9	85.4	
Adolescent	25.4	49.2	74.6	87.3	
Young adult	28.4	58.2	81.3	91.8	
Mature adult	29.6	55.6	78.7	94.4	
Old adult	23.5	76.5	88.2	94.1	0.05
Adult	28.6	54.7	77.0	89.2	
Male	30.8	71.7	87.5	94.2	0.01
Female	24.2	54.1	78.3	91.7	
Animal bones present:	28.1	53.7	79.4	91.2	
Sheep	32.7	52.7	70.9	87.3	
Cow/Ox	36.4	59.1	86.4	100.0	
Pig	39.1	65.2	95.7	100.0	
Horse	40.0	60.0	90.0	100.0	

Table 41 Frequency distribution of vessel shoulderedness for each grave-good

| | SHOULDEREDNESS (Cum.freq%) | | | SIG. LEVEL (Kolmogorov-Smirnov test) |
	0.9	1.0	1.1	
Total	22.9	55.8	84.4	
GRAVE-GOOD PRESENT:				
Bone fitting	36.4	72.7	97.0	
Bronze fragment	21.6	57.8	86.7	
Bronze sheet	17.6	52.8	81.5	
Bronze tweezers	26.2	63.7	87.5	
Brooch	9.6	38.5	81.7	0.01
Comb	23.3	54.3	84.9	
Crystal	22.6	54.8	93.5	
Glass	28.4	65.7	90.3	0.15
Glass beads	17.2	49.6	81.9	0.15
Glass vessel	14.6	58.3	81.3	
Iron fragment	19.7	53.5	78.9	
Iron rivet	28.6	60.3	92.1	
Ivory	22.4	57.8	90.5	
Miniature iron blade	25.3	63.9	83.1	
Miniature iron shears	27.3	59.5	82.6	
Miniature iron tweezers	27.3	56.2	79.3	
Playing piece	21.8	56.4	80.0	
Spindlewhorl	18.5	53.7	87.0	
Worked flint	13.5	51.4	94.6	

Table 42 Frequency distribution of vessel shoulderedness for each skeletal grouping

| | SHOULDEREDNESS (Cum.freq%) | | | SIG. LEVEL (Kolmogorov-Smirnov test) |
	0.9	1.0	1.1	
Total	22.9	55.8	84.4	
SKELETAL GROUP PRESENT:				
Infant	15.4	46.2	87.2	
Child	24.5	53.0	86.8	
Adolescent	20.6	42.9	79.4	
Young adult	18.7	53.0	85.8	
Mature adult	28.7	60.2	86.1	
Old adult	14.7	52.9	91.2	
Adult	26.5	54.0	80.1	
Male	31.7	62.5	88.3	
Female	22.3	54.1	86.6	
Animal bones present:	31.3	56.9	87.5	
Sheep	29.1	65.5	90.9	
Cow/Ox	50.0	68.2	100.0	0.1
Pig	34.8	65.2	95.7	
Horse	35.0	55.0	85.0	

Table 43 Frequency distribution of vessel neck restriction for each grave-good

	NECK RESTRICTION (Cum.freq%)				SIG. LEVEL
	0.6	0.8	1.0	1.2	(Kolmogorov-Smirnov test)
Total	19.2	40.5	65.9	84.4	
GRAVE-GOOD PRESENT:					
Bone fitting	12.1	30.3	54.5	84.8	
Bronze fragment	12.8	34.4	56.4	83.5	0.05
Bronze sheet	16.7	32.4	55.6	77.8	
Bronze tweezers	11.2	23.7	45.0	70.0	0.01
Brooch	15.4	36.5	60.6	82.7	
Comb	13.2	30.6	57.4	79.8	0.01
Crystal	19.4	48.4	64.5	74.2	
Glass	11.9	28.4	58.2	76.9	0.01
Glass beads	13.6	34.7	59.9	82.8	0.2
Glass vessel	12.5	31.3	52.1	79.2	
Iron fragment	14.1	29.6	57.7	83.1	0.1
Iron rivet	12.7	27.0	52.4	76.2	0.2
Ivory	11.2	31.0	60.3	84.5	
Miniature iron blade	7.2	22.9	53.0	73.5	0.05
Miniature iron shears	9.1	22.3	50.4	72.7	0.01
Miniature iron tweezers	6.6	16.5	48.8	70.2	0.01
Playing piece	5.5	21.8	49.1	63.6	0.05
Spindlewhorl	16.7	37.0	66.7	81.5	
Worked flint	5.4	27.0	45.9	70.3	0.15

Table 44 Frequency distribution of vessel shoulderedness for each skeletal grouping

	NECK RESTRICTION (Cum.freq%)				SIG. LEVEL
	0.6	0.8	1.0	1.2	(Kolmogorov-Smirnov test)
Total	19.2	40.5	65.9	84.4	
SKELETAL GROUP PRESENT:					
Infant	23.1	51.3	87.2	94.9	0.05
Child	19.2	42.4	70.2	90.1	
Adolescent	15.9	42.9	68.3	90.5	
Young adult	21.6	41.0	68.7	90.3	
Mature adult	16.7	37.0	62.0	81.5	
Old adult	26.5	50.0	67.6	82.4	0.15
Adult	20.9	37.6	66.6	83.3	
Male	15.8	30.8	63.3	79.2	
Female	21.0	42.7	68.2	86.0	
Animal bones present:	16.9	36.2	64.4	83.1	
Sheep	18.2	43.6	69.1	87.3	
Cow/Ox	18.2	36.4	59.1	72.7	
Pig	8.7	21.7	69.6	91.3	
Horse	20.0	40.0	60.0	70.0	

The restrictedness of the neck, however, is strongly correlated with a wide range of grave-goods, and skeletal groups. It is worth noting that this ratio only accounted for 5% of the variability in urn shape. The former two ratios represent 88% of the variability, but revealed fewer significant correlations. Clearly, the greatest physical differences between artefacts are not necessarily those which are most significant to the makers and users. All the miniatures, plus bronze tweezers, bronze and iron fragments, combs and iron rivets, glass, glass beads, playing pieces, and worked flints, are significantly correlated with these vessels which have a restricted neck and are less frequently found in wide-mouthed urns. Amongst the other grave-goods, brooches are certainly not linked to particular types of neck.

The association between narrow-necked urns and many grave-goods cannot just reflect that these vessels are somehow less likely to have lost their grave-goods in the ground. In that case the association should be with all grave-goods, with no exceptions. Similarly, these results suggest that worked flints are not simply accidental inclusions, having fallen into the urn from the surrounding matrix after deposition. Since the correlation is with "closed" rather than "open" urns (into which they should have been more likely to fall), they must be seen as deliberate grave-goods[1].

Finally, most age groups appear to be found across the range of neck types, except for the two extremes of age. In particular, infants tend to be buried in open-mouthed vessels, and are less common in narrow-necked pots. Whilst both infants and children are buried in small pots, infants are thus distinguished from children by being placed in such vessels. Similarly, old adults, as well as being buried in narrower pots, also tend to be given an urn with a narrow neck.

3.33 Deliberately-holed urns

We have observed that as many as 10% of vessels may be deliberately holed, although the meaning of this ritual remains unclear. Since it is only applied to a small and regular proportion of urns it may be used to signify a particular minority group. One is reminded of the special treatment of small numbers of inhumations such as decapitation and the flexing of the legs. Such messages are not available in the case of cremations, and alternative means of signifying their meaning would have to be found.

NOTE

[1] At Spong Hill, the correlation between flints and narrow-necked vessels was even stronger, significant at 0.05. In addition, the urns in which they were found were fairly widely distributed thoughout the sampled area of the cemetery, and did not appear to be concentrated in areas of prehistoric activity.

If several types of decoration are cross-tabulated with the presence of deliberate holes (table 45) none are significant at the 0.1level, although there does appear to be a tendency for a higher proportion of decorated vessels to have a hole.

Table 45 Associations of types of decoration with urns with deliberate holes

	Total No	Holed urns No	Row%	Sig
Total	1887	82	4.4	
Plastic decoration	740	35	4.7	0.59
Vertical bosses	573	31	5.4	0.17
Round bosses	142	7	2.8	0.89
Cordons	137	3	2.2	0.29
Stamped decoration	930	45	4.8	0.36

Table 46 Associations of identity groupings with urns with deliberate holes

	Total No	GROUP ZERO No	Row%	Sig	GROUP ONE No	Row%	Sig	GROUP TWO No	Row%	Sig
		IDENTITY GROUPING:								
Total	2440	1270	52.0		252	10.3		404	16.6	
Holed urns	112	49	43.8	0.09	7	6.3	0.2	19	17.0	1.0

However, when holed urns are cross-tabulated with the identity groups (table 46) there is a significant tendency for GROUP ZERO not to be buried in holed vessels. In other words there are more burials with grave-goods than would be expected by chance[1]. However, GROUP ONE do not tend to be buried in holed urns, and GROUP TWO occur in

NOTE

[1] At Spong Hill, however, precisely the opposite was found. For the pilot sample there was a tendency for GROUP ZERO to be buried in holed urns, significant at 0.06. Clearly, there are regional differences in the manner in which individuals buried in holed urns are treated.

Table 47 Associations of grave-goods with urns with deliberate holes

	Total No	Holed urns		
		No	Row%	Sig
Total	2440	111	4.6	
GRAVE-GOOD PRESENT:				
Bone fitting	33	1	3.0	0.99
Bronze fragment	217	13	6.0	0.39
Bronze sheet	108	14	13.0	0.001
Bronze tweezers	80	1	1.3	0.24
Brooch	96	4	4.2	1.0
Comb	309	15	4.9	0.94
Crystal	31	2	6.5	0.95
Glass	134	7	5.2	0.88
Glass beads	337	18	5.3	0.57
Glass vessel	48	2	4.2	1.0
Iron fragment	71	2	2.8	0.66
Iron rivet	63	3	4.8	1.0
Ivory	115	4	3.5	0.72
Miniature iron blade	83	3	3.6	0.87
Miniature iron shears	121	4	3.3	0.64
Miniature iron tweezers	121	4	3.3	0.64
Playing piece	55	3	5.5	1.0
Spindlewhorl	52	5	9.6	0.16
Worked flint	37	1	2.7	0.88

Table 48 Associations of skeletal remains with urns with deliberate holes

	Total No	Holed urns		
		No	Row%	Sig
Total	706	23	3.3	
SKELETAL GROUP PRESENT:				
Infant	39	–	–	0.48
Child	149	5	3.4	1.0
Adolescent	61	–	–	0.26
Young adult	134	7	5.2	0.25
Mature adult	108	2	1.9	0.55
Old adult	32	1	3.1	1.0
Adult	286	13	4.5	0.17
Male	119	3	2.5	0.83
Female	153	5	3.3	1.0
Animal bones present:	144	9	6.3	0.05

exactly the proportion that would be expected by chance. Therefore it must be other grave goods that are deposited in holed urns. This is confirmed when each of the popular grave-goods is cross-tabulated with the presence of deliberate holes (table 47). In particular, this table reveals that fragments of bronze and bronze sheet are associated with holed urns. Possibly this was because the objects placed in a holed vessel were also deliberately damaged, and this has prevented their identification.

The associations between deliberate holes and skeletal groups may offer some further clues about their meaning (table 48). No infants or adolescents have been found in holed vessels, but children occur as frequently as would be expected by chance. The holed urns tend to contain adults or young adults, but without any preference for males or females. The only link significant above 0.1, however, is the correlation between holed urns and the inclusion of animals. Taken with the correlation with the deposition of other grave-goods, this would argue against these being burials of social outcasts, or other deviants, prevented from returning from the spirit world. Rather these individuals are given preferential treatment at most sites and the insertion of a hole in the vessel must be viewed in this context.

3.4 The significance of vessel decoration

The decoration of Anglo-Saxon cremation urns has been described by a large number of attributes discussed in section 2. Like vessel form, variation in decoration has traditionally been explained according to a cultural-history model. In this section the relationship between decorative attributes and other attributes of the cremation will be discussed, in an attempt to identify alternative interpretations of vessel decoration.

About 77% of all urns in the sample have some form of decoration, which may range from simple bands of incised lines around the neck, to elaborate Buckelurnen. This enormous variety in decorative styles suggests that any simple division into plain and decorated vessels is a false one; there may be more in common between plain and simply decorated vessels, than between vessels with little decoration and those with considerable decoration. Therefore, the actual type and quantity of decoration must be considered.

There is also variation in the proportion of decorated vessels between sites, ranging from the Saxon site, Mucking, with less than 40% of vessels decorated, and Anglian sites such as Elsham, Lackford and Newark with over 80% (see table 9). Therefore some attention must be paid to regional variability.

Finally, the use of decoration itself must be related to the social identity of the individual(s) buried within it. Table 49 cross-tabulates the use of decoration with the presence of each of the most common classes of grave-good. The associations significant at the 0.11evel are underlined. Bronze tweezers, ivory and glass are more common in decorated vessels than would be expected by chance. In order to check if these links run through all types of decoration, and

Table 49 Associations of grave-good classes with use of decoration

	Total No	Decoration No	Row%	Sig
Total	2440	1887	77.3	
GRAVE-GOOD PRESENT:				
Bone fitting	33	30	90.9	0.1
Bronze fragment	217	173	79.7	0.43
Bronze sheet	108	88	81.5	0.35
Bronze tweezers	80	71	88.8	0.02
Brooch	96	72	75.0	0.66
Comb	309	246	79.6	0.34
Crystal	31	23	74.2	0.84
Glass	134	117	87.3	0.006
Glass beads	337	266	78.9	0.49
Glass vessel	48	38	79.2	0.9
Iron fragment	71	57	80.3	0.65
Iron rivet	63	54	85.7	0.15
Ivory	115	97	84.4	0.09
Miniature iron blade	83	67	80.7	0.54
Miniature iron shears	121	97	80.2	0.52
Miniature iron tweezers	121	98	81.0	0.38
Playing piece	55	46	83.6	0.33
Spindlewhorl	52	44	84.6	0.27
Worked flint	37	29	78.4	1.0

if there are other links with particular decorative classes which are masked at this level, it was necessary to examine each type of decoration individually.

3.41 Incised and impressed decoration

The most popular means of decorating a vessel was to inscribe or impress its surface with a pointed implement. Approximately 75% of vessels at each site, (with the exception of Mucking), have incised or impressed decoration. In fact, virtually every decorated vessel has some form of incised design, even if it is just a simple band of lines around the neck. The only common exceptions are simple bossed or lugged pots, which may have bosses without incised lines. There are also one or two instances of pots with stamped decoration but no incised lines, but these are less common as the incising is generally required to provide a framework for the stamped design.

The popularity of incised decoration may be understood in terms of both its ease of execution, and its potential for producing a wide range of easily visible variability in vessel style. Therefore the various types of incised pattern are an obvious place in which to look for design symbolism.

3.411 Influence on vessel decoration

Despite its flexibility, the use of incised decoration on a particular vessel appears to have implications for the other forms of decoration which could be applied. Table 50 presents the large number of associations between the major classes of incised decoration and categories of plastic decoration[1]. Some of these are determined by the fact that one form will tend to logically exclude or favour another. The strong association between plastic decoration and the use of vertical lines or single reversed chevrons, for example, merely indicates that once the decorative surface of a pot has been broken by the use of bosses, then the individual fields are suitable for the application of these types of incised designs. Similarly, such vessels are unsuitable for the application of continuous chevron patterns. Again, the positive associations between plastic decoration and the use of slashes, dots, circles and crosses simply reflects the use of these to decorate raised surfaces, as in "slashed cordons" or "slashed vertical bosses".

On the other hand, there are other associations which cannot easily be explained by design logic. Why, for example, should plastic decoration be negatively correlated with hanging arches, but positively linked with standing arches? There are cases where the lack of any significant association is equally interesting. Why, for example, is there not a positive link between single upright chevrons and plastic decoration, just as there is for reversed chevrons? Both would appear to be logically equivalent. In these cases an interpretation based on Anglo-Saxon iconography is certainly tempting.

Some explanations become more obvious when links with particular forms of plastic decoration are examined. For example, it can be seen that there is a negative correlation between vertical bosses and hanging arches, but no significant link with standing arches. For round bosses, on the other hand, there is a strong, positive association with standing arches, but no significant association with hanging arches. The latter may be explained by the use of standing arches to "outline" a round boss on many vessels, although why hanging arches are infrequently found with vertical bosses remains unclear.

There are also significant associations between bosses and cordons and other types of incised decoration, although the reasons are less clear. In particular, groups of diagonal lines sloping downwards to the right are positively linked with vertical and round bosses and cordons. Leftwards sloping diagonals, on the other hand, are not significantly associated with vertical bosses, despite exhibiting links with round bosses and cordons.

NOTE

[1] No figures are given for the use of horizontal lines since these are virtually identical to the figures for the use of incised decoration in general.

Table 50 Associations of classes of plastic decoration with classes of incised decoration

	Total No	Plastic decoration No Row%		Sig	Vertical bosses No Row%		Sig
Total	2440	740	39.2		573	30.4	
Incised decoration	1805	663	36.7	0.001	526	29.1	0.001
Vertical lines	761	465	61.1	0.001	411	54.0	0.001
Continuous chevron	571	92	16.2	0.001	60	10.6	0.001
Broken chevron	41	22	55.0	0.06	15	37.5	0.42
Upright chevron	121	50	41.3	0.69	42	34.7	0.33
Reversed chevron	117	67	57.8	0.001	53	45.7	0.001
Diagonals to left	164	69	42.6	0.41	54	33.3	0.45
Diagonals to right	125	58	46.4	0.11	47	37.6	0.09
Curvilinear	32	13	40.6	1.0	7	21.9	0.39
Hanging arch	133	35	26.3	0.002	26	19.5	0.007
Standing arch	164	80	48.8	0.01	56	34.1	0.31
Slashes	246	163	66.3	0.001	120	48.8	0.001
Dots	316	138	43.7	0.09	106	33.5	0.2
Circle	22	19	86.4	0.001	17	77.3	0.001
Swastika	28	15	53.6	0.17	12	42.9	0.22
Cross	71	38	53.5	0.02	31	43.7	0.02
Cross on base	8	2	25.0	0.64	2	25.0	1.0

	Total No	Round bosses No Row%		Sig	Cordons No Row%		Sig
Total	2440	142	7.5		137	7.3	
Incised decoration	1805	126	7.0	0.001	133	7.4	0.55
Vertical lines	761	74	9.7	0.004	84	11.0	0.001
Continuous chevron	571	10	1.8	0.001	19	3.4	0.001
Broken chevron	41	3	7.5	1.0	8	20.0	0.005
Upright chevron	121	8	6.6	0.83	10	8.3	0.8
Reversed chevron	117	19	16.4	0.001	17	14.7	0.003
Diagonals to left	164	22	13.6	0.004	21	13.0	0.006
Diagonals to right	125	20	16.0	0.001	15	12.0	0.05
Curvilinear	32	4	12.5	0.46	3	9.4	0.9
Hanging arch	133	10	7.5	1.0	9	6.8	0.96
Standing arch	164	36	22.0	0.001	26	15.9	0.001
Slashes	246	54	22.0	0.001	89	36.2	0.001
Dots	316	32	10.1	0.07	36	11.4	0.003
Circle	22	13	59.1	0.001	6	27.3	0.001
Swastika	28	9	32.1	0.001	5	17.9	0.07
Cross	71	10	14.1	0.06	11	15.5	0.01
Cross on base	8	–	–	0.89	–	–	0.91

Table 51 Associations of urns with stamped decoration with classes of incised decoration

	Total No	Stamped decoration No	Row%	Sig
Total	1887	930	49.3	
Horizontal lines	1781	916	51.4	0.001
Vertical lines	761	357	46.9	0.1
Continuous chevron	567	281	49.6	0.89
Broken chevron	40	18	45.0	0.7
Upright chevron	121	75	62.0	0.005
Reversed chevron	116	56	48.3	0.89
Diagonals to left	162	46	28.4	0.001
Diagonals to right	125	42	33.6	0.001
Curvilinear	32	16	50.0	1.0
Hanging arch	133	91	68.4	0.001
Standing arch	164	52	31.7	0.001
Slashes	246	109	44.3	0.11
Dots	316	77	24.4	0.001
Circle	22	6	27.3	0.06
Swastika	28	6	21.4	0.005
Cross	71	31	43.7	0.4
Cross on base	8	6	75.0	0.27

In addition, there are differences in the extent to which the different incised motifs are used with stamped decoration. Table 51 cross-tabulates each incised motif against vessels with any stamped decoration. There are some interesting variations, not all of which can be explained by technical aspects of design. Urns with stamped decoration are significantly less likely to have vertical incised lines, circles and crosses. They are more likely to have horizontal incised lines, and upright chevrons, although there is not a significant relationship with reversed chevrons. Diagonal sloping lines, whether to the left or right, are less common on stamped vessels; hanging arches are more common, whilst standing arches are less so.

The different significance attached to "left hand" and "right hand" diagonals and to upright and reversed chevrons and arches, suggests that those may be being used to represent simple binary oppositions. The social significance of these dichotomies will become clearer if links between incised decoration and grave-goods are considered.

3.412 Incised motifs and vessel contents

Most grave-goods exhibit distinctive links with categories of incised decoration (table 52a-e). By implication, it is possible to predict from the design of a funerary vessel that it is more likely to contain

Table 52(a) Associations of grave-good classes with types of incised decoration

	Total	Horizontal lines			Vertical lines			Continuous chevron			Broken chevron		
	No	No	Row%	Sig	No	Row%	Sig	No	Row%	Sig	No	Row%	Sig
Total	2440	1781	73.0		761	31.2		571	23.3		41	1.6	
GRAVE-GOOD PRESENT:													
Bone fitting	33	29	87.9	0.08	12	36.4	0.65	9	27.3	0.73	1	3.0	1.0
Bronze fragment	217	163	75.1	0.51	69	31.8	0.89	55	25.5	0.48	4	1.8	1.0
Bronze sheet	108	81	75.0	0.71	38	35.2	0.42	29	26.9	0.43	1	0.9	0.83
Bronze tweezers	80	70	87.5	0.005	40	50.0	0.001	22	27.5	0.44	1	1.2	1.0
Brooch	96	67	69.8	0.55	26	27.1	0.44	21	22.1	0.88	-	-	0.38
Comb	309	235	76.1	0.21	102	33.0	0.5	77	25.0	0.47	5	1.6	1.0
Crystal	31	19	61.3	0.2	9	29.0	0.95	3	9.7	0.11	-	-	0.99
Glass	134	112	83.6	0.006	48	35.8	0.27	34	25.4	0.63	3	2.2	0.83
Glass beads	337	253	75.1	0.39	114	33.8	0.29	69	20.5	0.23	5	1.5	1.0
Glass vessel	48	37	77.1	0.63	19	39.6	0.27	9	18.7	0.56	-	-	0.75
Iron fragment	71	52	73.2	1.0	23	32.4	0.93	15	21.1	0.77	-	-	0.53
Iron rivet	63	52	82.5	0.11	21	33.3	0.82	14	22.2	0.96	1	1.6	1.0
Ivory	115	93	80.9	0.07	38	33.0	0.74	32	28.1	0.26	-	-	0.3
Miniature iron blade	83	64	77.1	0.46	35	42.2	0.04	11	13.3	0.04	-	-	0.45
Miniature iron shears	121	92	76.0	0.5	48	39.7	0.05	23	19.0	0.3	-	-	0.28
Miniature iron tweezers	121	94	77.7	0.28	54	44.6	0.002	22	18.2	0.21	2	1.7	1.0
Playing piece	55	46	83.6	0.1	23	41.8	0.12	14	25.5	0.82	-	-	0.67
Spindlewhorl	52	40	76.9	0.62	20	38.5	0.32	12	23.1	1.0	2	3.8	0.48
Worked flint	37	28	75.7	0.85	8	21.6	0.28	10	27.0	0.73	1	2.7	1.0

some grave-goods, rather than others, without any previous knowledge of the contents. Only bronze fragments, glass vessels and spindlewhorls, show no associations which are significant at the 0.1 level. In the case of glass vessels and spindlewhorls this could be the result of small sample size; for the bronze fragments, however, it must mean that they are just not reflected in the incised decoration, as they are present in a large number of vessels.

Other grave-goods show specific correlations with just one or two aspects of incised decoration. Bone fittings, for example, were found in just 33 urns, and the only significant correlation is with the use of horizontal lines. Other grave-goods, such as bronze tweezers and miniature toilet implements, exhibit correlations with a wide range of incised motifs.

Conversely, some motifs appear to be richly symbolic and are correlated with many types of grave-goods; others reveal no significant links. Vessels with horizontal lines contain more bone fittings, bronze tweezers, glass fragments and ivory, than could be expected by chance. Those with vertical lines also contain more bronze tweezers, but in addition, they are associated with miniature blades, shears and tweezers.

The use of a continuous chevron, on the other hand, means that a vessel is less likely to contain miniature toilet implements, although only the negative correlation with blades is significant. The use of a broken chevron does not appear to be significant, although there are only 41 instances of it amongst 2440 vessels in the sample.

When one turns to instances of single upright and reversed chevrons, (table 52b), these vessels contain the number of miniatures that one would expect according to chance, yet they are positively associated with bronze tweezers and iron rivets. In this case, both the upright and the reversed chevrons reflect the same trend, and the correlation can be strengthened by combining them. In other words, here it is the use of the chevron that is important, not whether it is pointing up or down.

Table 52(b) Associations of grave-good classes with types of incised decoration

	Total	Upright chevron			Reversed chevron			Diagonals to left			Diagonals to right		
	No	No	Row%	Sig	No	Row%	Sig	No	Row%	Sig	No	Row%	Sig
Total	2440	121	5.0		117	4.8		164	6.7		125	5.1	
GRAVE-GOOD PRESENT:													
Bone fitting	33	-	-	0.36	1	3.0	0.95	1	3.0	0.63	1	3.0	0.88
Bronze fragment	217	11	5.1	1.0	10	4.6	1.0	11	5.1	0.4	6	2.8	0.14
Bronze sheet	108	3	2.8	0.4	6	5.6	0.87	7	6.5	1.0	3	2.8	0.36
Bronze tweezers	80	+ 8	10.0	0.06*	8	10.0	0.05*	6	7.5	0.93	4	5.0	1.0
Brooch	96	3	3.1	0.54	8	8.3	0.15	5	5.2	0.74	6	6.2	0.76
Comb	309	16	5.2	0.97	19	6.1	0.27	31	10.1	0.01	16	5.2	1.0
Crystal	31	1	3.2	0.98	2	6.5	0.98	1	3.2	0.69	-	-	0.37
Glass	134	7	5.2	1.0	3	2.3	0.24	11	8.3	0.55	9	6.7	0.51
Glass beads	337	11	3.3	0.16	22	6.5	0.13	25	7.4	0.61	19	5.6	0.74
Glass vessel	48	1	2.1	0.55	2	4.2	1.0	4	8.5	0.82	1	2.1	0.53
Iron fragment	71	3	4.2	0.99	4	5.6	0.94	6	8.5	0.71	5	7.0	0.64
Iron rivet	63	+ 7	11.1	0.05*	8	12.7	0.007*	4	6.3	1.0	5	7.9	0.46
Ivory	115	8	7.0	0.43	6	5.2	0.99	6	5.3	0.68	5	4.3	0.87
Miniature iron blade	83	5	6.0	0.84	5	6.0	0.77	10	12.0	0.07	5	6.0	0.9
Miniature iron shears	121	6	5.0	1.0	7	5.8	0.74	12	10.0	0.19	6	5.0	1.0
Miniature iron tweezers	121	6	5.0	1.0	7	5.8	0.74	17	14.2	0.001	12	9.9	0.03
Playing piece	55	3	5.5	1.0	4	7.3	0.57	11	20.0	0.001*	8	14.5	0.004*
Spindlewhorl	52	2	3.8	0.96	1	1.9	0.52	5	9.6	0.56	3	5.8	1.0
Worked flint	37	1	2.7	0.8	1	2.7	0.84	4	10.8	0.49	5	13.5	0.05*

+ Upright and reversed chevron combined because of low cell frequency:

		Chevron		
		No	Row%	Sig
		214	8.8	
Bronze tweezers	80	15	18.8	0.003
Iron rivet	63	11	17.5	0.03

Table 52(c) Associations of grave-good classes with types of incised decoration

	Total	Continuous curvilinear			Hanging arch			Standing arch		
	No	No	Row%	Sig	No	Row%	Sig	No	Row%	Sig
Total	2440	32	1.3		133	5.5		164	6.7	
GRAVE-GOOD PRESENT:										
Bone fitting	33	-	-	1.0	3	9.1	0.59	4	12.1	0.37
Bronze fragment	217	-	-	0.14	9	4.1	0.47	14	6.5	0.98
Bronze sheet	108	-	-	0.43	4	3.7	0.55	10	9.3	0.38
Bronze tweezers	80	2	2.5	0.65	3	3.7	0.67	9	11.2	0.16
Brooch	96	-	-	0.49	6	6.2	0.91	7	7.3	0.99
Comb	309	3	1.0	0.76	18	5.8	0.85	31	10.0	0.02
Crystal	31	-	-	1.0	2	6.5	1.0	2	6.5	1.0
Glass	134	4	3.0	0.17	7	5.2	1.0	14	10.4	0.11
Glass beads	337	6	1.8	0.58	13	3.9	0.21	18	5.3	0.33
Glass vessel	48	2	4.2	0.27	1	2.1	0.47	3	6.2	1.0
Iron fragment	71	2	2.8	0.55	5	7.0	0.74	10	14.1	0.02*
Iron rivet	63	1	1.6	1.0	1	1.6	0.28	9	14.3	0.03*
Ivory	115	1	0.9	0.99	6	5.2	1.0	8	7.0	1.0
Miniature iron blade	83	1	1.2	1.0	4	4.8	0.99	12	14.5	0.008
Miniature iron shears	121	2	1.7	1.0	10	8.3	0.23	14	11.6	0.05
Miniature iron tweezers	121	3	2.5	0.45	6	5.0	0.97	17	14.0	0.002
Playing piece	55	1	1.8	1.0	3	5.5	1.0	4	7.3	1.0
Spindlewhorl	52	-	-	0.82	2	3.8	0.84	2	3.8	0.58
Worked flint	37	1	2.7	0.98	2	5.4	1.0	6	16.2	0.05*

Table 52(d) Associations of grave-good classes with types of incised decoration

	Total	Slashes			Dots		
	No	No	Row%	Sig	No	Row%	Sig
Total	2440	246	10.1		316	13.0	
GRAVE-GOOD PRESENT:							
Bone fitting	33	5	15.2	0.5	6	18.2	0.52
Bronze fragment	217	21	9.7	0.93	33	15.2	0.35
Bronze sheet	108	11	10.2	1.0	22	20.4	0.03
Bronze tweezers	80	10	12.5	0.59	18	22.5	0.02
Brooch	96	8	8.3	0.7	19	19.8	0.06
Comb	309	42	13.6	0.03	54	17.5	0.02
Crystal	31	6	19.4	0.15	1	3.2	0.18
Glass	134	13	9.7	1.0	21	15.7	0.41
Glass beads	337	46	13.6	0.03	54	16.0	0.09
Glass vessel	48	6	12.5	0.75	7	14.6	0.9
Iron fragment	71	9	12.7	0.59	17	23.9	0.009
Iron rivet	63	5	7.9	0.72	9	14.3	0.9
Ivory	115	8	7.0	0.33	19	16.5	0.31
Miniature iron blade	83	12	14.5	0.25	14	16.9	0.36
Miniature iron shears	121	11	9.1	0.83	24	19.8	0.03
Miniature iron tweezers	121	19	15.7	0.05	23	19.0	0.06
Playing piece	55	11	20.0	0.03	7	12.7	1.0
Spindlewhorl	52	4	7.7	0.73	9	17.3	0.46
Worked flint	37	3	8.1	0.9	1	2.7	0.1

Table 52(e) Associations of grave-good classes with types of incised decoration

	Total No	Circle No	Row%	Sig	Swastika No	Row%	Sig	Cross No	Row%	Sig	Cross on base No	Row%	Sig
Total	2440	22	0.9		28	1.1		70	2.9		8	0.3	
GRAVE-GOOD PRESENT:													
Bone fitting	33	-	-	1.0	1	3.0	0.84	2	6.0	0.57	-	-	1.0
Bronze fragment	217	2	0.9	1.0	2	0.9	1.0	7	3.2	0.94	1	0.5	1.0
Bronze sheet	108	2	1.9	0.58	2	1.9	0.81	9	8.3	0.002*	-	-	1.0
Bronze tweezers	80	-	-	0.79	1	1.3	1.0	5	6.3	0.14	-	-	1.0
Brooch	96	1	1.0	1.0	-	-	0.56	1	1.0	0.43	-	-	1.0
Comb	309	3	1.0	1.0	5	1.6	0.53	7	2.3	0.58	1	0.3	1.0
Crystal	31	2	6.5	0.02*	2	6.5	0.05	-	-	0.67	-	-	1.0
Glass	134	2	1.5	0.78	2	1.5	1.0	7	5.2	0.17	1	0.8	0.93
Glass beads	337	3	0.9	1.0	7	2.1	0.15	13	3.9	0.35	1	0.3	1.0
Glass vessel	48	1	2.1	0.92	2	4.2	0.19	3	6.3	0.34	-	-	1.0
Iron fragment	71	2	2.8	0.28	-	-	0.72	6	8.5	0.01*	1	1.4	0.57
Iron rivet	63	1	1.6	1.0	2	3.2	0.35	3	4.8	0.61	-	-	1.0
Ivory	115	2	1.7	0.64	3	2.6	0.29	7	6.1	0.07*	1	0.9	0.84
Miniature iron blade	83	-	-	0.77	1	1.2	1.0	2	2.4	1.0	1	1.2	0.66
Miniature iron shears	121	-	-	0.56	-	-	0.44	2	1.7	0.57	-	-	1.0
Miniature iron tweezers	121	1	0.8	1.0	2	1.7	1.0	4	3.3	1.0	2	1.7	0.07*
Playing piece	55	3	5.5	0.004*	1	1.8	1.0	1	1.8	0.94	-	-	1.0
Spindlewhorl	52	-	-	1.0	-	-	1.0	2	3.9	1.0	-	-	1.0
Worked flint	37	-	-	1.0	-	-	1.0	3	8.1	0.16	-	-	1.0

Table 53 Associations of identity groupings with types of incised decoration

IDENTITY GROUPING:

	Total No	GROUP ZERO No	Row%	Sig	GROUP ONE No	Row%	Sig	GROUP TWO No	Row%	Sig
Total	2440	1270	52.0		252	10.3		404	16.6	
Vertical lines	761	369	48.5	0.02	116	15.2	0.001	131	17.2	0.6
Continuous chevron	571	307	54.1	0.28	55	9.7	0.62	90	15.9	0.67
Broken chevron	41	25	62.5	0.24	3	7.5	0.74	5	12.5	0.63
Upright chevron	121	69	57.0	0.3	16	13.2	0.36	15	12.4	0.26
Reversed chevron	117	56	48.3	0.46	16	13.8	0.27	24	20.7	0.27
Diagonals to left	164	71	43.8	0.04	29	17.9	0.002	26	16.0	0.95
Diagonals to right	125	58	46.4	0.23	18	14.4	0.17	20	16.0	0.96
Curvilinear	32	14	43.8	0.44	5	15.6	0.49	6	18.8	0.92
Hanging arch	133	66	49.6	0.63	16	12.0	0.61	16	12.0	0.19
Standing arch	164	69	42.1	0.01	30	18.3	0.001	23	14.0	0.43
Slashes	246	108	43.9	0.009	37	15.0	0.01	51	20.7	0.08
Dots	316	136	43.0	0.001	49	15.5	0.002	64	20.3	0.07
Circle	22	9	40.9	0.4	1	4.5	0.59	5	22.7	0.62
Swastika	28	8	28.6	0.02	3	10.7	1.0	8	28.6	0.14
Cross	71	27	38.0	0.02	12	16.9	0.1	17	23.9	0.12
Cross on base	8	4	50.0	1.0	2	25.0	0.43	1	12.5	1.0

Similarly, pots with diagonal lines sloping to both left and right tend to have more miniature iron tweezers, and perhaps more playing pieces, than one would expect. Yet if the lines slope leftwards, the vessels are also more likely to contain combs; whilst if they slope to the right, there is no such link. Apparently, in the case of combs, the direction of slope is important, whilst with tweezers and playing pieces, it is not. Furthermore, for chevrons, bone tweezers are appropriate, whilst if the chevrons are split in half, then iron tweezers are more suitable.

Table 52c presents the links with various curvilinear forms of incised decoration. The use of a continuous curvilinear "wave" is uncommon, and reveals no significant links. Hanging arches, however, whilst much more popular, still do not appear to be related to the choice of grave-goods. The use of standing arches, by contrast, indicates that the vessels are more likely to contain combs and miniature toilet implements, and also perhaps iron rivets, iron fragments and worked flints. In fact, a vessel with a standing arch is twice as likely to contain a pair of miniature iron tweezers as is another vessel. Clearly, the standing arch was seen as a significant motif.

The links with the use of slashes and dots are shown in table 52d. Vessels with incised slashes are more likely to contain combs, glass beads, iron tweezers and playing pieces, than other urns. The use of impressed dots is even more distinguishing. These vessels are more likely to contain bronze sheet fragments, bronze tweezers, brooches, combs, glass beads, iron fragments, and miniature iron shears and tweezers.

The cross-tabulations for a few unusual incised motifs are presented in table 52e. Few occur in large enough numbers to overcome problems of minimum cell frequency, but it can be seen that some results suggest positive links.

Finally, we may combine grave-goods into the groups derived by PCA (table 53). Vessels with vertical lines, diagonal lines sloping to the left, standing arches, slashes and dots, swastikas and crosses are each less likely to belong to GROUP ZERO. The same classes, minus the swastikas and crosses, are especially likely to belong to GROUP ONE, the miniature toilet sets group. Urns with slashes and dots are also more likely to contain toilet sets. Urns with slashes and dots are also more likely to contain the glass beads and ivory which distinguish GROUP TWO.

So far, all the links described are for the complete assemblage of 2440 urns. One means of investigation would be to subdivide the sample according to cemetery in order to check if there was inter-site variation. Unfortunately this procedure also reduces the number of urns per sub-sample so that one encounters problems of low numbers when testing for significance levels. Nevertheless, it was possible to see that the trends appeared to apply to each site with one or two variations. Only at Spong Hill was the number of vessels large enough to allow significance levels to be calculated, yielding the following results significant at the 0.1 level.

Vessels with vertical lines were more likely to contain bronze tweezers and miniature iron toilet implements, as for the total sample. Vessels with impressed dots are more likely to contain brooches, combs, glass beads and miniature iron shears. No other results were significant at the 0.1 level.

It has been observed (section 3.2) that there is an ambiguous relationship between grave-goods and simple age or sex of an individual. For urns where a skeletal identification was possible, major classes of incised decoration were cross-tabulated with skeletal groupings, (table 54). The numbers involved are generally too small to yield significant results, although one or two links may be noted. Firstly, vessels with lines sloping to the right are about 75% less likely to contain children than are other vessels; whilst vessels with slashes are about half as likely to contain either children or young adults. Secondly, vessels with hanging arches are about half as likely to contain adults, but where they do, then there is a greater likelihood that these will be female rather than male. Vessels with either upright or reversed chevrons are also more likely to contain females. Finally, the use of horizontal or vertical lines, lines sloping down to the right and crosses, are each likely to denote that the vessel contains cremated animal bones as well.

3.413 Arrangement of incised decoration

To summarize so far, each of the major categories of incised decoration appears to have been used to signify particular aspects of the social identity of individuals buried within the vessels, although there are more links between incised motifs and grave-goods than with skeletal attributes. We must now examine if finer aspects of incised decoration are also used to mark social identity. A considerable amount of information about the detailed use of incised decoration was recorded for the Phase One pilot sample of 466 urns from Elsham and Spong Hill (see Appendix 3). This included data about the layout of the decoration, and about the actual numbers of lines and groups of lines applied. It is now necessary to determine the meaning, if any, of each of these aspects of incised decoration.

Ten ways of applying impressed dots, and four ways of applying slashes were cross-tabulated with each of the most popular grave-goods. The possible ways of using dots which were identified are:

i)	In continuous horizontal line
ii)	In broken horizontal line
iii)	In broken horizontal line alternating with another motif
iv)	In solid triangle
v)	In open triangle
vi)	In circle
vii)	In arch
viii)	Enclosed in triangular panel
ix)	Enclosed in arched panel
x)	Enclosed in rectangular panel

Table 54 Associations of skeletal groupings with classes of incised decoration

SKELETAL GROUPING:

	Animal			Infant			Child			Adolescent		
	No	Row%	Sig	No	Row%	Sig	No	Row%	Sig	No	Row%	Sig
Total	144	20.4		39	5.5		149	21.1		61	8.6	
Horizontal lines	115	23.3	0.005	25	5.1	0.52	103	20.9	0.88	42	8.5	0.96
Vertical lines	56	27.2	0.006	11	5.3	1.0	42	20.4	0.84	16	7.8	0.7
Continuous chevron	33	22.3	0.6	4	2.7	0.14	28	18.9	0.53	14	9.5	0.82
Broken chevron	2	20.0	1.0	1	10.0	1.0	1	10.0	0.63	-	-	0.68
Upright chevron	8	26.7	0.52	1	3.3	0.9	7	23.3	0.94	3	10.0	1.0
Reversed chevron	8	23.5	0.79	-	-	0.29	5	14.7	0.47	2	5.9	0.78
Diagonals to left	12	24.0	0.64	2	4.0	0.87	10	20.0	0.99	1	2.0	0.14
Diagonals to right	13	37.1	0.02	2	5.7	1.0	2	5.7	0.04	3	8.6	1.0
Curvilinear	4	28.6	0.67	-	-	0.75	3	21.4	1.0	1	7.1	1.0
Hanging arch	8	22.9	0.88	1	2.9	0.74	11	31.4	0.19	4	11.4	0.77
Standing arch	4	10.3	0.16	3	7.7	0.8	6	15.4	0.49	3	7.7	1.0
Slashes	15	22.7	0.74	4	6.1	1.0	7	10.6	0.04	8	12.1	0.41
Dots	14	18.7	0.81	4	5.3	1.0	17	22.7	0.84	5	6.7	0.67
Circle	2	28.6	0.95	-	-	1.0	-	-	0.36	-	-	0.89
Swastika	5	33.3	0.35	-	-	0.71	1	6.7	0.29	1	6.7	1.0
Cross	10	38.5	0.04	2	7.7	0.96	5	19.2	1.0	1	3.8	0.6
Cross on base	2	40.0	0.59	-	-	1.0	1	20.0	1.0	3	60.0	0.001*

	Young adult			Mature adult			Old adult			Adult			Male			Female		
	No	Row%	Sig	No	Row%	Sig	No	Row%	Sig	No	Row%	Sig	No	Row%	Sig	No	Row%	Sig
Total	134	19.0		108	15.3		32	4.5		286	40.5		119	16.9		153	21.7	
Horizontal lines	97	19.6	0.57	79	16.0	0.5	25	5.1	0.41	186	37.7	0.02	82	16.6	0.87	111	22.5	0.49
Vertical lines	33	16.0	0.24	29	14.1	0.64	10	4.9	0.95	93	45.1	0.13	42	20.4	0.13	39	18.9	0.3
Continuous chevron	30	20.3	0.75	28	18.9	0.22	6	4.1	0.92	55	37.2	0.42	18	12.2	0.12	38	25.7	0.23
Broken chevron	4	40.0	0.19	2	20.0	1.0	-	-	1.0	3	30.0	0.72	3	30.0	0.49	4	40.0	0.3
Upright chevron	9	30.0	0.18	4	13.3	0.96	2	6.7	0.9	9	30.0	0.31	4	13.3	0.78 +	8	26.7	0.65
Reversed chevron	8	23.5	0.64	4	11.8	0.75	3	8.8	0.42	13	38.2	0.92	7	20.6	0.72 +	10	29.4	0.35
Diagonals to left	10	20.0	1.0	7	14.0	0.95	2	4.0	1.0	22	44.0	0.71	11	22.0	0.42	8	16.0	0.41
Diagonals to right	9	25.7	0.41	6	17.1	0.94	1	2.9	0.94	16	45.7	0.64	9	25.7	0.23	8	22.9	1.0
Curvilinear	3	21.4	1.0	5	35.7	0.08*	-	-	0.86	3	21.4	0.23	4	28.6	0.41	4	28.6	0.76
Hanging arch	10	28.6	0.21	4	11.4	0.68	2	5.7	1.0	8	22.9	0.05	3	8.6	0.27	12	34.3	0.1
Standing arch	8	20.5	0.97	3	7.7	0.26	1	2.6	0.83	20	51.3	0.21	4	10.3	0.36	12	30.8	0.22
Slashes	7	10.6	0.1	11	16.7	0.89	4	6.1	0.75	27	40.9	1.0	11	16.7	1.0	14	21.2	1.0
Dots	12	16.0	0.59	7	9.3	0.18	3	4.0	1.0	33	44.0	0.6	17	22.7	0.21	14	18.7	0.6
Circle	2	28.6	0.87	2	28.6	0.65	-	-	1.0	3	42.9	1.0	2	28.6	0.75	1	14.3	0.99
Swastika	1	6.7	0.37	8	53.3	0.001*	-	-	0.82	3	20.0	0.17	5	33.3	0.17	4	26.7	0.88
Cross	7	26.9	0.43	4	15.4	1.0	-	-	0.52	14	53.8	0.23	5	19.2	0.95	5	19.2	0.95
Cross on base	2	40.0	0.53	1	20.0	1.0	-	-	1.0	2	40.0	1.0	-	-	0.68	1	20.0	1.0

+ Upright and reversed chevron combined:

	Female		
	No	Row%	Sig
Chevron	18	31.6	0.08

Slashes are frequently used in the following ways:

i)   In continuous horizontal line
ii)   In broken horizontal line
iii)   In broken horizontal line alternating with another
       motif
iv)   In solid triangle

The results have not been tabulated here because not a single positive or negative correlation was found to be significant at the 0.1 level. The same categories of dots and slashes were also cross-tabulated with the skeletal groupings at Elsham. Again, no significant links were found. Clearly, whilst it has been demonstrated that the use of both dots and slashes is used to signify the identity of the occupant of a vessel, the actual manner in which they are applied is of no importance, or at least does not signify anything that can be detected.

In addition, the following information about numbers of fields of incised decoration was examined:

i)   Number of horizontal incised fields
ii)   Number of vertical incised fields
iii)   Number of chevrons in a continuous field
iv)   Number of single upright chevrons
v)   Number of single reversed chevrons
vi)   Number of groups of lines sloping down to the left
vii)   Number of groups of lines sloping down to the right
viii) Number of hanging arches
ix)   Number of standing arches

Finally, information about the average number of lines per field was examined.

i)   Average number of lines in a horizontal field
ii)   Average number of lines in a vertical field
iii)   Average number of lines in a continuous field
iv)   Average number of lines in an upright chevron
v)   Average number of lines in a reversed chevron
vi)   Average number of lines in a group sloping downwards
       to the left
vii)   Average number of lines in a group sloping downwards
       to the right
viii) Average number of lines in a hanging arch
ix)   Average number of lines in a standing arch

The cumulative frequency distribution for each of these categories containing each of the most popular grave-goods was compared against the distribution of the pilot sample as a whole. The Kolmogorov-Smirnov test was used to check if any differences in frequency graphs were statistically significant.

Again, the full results have not been tabulated here, because very few were significant. In fact, out of 221 distributions, the only ones which differed significantly from the overall sample are shown in table 55.

Table 55 Elsham and Spong Hill – significant links between grave-goods and number of lines

	NUMBER OF MOTIFS															SIGNIFICANCE LEVEL (Kolmogorov-Smirnov test)
	1	2	3	4	5	6	7	8	9	10	11	12	13	14	15	
Chevrons in continuous field:																
Total sample			3	12	14	20	25	~19	9	14	2	3	1		2	
Bronze sheet				1		1		5	1	1			1			0.1
Glass vessel										2						0.1
Single reversed chevrons:																
Total sample	2	6	3	6	5	5	2	3	1	1						
Glass beads		1		1	1	1	2	2		1						0.2
Miniature iron blade		3		1												0.2
Miniature iron shears		3														0.05
Hanging arches:																
Total sample	1		1	8	2	4	6	1	3	4	4	1	2		1	
Miniature iron tweezers			1	1	1											0.1
Standing arches:																
Total sample	1		1	4	6	12	5	4	3	3						
Bronze sheet							1		2							0.15
Miniature iron tweezers	1				1		2	2	1	2						0.1

Table 56 Elsham and Spong Hill – links between grave-goods and total number of chevrons

	NUMBER OF CHEVRONS																				SIGNIFICANCE LEVEL (Kolmogorov-Smirnov test)
	1	2	3	4	5	6	7	8	9	10	11	12	13	14	15	16	17	18	19	20	
Total sample	1	5	6	20	22	25	29	20	9	18	3	4	1	2	2	3		1	2	1	
Bronze fragment				4	1	3	5	6			1		1	1	1			1			
Bronze sheet	1		1	2		7	1	2			1										0.1
Brooch						3	7		1		1		1	1							0.01
Comb	2	1	5	1		4	10	5		5	1		1						1		
Crystal								3													0.2
Glass beads	1		4	6	5	12	12		4	1	1			1				1			
Glass vessel			1	2	1				2												
Iron rivet			1		2	2	3		4												
Ivory				2	2	4	3		2					1							
Miniature iron blade	2	2		1	2	2	3		1												
Miniature iron shears	2	3	4		3	1	2		1		1										0.05
Miniature iron tweezers	2	1	3	2	3	5	4		2												
Spindlewhorl			1	1		2													1		
Worked flint	1		1	1	1		4														

The number of horizontal and vertical fields, of upright chevrons, and of groups of diagonal lines sloping to left and to right, does not appear to bear any relationship to the grave-goods included in the vessel. Each of the other classes of decoration reveals no more than one or, at most, two correlations with particular grave-goods. However, none are significant at high levels, and when one considers the total number of tests performed, they are really no more than would be expected by chance, (bearing in mind that a 0.1 level implies that this could happen by chance one time out of ten anyway). The number of each of these classes of motif was also checked for correlations with any of the human skeletal groupings at Elsham, and with PCA identity groupings at either site. No significant correlations were found.

It appeared, therefore, that whilst the use of a motif might reflect the "occupant" of a vessel, the actual number of such motifs, and the number of lines making up the motif, did not seem to be related to the social identity of the deceased. In only one case (miniature iron shears and number of reversed chevrons) was the number of motifs significant at the 0.05 level, and in only one case (average number of lines in a horizontal field and combs), was the number of lines significant at the 0.05 level. Whatever this level of variability was related to, it did not appear to be any measurable aspect of social identity.

Nevertheless, it was considered necessary to investigate the two possible correlations further, in case they were significant. A new variable was created representing the total number of chevrons on a vessel, including both upright and reversed chevrons, and those in continuous bands. This variable served to increase the number of vessels which could be included in a single test, and overcame the problems of overlap between the three classes of design. The new variable was correlated against grave-goods for the pilot sample from Elsham and Spong Hill, and against skeletal groupings from Elsham. The results are shown in table 56. Miniature shears again produced a significant result, many being concentrated in vessels with less than five chevrons. Brooches, and bronze sheets were also found to be non-randomly distributed, being concentrated in vessels with more than seven or eight chevrons. This number of correlations may be more than would be expected by chance for the number of tests performed. One might conclude that whilst particular classes of chevron may mean something, the overall number of chevrons, of any class, is also related to social identity. However, one must be careful that what is being measured is an independent variable. The number of chevrons which may be incised upon a vessel is related to the size and diameter of that vessel. Could it be, then, that the correlations identified are really between social identity and vessel form, which we have already seen to be related to the deceased (section 3.3). As there is little evidence for believing that the number of any motif applied is otherwise significant, this would appear to be the logical conclusion. It might only be refuted by investigating a much greater number of vessels than was included in the pilot study. However, it was decided that since the number of chevrons could not be gleaned from published reports, it was not practical to record this variable in Phase Two.

The second variable which it has been suggested could be related to social identity, <u>was</u> capable of investigation in Phase Two. The number of lines in horizontal bands around the neck of a vessel can generally be counted from published drawings. Therefore, this variable was measured for each of the 2440 vessels in Phase Two which had horizontal incised decoration. Tests were repeated to check if vessels containing each of the possible grave-goods tended to have more or less lines in horizontal bands than usual. Again, vessels containing combs were found to be non-randomly distributed (significant at 0.01 level), as they tended to be found in vessels which had a large number of lines in each horizontal band. Perhaps the close set bands of massed lines around the neck of a vessel in some way represent the rows of teeth of a comb. All other grave-goods were apparently randomly distributed, although when tests were repeated for all urns with skeletal identifications in the Phase Two sample, there appeared to be a tendency for mature adults to be concentrated in vessels which averaged more than three lines per band (significant at 0.1 level).

The meaning of horizontal lines was therefore examined further. Vessels were split into two groups according to whether they had more bands of lines which totalled an odd number, or more which totalled an even number. It will be suggested (section 3.42), that Anglo-Saxons had a conception of even and odd numbers. It was hypothesised that the opposition between even and odd might have represented a transformation of some other opposition in Anglo-Saxon society: male vs female, young vs old etc? It was found that more vessels (58%) had more odd numbers of lines per band than had more even numbers. The two groups were cross-tabulated with each of the most popular grave-goods (table 57). Two grave-goods tended to be found more often with vessels with more odd groups of lines: bronze sheets were correlated with vessels with more odd groups, and combs were associated with vessels with more even groups. Skeletal groups were also cross-tabulated, but none provided significant results. The total assemblage was then subdivided by site and the cross-tabulations were repeated. On the whole the individual sub-samples were now too small, but at Sancton and Spong Hill, the association between combs and even numbers was repeated (significant at the 0.1 level). The result for bronze sheet was only significant at Spong Hill, but an additional correlation, between bronze fragments and vessels with more odd groups of lines, was revealed at Loveden Hill.

It must be borne in mind, however, that with such large numbers of cross-tabulations being performed, one would expect one or two "significant" results by the laws of probability. With the case of combs, there are rather more links than could reasonably be expected by chance, and these items might repay further investigation with other samples.

In conclusion, these tests have shown that there appear to be different levels of variability in the use of incised decoration. On the broadest level, the choice of decorative motif is related to the social identity of the deceased. The use of horizontal lines, vertical lines, continuous chevrons, single chevrons, diagonal lines, standing arches, slashes and dots, has been shown to be correlated

Table 57 Associations of grave-good classes with use of odd and even
numbers of lines

	ODD		EVEN		
	No	Row%	No	Row%	Sig
Total	882	58.1	635	41.9	
GRAVE-GOOD PRESENT:					
Bronze fragment	91	64.1	51	35.9	0.16
Bronze sheet	49	72.1	19	27.9	0.02
Bronze tweezers	30	52.6	27	47.4	0.47
Brooch	37	67.3	18	32.7	0.2
Comb	100	50.5	98	49.5	0.02
Crystal	13	68.4	6	31.6	0.5
Glass	56	60.2	37	39.8	0.76
Glass beads	126	59.4	86	40.6	0.74
Glass vessel	16	55.2	13	44.8	0.89
Iron fragment	26	59.1	18	40.9	1.0
Iron rivet	24	53.3	21	46.7	0.61
Ivory	51	62.2	31	37.8	0.52
Miniature iron blade	36	66.7	18	33.3	0.25
Miniature iron shears	49	60.5	32	39.5	0.75
Miniature iron tweezers	51	60.7	33	39.3	0.71
Playing piece	20	52.6	18	47.4	0.6
Spindlewhorl	22	64.7	12	35.3	0.54
Worked flint	17	68.0	8	32.0	0.42

Table 58 Spong Hill: variation in number of lines and fields of
incised decoration within stamp groups

		STANDARD DEVIATION FOR STAMP GROUP:																			
	TOTAL	1	4	5	6	7	8	10	11	14	15	17	19	20	22	26	28	31	38	41	42
Number of fields:																					
Of horizontal lines	1.15	0.6	1.0	0.0	0.0	2.5	0.0	0.7	0.7	0.0	0.0	1.0	0.0	1.0	0.7	0.0	0.0	0.6	0.7	0.7	0.6
Of vertical lines	5.6			2.9		1.4	0.0										1.4		1.5	0.7	2.1	1.7
Of chevrons	3.33		1.0		0.0	2.6	0.7				1.4	1.5		0.0	2.1	0.7	1.4					
Number of lines:																					
+ Horizontal	1.62	0.6	0.5	0.6	0.0	0.9	1.0	0.0	0.0	0.0	0.0	1.0	0.0	0.0	0.0	0.0	0.0	0.6	0.7	0.7	0.6
Vertical	3.95			3.0		1.0	0.0										0.7		1.0	0.0	1.4	1.5
Continuous chevron	1.2		0.6								2.1	0.6		0.7	0.7							
Reversed chevron	1.2					0.7																
Standing arch	1.2					0.6																
Hnaging arch	1.0					0.0																

+ Average for all horizontal fields, where more than one.

with whether or not an individual is buried with grave-goods, and which particular grave-goods are included. With the possible exception of combs, however, the number of each of the motifs applied, and the number of lines making up each motif, does not appear to bear any relationship to the use of grave-goods. It is more likely, therefore, that variation in attributes is related to some other aspect of the manufacture and use of the cremation urns. Since this variability is of a finer level of detail and is generally less visible, one might suppose that it is related to more localised factors of manufacture and use. Intuitively, it might be suggested that it is related to the style of individual potters or group of potters. The potters' groups, distinguished by the use of identical stamp dies, provide one means of testing this hypothesis. If the number of fields of decoration, and the number of lines per field, are related to the style of particular potters, then one would expect there to be less variation within groups than between groups. A small test was carried out for the twenty-one stamp groups identified at Spong Hill and Elsham recorded in the pilot study. The standard deviation for each of these quantitative variables was measured for all the pots from each site, and compared against the standard deviation within each stamp group (table 58). In only one case (for the number of horizontal incised fields) was there greater variation in these attributes within a stamp group than between stamp groups. The results of this test therefore seem to support the hypothesis that in general the number of field of lines, and the number of lines per field, are related to individual style. Stylistic variability at this level is not related to the social identity of the deceased, but it does appear to be related to the identity of the potter.

3.42 Plastic decoration

The use of "plastic" decoration has been noted on approximately one-third of the total sample. We have already observed that the use of various classes of plastic decoration is related to the types of incised decoration which are being used. Table 59 demonstrates that it is also related to the use of stamped decoration. In fact, there is an inverse relationship between the two, and if stamped decoration is used, then plastic decoration is less likely to be applied. Round bosses, in particular, are significantly less likely to be used if a vessel is stamped. In order to examine the meaning of plastic decoration and its use, it was cross-tabulated with each of the commonly occurring grave-goods (table 60). It is apparent that urns with plastic decoration are also more likely to contain certain grave-goods. Miniature iron blades, iron tweezers and bronze tweezers are positively linked with plastic decoration, as are bronze sheet fragments, crystal and glass beads and playing pieces. For those vessels with skeletal identifications, the skeletal groupings were also cross-tabulated with the use of plastic decoration (table 61). Child burials and female adults are both less likely to be buried in vessels with plastic decoration, whilst there is a positive link between cremated cow offerings and the use of plastic decoration.

Table 59 Associations of urns with stamped decoration with classes of
plastic decoration

	Total No	Stamped decoration No	Row%	Sig
Total	1887	930	49.3	
Plastic decoration	740	335	45.3	0.006
Vertical bosses	573	274	47.8	0.43
Round bosses	142	59	41.5	0.07
Cordons	137	68	49.6	1.0

Table 60 Associations of grave-good classes with use of plastic
decoration

	Total No	Plastic decoration No	Row%	Sig
Total	2440	738	30.3	
GRAVE-GOOD PRESENT:				
Bone fitting	33	13	39.4	0.35
Bronze fragment	217	63	29.0	0.72
Bronze sheet	108	41	38.0	0.09
Bronze tweezers	80	33	41.2	0.04
Brooch	96	29	30.2	1.0
Comb	309	101	32.7	0.36
Crystal	31	15	48.4	0.05
Glass	134	41	30.6	1.0
Glass beads	337	117	34.7	0.07
Glass vessel	48	13	27.1	0.73
Iron fragment	71	26	36.6	0.3
Iron rivet	63	20	31.7	0.92
Ivory	115	31	27.0	0.48
Miniature iron blade	83	33	39.8	0.08
Miniature iron shears	121	44	36.4	0.17
Miniature iron tweezers	121	47	38.8	0.05
Playing piece	55	25	45.5	0.02
Spindlewhorl	52	19	36.5	0.4
Worked flint	37	11	29.7	1.0

Table 61 Associations of skeletal groups with use of plastic
decoration

	Total No	Plastic decoration		
		No	Row%	Sig
Total	706	195	27.6	
SKELETAL GROUP PRESENT:				
Infant	39	12	30.8	0.79
Child	149	26	17.4	0.003
Adolescent	61	20	32.8	0.43
Young adult	134	31	23.1	0.24
Mature adult	108	28	25.9	0.76
Old adult	32	11	34.4	0.5
Adult	286	88	30.8	0.15
Male	119	37	31.1	0.41
Female	153	33	21.6	0.07
Animal bones present:	144	41	28.5	0.88
Sheep	50	10	20.0	0.28
Cow / Ox	20	10	50.0	0.04
Pig	21	7	33.3	0.73
Horse	18	8	44.4	0.18

Table 62 Associations of grave-good classes with types of plastic
decoration

	Total	Vertical Bosses			Round Bosses			Cordons		
	No	No	Row%	Sig	No	Row%	Sig	No	Row%	Sig
Total	2440	573	23.5		142	5.8		137	5.6	
GRAVE-GOOD PRESENT:										
Bone fitting	33	10	30.3	0.47	4	12.1	0.24	5	15.2	0.04*
Bronze fragment	217	47	21.7	0.57	6	2.8	0.06	16	7.4	0.31
Bronze sheet	108	30	27.8	0.34	12	11.1	0.03	6	5.6	1.0
Bronze tweezers	80	30	37.5	0.004	10	12.5	0.02*	9	11.2	0.05*
Brooch	96	19	19.8	0.46	7	7.3	0.69	5	5.2	1.0
Comb	309	75	24.3	0.75	26	8.4	0.05	19	6.1	0.72
Crystal	31	12	38.7	0.07	1	3.2	0.81	3	9.7	0.55
Glass	134	29	21.6	0.68	9	6.7	0.79	8	6.0	1.0
Glass beads	337	83	24.6	0.64	18	5.3	0.78	26	7.7	0.09
Glass vessel	48	10	20.8	0.79	3	6.2	1.0	4	8.3	0.61
Iron fragment	71	19	26.8	0.6	10	14.1	0.006*	4	5.6	1.0
Iron rivet	63	16	25.4	0.83	6	9.5	0.32	4	6.3	1.0
Ivory	115	27	23.5	1.0	4	3.5	0.37	6	5.2	1.0
Miniature iron blade	83	27	32.5	0.07	6	7.2	0.75	11	13.3	0.005*
Miniature iron shears	121	35	28.9	0.18	12	9.9	0.08	14	11.6	0.007
Miniature iron tweezers	121	36	29.8	0.12	9	7.4	0.56	13	10.7	0.02
Playing piece	55	22	40.0	0.006	7	12.7	0.06*	6	10.9	0.15
Spindlewhorl	52	15	28.8	0.44	2	3.8	0.75	2	3.8	0.8
Worked flint	37	8	21.6	0.94	2	5.4	1.0	2	5.4	1.0

The next stage was to examine if these links were with plastic decoration in general, or only with particular types. Three specific types of plastic decoration occurred in sufficient numbers to allow them to be meaningfully cross-tabulated with skeletal and grave-good attributes. They were vertical bosses, round bosses and cordons (table 62). Vertical bosses are positively linked with miniature iron blades, bronze tweezers, crystal and playing pieces. Round bosses are linked with miniature iron shears, bronze sheet fragments and combs, and exhibit a negative relationship with bronze fragments. Cordons are positively linked with miniature iron tweezers, iron shears and glass beads. Most of these links also applied to the use of plastic decoration as a whole. That each association was not significant for each type of plastic decoration may to some extent be due to the reduced sample size.

We may conclude, therefore, that in general it is the use of plastic decoration as a whole which is significant in marking burials of particular groups of people, and that the specific form of decoration is largely immaterial. The only links between grave-goods and particular types of plastic decoration, which were not apparent for all plastic decoration, are the positive links between round bosses and combs (which are not associated with vertical bosses at all), and the negative relationship with bronze fragments. Both these associations were marked at the higher level.

The same pattern is repeated for the associations between types of plastic decoration and skeletal groupings (table 63). The negative relationship with children is repeated for vertical and round bosses, whilst that with adult females is no longer significant at the smaller sample level. There are no significant links between the use of cordons and any of the skeletal groupings.

The use of any form of plastic decoration increases the elaborate appearance of a vessel. It appears that the Pagan Anglo-Saxons chose to distinguish the burials of social identities given particular grave-goods with plastic decoration. We can say little about the nature of these social groups, apart from the fact that they were less likely to be children or adult females, and that they were frequently buried with a variety of miniature toilet implements, bronze sheet fragments, playing pieces, crystal and glass beads.

During Phase One, several links between specific numbers of bosses used on a pot and the contents had been suggested at Elsham and Spong Hill. It was decided to examine this relationship more closely with the larger sample available in Phase Two.

Using the Kolmogorov-Smirnov test, the number of bosses per urn, for those containing specific grave-goods, was compared against the total sample. For vertical bosses, the only difference significant at the 0.1 level was for urns containing bronze tweezers which were concentrated in vessels with more than seven bosses.

The number of round bosses per urn was itself different from the number of vertical bosses, significant at the 0.01 level. The number of round bosses appeared to have been consciously selected in the case

Table 63 Associations of skeletal groups with types of plastic decoration

	Total	Vertical Bosses			Round Bosses			Cordons		
	No	No	Row%	Sig	No	Row%	Sig	No	Row%	Sig
Total	706	150	21.2		38	5.4		34	4.8	
SKELETAL GROUP PRESENT:										
Infant	39	8	20.5	1.0	2	5.1	1.0	3	7.7	0.63
Child	149	19	12.8	0.006	3	2.0	0.07	6	4.0	0.77
Adolescent	61	17	27.9	0.25	2	3.3	0.64	1	1.6	0.37
Young adult	134	23	17.2	0.24	7	5.2	1.0	3	2.2	0.19
Mature adult	108	24	22.2	0.89	7	6.5	0.75	5	4.6	1.0
Old adult	32	10	31.3	0.23	-	-	0.33	2	6.3	1.0
Adult	286	68	23.8	0.21	18	6.3	0.47	17	5.9	0.33
Male	119	31	26.1	0.2	8	6.7	0.63	6	5.0	1.0
Female	153	28	18.3	0.37	8	5.2	1.0	5	3.3	0.43
Animal bones present:	144	31	21.5	1.0	7	4.9	0.92	5	3.5	0.53
Sheep	50	7	14.0	0.26	1	2.0	0.44	2	4.0	1.0
Cow / Ox	20	9	45.0	0.02*	1	5.0	1.0	1	5.0	1.0
Pig	21	5	23.8	0.98	1	4.8	1.0	1	4.8	1.0
Horse	18	7	38.9	0.12	1	5.6	1.0	1	5.6	1.0

Table 64 Spong Hill: variation in number of vertical bosses within stamp groups

	No. of urns	STANDARD DEVIATION for Number of vertical bosses
TOTAL	381	3.966
Stamp group		
5	3	0.0
7	17	1.309
8	4	1.155
17	3	0.707
31	3	1.155
38	2	0.707
42	3	0.0

of 3 grave-goods: miniature iron blades, concentrated in vessels with a large number of round bosses (significant at 0.05 level), bone fittings, also concentrated in vessels with many bosses (significant at the 0.05 level), and spindlewhorls, concentrated in vessels with few bosses (significant at the 0.1 level). The meaning of these results is difficult to interpret. There is the possibility that these few correlations, whilst statistically significant, may still have occurred by chance. Nevertheless, since the number of bosses is related to the overall level of decoration of a vessel, it may be that these links illustrate the preference for putting individuals who were accorded these grave-goods in highly decorated pots.

Interpretations stressing the symbolic nature of decoration might seek significance in the actual number of bosses, which was not examined. However, it is more likely that this relates to purely stylistic considerations. In section 3.41 it was found that whereas the types of incised decoration were related to the occupant of the cremation urns, the actual number of fields, and the number of lines per field, generally appeared to be related to the individual potter, or "school" of potters. Table 64 compares the standard deviation for the number of bosses per vessel for each of the potter groups identified at Spong Hill to the standard deviation for the site as a whole. In each case there is less variation in the number of bosses applied within potters' groups than between them, supporting the idea that this is a reflection of an individual level of variation.

3.43 Stamped decoration

Stamped designs are frequently used to embellish a vessel with incised or plastic decoration, but are rarely used on their own. They are most commonly used in horizontal or vertical bands, or to fill triangular panels, usually within an incised outline. Alternatively, they may be used to cover the raised surfaces of bosses and cordons. We have already seen that stamps may be used on between 10% and 60% of the vessels from any one site, and that there is also great variability in the number of stamps applied.

There is considerable potential for the use of stamped motifs as symbolic markers, and indeed, designs such as the swastika and wyrm have been seen as openly symbolic. There is, moreover, an enormous variety of designs which may be reproduced on the head of a stamp. In this section, we shall attempt to examine if these designs have any meaning, and if so, what that meaning might be.

Firstly, the use of stamps was cross-tabulated with each of the commonly occurring grave-goods (table 65). Once again, miniature tweezers and blades stand out as significant, for they are less likely to be found in stamped urns than are other grave goods. Glass vessels, on the other hand, are especially likely to be found in stamped vessels. The use of stamps was also cross-tabulated with the individual skeletal groups (table 66). Perhaps surprisingly, the only significant link was that urns with animals in them were slightly more likely to be decorated with stamps. The age and sex of the individual buried appears to have been irrelevant in determining whether they

Table 65 Associations of grave-good classes with use of stamped decoration

	Total No	Stamped decoration		
		No	Row%	Sig
Total	2440	930	38.1	
GRAVE-GOOD PRESENT:				
Bone fitting	33	11	33.3	0.7
Bronze fragment	217	37	35.5	0.44
Bronze sheet	108	42	38.9	0.95
Bronze tweezers	80	37	46.2	0.16
Brooch	96	31	32.3	0.28
Comb	309	109	35.3	0.31
Crystal	31	13	41.9	0.8
Glass	134	60	44.8	0.12
Glass beads	337	118	35.0	0.23
Glass vessel	48	27	56.2	0.01
Iron fragment	71	24	33.8	0.53
Iron rivet	63	26	41.3	0.7
Ivory	115	46	40.0	0.75
Miniature iron blade	83	22	26.5	0.04
Miniature iron shears	121	39	32.2	0.2
Miniature iron tweezers	121	34	28.1	0.03
Playing piece	55	23	41.8	0.66
Spindlewhorl	52	24	46.2	0.29
Worked flint	37	9	24.3	0.12

Table 66 Associations of skeletal groups with use of stamped decoration

	Total No	Stamped decoration		
		No	Row%	Sig
Total	706	241	34.1	
SKELETAL GROUP PRESENT:				
Infant	39	9	23.1	0.19
Child	149	45	30.2	0.3
Adolescent	61	24	39.3	0.45
Young adult	134	48	35.8	0.72
Mature adult	108	37	34.3	1.0
Old adult	32	14	43.7	0.33
Adult	286	99	34.6	0.89
Male	119	36	30.3	0.38
Female	153	59	38.6	0.23
Animal bones present:	144	59	41.0	0.07

should be buried in a stamped urn. The same test was also carried out
for sub-samples on each site, but the numbers involved were usually
too small to indicate any regional variations. The only significant
links   were   between glass vessels and stamping at Spong Hill
(significant at 0.05, and a tendency for combs not to be in stamped
vessels at Lackford (significant at 0.1).

3.431 Stamp form and design

Having established that the use of stamped decoration was related to
the grave-goods present, it was decided to test if particular stamped
motifs were used exclusively with particular grave-goods. Each of 65
stamped   motifs   (those   occurring   four   or   more   times) was
cross-tabulated with each of 32 grave-goods.   In fact no exclusive
links were found, and since problems of minimum cell frequency put the
results in doubt, they are not tabulated here.   However, both types
A14 and A18 were linked with urns without grave-goods (significant at
the 0.05 level).

The next stage, therefore, was to enlarge the groups by combining
all stamps of the same form or design types<1>. Stamp form A in
general was found to be linked with urns without grave-goods.
Cross-tabulations were performed between common grave-goods and stamp
form types A-K (table 67)<2>.   In two cases, there is a result
significant at the 0.1 level. Urns with glass beads are unlikely to
be decorated with form A (circular stamps) and with form K (wyrm
stamps). These may just be chance results, but it is interesting that
(round) glass beads should be less frequently buried in vessels
decorated with round stamps.

The cross-tabulation between grave-goods and stamp designs are
presented in table 68. Only design types constituting more than 5% of
the total are included.   Three groups consist of combined types:

NOTE

<1> PCA was also applied to all of the 930 vessels
with   stamped   decoration. If particular stamped
designs occurred regularly together then this
technique   would   isolate   groups of commonly
co-occurring stamps which could be treated as combined
goods.   However the plot of the correlation
coefficient indicated that there was no break, and
therefore, no regular associations of stamp types.

NOTE

<2> Types B, L and M were omitted because even when
all these types were combined, the resulting groups
were still too small.

Table 67 Associations of grave-goods with use of stamp forms

	Total No	A No RowZ Sig	C No RowZ Sig	D No RowZ Sig	E No RowZ Sig	F No RowZ Sig
Total	930	627 67.4	35 3.8	103 11.1	180 19.4	34 3.7
GRAVE-GOOD PRESENT:						
Bone fitting	11	8 72.7 0.96	- - 1.0	1 9.1 1.0	3 27.3 0.78	- - 1.0
Bronze fragment	77	54 70.1 0.69	4 5.2 0.71	6 7.8 0.44	16 20.8 0.86	3 3.9 1.0
Bronze sheet	42	25 59.5 0.34	3 7.1 0.45	5 11.9 1.0	8 19.0 1.0	1 2.4 0.98
Bronze tweezers	37	26 70.3 0.84	- - 0.43	5 13.5 0.83	5 13.5 0.48	3 8.1 0.31
Brooch	31	17 54.8 0.19	1 3.2 1.0	3 9.7 1.0	5 16.1 0.82	- - 0.54
Comb	109	78 71.6 0.37	5 4.6 0.84	13 11.9 0.9	20 18.3 0.86	2 1.8 0.42
Crystal	13	10 76.9 0.66	1 7.7 0.99	- - 0.4	- - 0.15	- - 1.0
Glass	60	38 63.3 0.58	2 3.3 1.0	7 11.7 1.0	16 26.7 0.19	4 6.7 0.35
Glass beads	118	71 60.2 0.09	5 4.2 0.98	15 12.7 0.65	22 18.6 0.93	4 3.4 1.0
Glass vessel	27	17 63.0 0.77	2 7.4 0.62	7 25.9 0.03*	7 25.9 0.53	- - 0.61
Iron fragment	24	16 66.7 1.0	2 8.3 0.52	5 20.8 0.23	6 25.0 0.66	- - 0.68
Iron rivet	26	18 69.2 1.0	- - 0.62	8 30.8 0.003*	6 23.1 0.81	2 7.7 0.56
Ivory	46	33 71.7 0.63	1 2.2 0.85	3 6.5 0.44	12 26.1 0.32	- - 0.34
Miniature iron blade	22	14 63.6 0.88	2 9.1 0.45	2 9.1 1.0	2 9.1 0.34	1 4.5 1.0
Miniature iron shears	39	27 69.2 0.94	1 2.6 1.0	3 7.7 0.67	9 23.1 0.69	2 5.1 0.95
Miniature iron tweezers	34	26 76.5 0.34	- - 0.47	3 8.8 0.88	7 20.6 1.0	4 11.8 0.04*
Playing piece	23	13 56.5 0.37	- - 0.69	5 21.7 0.19	9 39.1 0.03*	1 4.3 1.0
Spindlewhorl	24	18 75.0 0.57	- - 0.66	1 4.2 0.45	6 25.0 0.65	- - 0.68
Worked flint	9	8 88.9 0.31	- - 1.0	3 33.3 0.11	3 33.3 0.52	- - 1.0

	Total No	G No RowZ Sig	H No RowZ Sig	I No RowZ Sig	J No RowZ Sig	K No RowZ Sig
Total	930	97 10.4	69 7.4	51 5.5	86 9.2	138 14.8
GRAVE-GOOD PRESENT:						
Bone fitting	11	1 9.1 1.0	4 36.4 0.002*	1 9.1 1.0	1 9.1 1.0	3 27.3 0.46
Bronze fragment	77	6 7.8 0.55	4 5.2 0.58	1 1.3 0.16	6 7.8 0.8	12 15.6 0.98
Bronze sheet	42	3 7.1 0.65	1 2.4 0.33	2 4.8 1.0	3 7.1 0.83	3 7.1 0.23
Bronze tweezers	37	8 21.6 0.05*	4 10.8 0.63	4 10.8 0.28	2 5.4 0.59	7 18.9 0.63
Brooch	31	6 19.4 0.17	3 9.7 0.9	2 6.5 1.0	3 9.7 1.0	5 16.1 1.0
Comb	109	15 13.8 0.28	11 10.1 0.36	4 3.7 0.5	8 7.3 0.57	16 14.7 1.0
Crystal	13	1 7.7 1.0	4 30.8 0.007*	2 15.4 0.33	2 15.4 0.77	2 15.4 1.0
Glass	60	9 15.0 0.33	2 3.3 0.32	4 6.7 0.9	4 6.7 0.63	12 20.0 0.33
Glass beads	118	12 10.2 1.0	10 8.5 0.78	6 5.1 1.0	14 11.9 0.38	10 8.5 0.05
Glass vessel	27	3 11.1 1.0	2 7.4 1.0	5 18.5 0.01*	4 14.8 0.5	7 25.9 0.17
Iron fragment	24	1 4.2 0.5	- - 0.31	2 8.3 0.87	1 4.2 0.61	- - 0.08*
Iron rivet	26	5 19.2 0.25	4 15.4 0.23	1 3.8 1.0	2 7.7 1.0	3 11.5 0.84
Ivory	46	3 6.5 0.52	2 4.3 0.6	4 8.7 0.52	1 2.2 0.15	9 19.6 0.48
Miniature iron blade	22	4 18.2 0.4	1 4.5 0.91	1 4.5 1.0	- - 0.25	2 9.1 0.64
Miniature iron shears	39	6 15.4 0.44	2 5.1 0.81	2 5.1 1.0	- - 0.08*	3 7.7 0.29
Miniature iron tweezers	34	4 11.8 1.0	1 2.9 0.5	1 2.9 0.78	- - 0.11	2 5.9 0.21
Playing piece	23	2 8.7 1.0	2 8.7 1.0	2 8.7 0.83	2 8.7 1.0	3 13.0 1.0
Spindlewhorl	24	1 4.2 0.5	1 4.2 0.82	2 8.3 0.87	2 8.3 1.0	5 20.8 0.59
Worked flint	9	- - 0.63	- - 0.83	- - 1.0	1 11.1 1.0	1 11.1 1.0

Table 68 Associations of grave-goods with use of stamp designs

	Total No	1 No RowZ Sig	2 No RowZ Sig	3/4/5 No RowZ Sig	6 No RowZ Sig	7 No RowZ Sig
Total	930	161 17.3	235 25.3	276 29.7	67 7.2	260 28.0
GRAVE-GOOD PRESENT:						
Bone fitting	11	2 18.2 1.0	4 36.4 0.62	7 63.6 0.03*	1 9.1 1.0	4 36.4 0.77
Bronze fragment	77	16 20.8 0.5	18 23.4 0.79	24 31.2 0.87	6 7.8 1.0	19 24.7 0.59
Bronze sheet	42	6 14.3 0.75	8 19.0 0.44	10 23.8 0.5	4 9.5 0.77	11 26.2 0.93
Bronze tweezers	37	8 21.6 0.63	11 29.7 0.67	12 32.4 0.85	2 5.4 0.91	11 29.7 0.95
Brooch	31	4 12.9 0.68	8 25.8 1.0	8 25.8 0.81	4 12.9 0.38	9 29.0 1.0
Comb	109	27 24.8 0.04	30 27.5 0.65	25 22.9 0.13	11 10.1 0.3	27 24.8 0.5
Crystal	13	1 7.7 0.58	6 46.2 0.16	6 46.2 0.32	1 7.7 1.0	2 15.4 0.48
Glass	60	7 11.7 0.31	14 23.3 0.84	21 35.0 0.43	6 10.0 0.54	24 40.0 0.05
Glass beads	118	21 17.8 0.99	30 25.4 1.0	21 26.3 0.45	15 12.7 0.02	31 26.3 0.74
Glass vessel	27	4 14.8 0.93	7 25.9 1.0	13 48.1 0.06	5 18.5 0.05*	10 37.0 0.4
Iron fragment	24	6 25.0 0.46	6 25.0 1.0	4 16.7 0.24	1 4.2 0.86	4 16.7 0.31
Iron rivet	26	4 15.4 1.0	7 26.9 1.0	8 30.8 1.0	4 15.4 0.21	6 23.1 0.73
Ivory	46	8 17.4 1.0	10 21.7 0.7	13 28.3 0.96	4 8.7 0.91	13 28.3 1.0
Miniature iron blade	22	2 9.1 0.46	2 9.1 0.13	9 40.9 0.35	2 9.1 1.0	3 13.6 0.2
Miniature iron shears	39	6 15.4 0.91	5 12.8 0.1	10 25.6 0.7	3 7.7 1.0	8 20.5 0.38
Miniature iron tweezers	34	4 11.8 0.52	5 14.7 0.21	9 26.5 0.82	2 5.9 1.0	11 32.4 0.7
Playing piece	23	4 17.4 1.0	4 17.4 0.52	5 21.7 0.54	3 13.0 0.49	8 34.8 0.62
Spindlewhorl	24	- - 0.05*	10 41.7 0.1	7 29.2 1.0	2 8.3 1.0	7 29.2 1.0
Worked flint	9	3 33.3 0.4	4 44.4 0.35	3 33.3 1.0	2 22.2 0.27	3 33.3 1.0

	Total No	11 No RowZ Sig	13 No RowZ Sig	16 No RowZ Sig	Segmented No RowZ Sig	Cruciform No RowZ Sig
Total	930	207 22.3	52 5.6	141 15.2	317 34.1	324 34.8
GRAVE-GOOD PRESENT:						
Bone fitting	11	1 9.1 0.49	1 9.1 1.0	1 9.1 0.89	6 54.5 0.26	2 18.2 0.4
Bronze fragment	77	16 20.8 0.86	3 3.9 0.68	15 19.5 0.35	22 28.6 0.35	22 28.6 0.28
Bronze sheet	42	8 19.0 0.75	2 4.8 1.0	6 14.3 1.0	13 31.0 0.79	12 28.6 0.48
Bronze tweezers	37	6 16.2 0.48	3 8.1 0.75	9 24.3 0.18	14 37.8 0.75	10 27.0 0.4
Brooch	31	8 25.8 0.78	2 6.5 1.0	2 6.5 0.27	9 29.0 0.68	12 38.7 0.79
Comb	109	25 22.9 0.95	10 9.2 0.13	17 15.6 1.0	35 32.1 0.72	38 34.9 1.0
Crystal	13	4 30.8 0.68	1 7.7 1.0	5 38.5 0.05*	3 23.1 0.58	5 38.5 1.0
Glass	60	16 26.7 0.49	2 3.3 0.62	9 15.0 1.0	27 45.0 0.09	21 35.0 1.0
Glass beads	118	22 18.6 0.37	7 5.9 1.0	15 12.7 0.51	36 30.5 0.44	36 30.5 0.34
Glass vessel	27	3 11.1 0.24	3 11.1 0.4	1 3.7 0.16	11 40.7 0.59	10 37.0 0.97
Iron fragment	24	4 16.7 0.68	1 4.2 1.0	2 8.3 0.51	6 25.0 0.46	7 29.2 0.71
Iron rivet	26	6 23.1 1.0	1 3.8 1.0	6 23.1 0.39	7 26.9 0.57	9 34.6 1.0
Ivory	46	16 34.8 0.06	2 4.3 0.96	7 15.2 1.0	16 34.8 1.0	19 41.3 0.43
Miniature iron blade	22	2 9.1 0.21	3 13.6 0.23	5 22.7 0.48	6 27.3 0.65	5 22.7 0.33
Miniature iron shears	39	9 23.1 1.0	3 7.7 0.82	9 23.1 0.24	11 28.2 0.54	13 33.3 0.98
Miniature iron tweezers	34	9 26.5 0.7	1 2.9 0.76	6 17.6 0.87	12 35.3 1.0	12 35.3 1.0
Playing piece	23	8 34.8 0.23	1 4.3 1.0	2 8.7 0.56	10 43.5 0.46	9 39.1 0.83
Spindlewhorl	24	5 20.8 1.0	1 4.2 1.0	4 16.7 1.0	9 37.5 0.89	6 25.0 0.42
Worked flint	9	2 22.2 1.0	- - 1.0	- - 0.42	3 33.3 1.0	3 33.3 1.0

repeated designs (3-5), segmented designs, and all crosses, were grouped together in order to raise numbers in each cell. Several significant links are apparent, although there are still problems of minimum cell frequency. Firstly, urns decorated with form type 1 (solid figures), are more likely to include combs than would be expected. Urns with a multiple form type (3-5) are more likely to be buried with glass vessels; gridded design (7) are correlated with glass fragments and simple crosses (11) are correlated with ivory. An attempt was made to test these links for individual sites, but the numbers involved were too small to yield any significant results.

As well as looking at links between grave-goods and stamped motifs, each of the skeletal groupings was cross-tabulated with the 65 most popular stamped motifs. Tables were produced for all vessels with stamped decoration for which a skeletal identification had been made. Urns with "possible" and "probable" identifications were counted as positive in order to maximise any links. A few correlations were significant at the 0.1 level. In particular, A11 was positively linked with young adults (at 0.05), E7 with females (at 0.1), and J2 was negatively associated with adult burials (at 0.1). This degree of correlation could easily have arisen through random chance.

In order to increase the degree of certainty, stamps of the same form and design types were combined (table 69). Vessels decorated with "wyrm" shaped stamps (Group K) were found to be less likely to contain young adults. Vessels with a cruciform shaped stamp (Group J) are less likely to contain individuals within the general adult category, and finally, those with rectangular stamps (Group E) appear to be linked with female burials. Table 70 presents cross-tabulations between skeletal groupings and those stamp design types 1-18 which constituted more than 5% of the total. Several correlations are significant at the 0.1 level. Stamps consisting of a repeated motif (Groups 3-5) are more likely to be used to decorate vessels containing child burials. They are also positively correlated with females, but negatively correlated with males. Stamps consisting of an outline figure (Group 2), are correlated with the burial of adolescents. Young adults are likely to be buried in vessels with a simple cross (Group 11) and with vessels bearing any of the cruciform group of stamps (Group 18).

These results allow us to draw several conclusions about the use of stamped decoration. Firstly, there are more links between combined stamp types than with individual motifs. Apparently the general shape or design is more important than the specific motif. Secondly, the internal logic of the design can be seen to have been just as significant as the external shape. These results justify the use of the two-tier classification system, taking both aspects of stamped decoration into account. Thirdly, there also appear to be more links between stamp type and skeletal groupings than there were with grave-goods. The particular aspects of age and sex which appear to be singled out include the burial of young adults and females, although children are also marked.

Table 69 Associations of skeletal groups with use of stamp forms

	Total No	A No Row% Sig	C No Row% Sig	D No Row% Sig	E No Row% Sig	F No Row% Sig
Total	241	157 65.1	12 5.0	29 12.0	41 17.0	10 4.1
SKELETAL GROUP PRESENT:						
Infant	9	6 66.7 1.0	1 11.1 0.94	2 22.2 0.66	2 22.2 1.0	1 11.1 0.83
Child	45	30 66.7 0.95	2 4.4 1.0	5 11.1 1.0	5 11.1 0.34	3 6.7 0.6
Adolescent	24	17 70.8 0.7	3 12.5 0.2	2 8.3 0.8	4 16.7 1.0	1 4.2 1.0
Young adult	48	37 77.1 0.08	2 4.2 1.0	3 6.2 0.26	8 16.7 1.0	3 6.2 0.68
Mature adult	37	19 51.4 0.08	1 2.7 0.78	6 16.2 0.57	7 18.9 0.92	1 2.7 0.98
Old adult	14	9 64.3 1.0	1 7.1 1.0	3 21.4 0.49	5 35.7 0.12	- - 0.91
Adult	99	62 62.6 0.58	3 3.0 0.39	13 13.1 0.81	13 13.1 0.24	2 2.0 0.29
Male	36	23 63.9 1.0	- - 0.28	3 8.3 0.64	6 16.7 1.0	2 5.6 1.0
Female	59	35 59.3 0.36	1 1.7 0.32	8 13.6 0.85	16 27.1 0.07	3 5.1 0.97

	Total No	G No Row% Sig	H No Row% Sig	I No Row% Sig	J No Row% Sig	K No Row% Sig
Total	241	36 14.9	19 7.9	7 2.9	18 7.5	36 14.9
SKELETAL GROUP PRESENT:						
Infant	9	- - 0.42	1 11.1 1.0	- - 1.0	- - 0.82	1 11.1 1.0
Child	45	5 11.1 0.57	2 4.4 0.52	3 6.7 0.24	3 6.7 1.0	6 13.3 0.92
Adolescent	24	1 4.2 0.21	3 12.5 0.63	2 8.3 0.3	1 4.2 0.81	8 33.3 0.02*
Young adult	48	5 10.4 0.45	3 6.2 0.87	- - 0.39	4 8.3 1.0	3 6.2 0.1
Mature adult	37	8 21.6 0.32	2 5.4 0.78	1 2.7 1.0	4 10.8 0.62	4 10.8 0.61
Old adult	14	3 21.4 0.75	3 21.4 0.15	- - 1.0	3 21.4 0.13	- - 0.22
Adult	99	16 16.2 0.79	7 7.1 0.88	5 5.1 0.21	3 3.0 0.05	18 18.2 0.32
Male	36	5 13.9 1.0	3 8.3 1.0	1 2.8 1.0	2 5.6 0.9	3 8.3 0.34
Female	59	11 18.6 0.48	6 10.2 0.64	- - 0.28	4 6.8 1.0	5 8.5 0.16

Table 70 Associations of skeletal groups with use of stamp designs

	Total No	1 No Row% Sig	2 No Row% Sig	3/4/5 No Row% Sig	6 No Row% Sig	7 No Row% Sig
Total	241	36 14.9	64 26.6	65 27.0	16 6.6	83 34.4
SKELETAL GROUP PRESENT:						
Infant	9	1 11.1 1.0	3 33.3 0.93	3 33.3 0.96	1 11.1 1.0	2 22.2 0.67
Child	45	4 8.9 0.3	12 26.7 1.0	19 42.2 0.02	2 4.4 0.75	13 28.9 0.49
Adolescent	24	6 25.0 0.25	12 50.0 0.01	6 25.0 1.0	1 4.2 0.94	7 29.2 0.73
Young adult	48	6 12.5 0.76	10 20.8 0.41	13 27.1 1.0	3 6.2 1.0	18 37.5 0.74
Mature adult	37	6 16.2 1.0	11 29.7 0.79	10 27.0 1.0	- - 0.16	16 43.2 0.3
Old adult	14	1 7.1 0.65	4 28.6 1.0	3 21.4 0.86	- - 0.64	6 42.9 0.69
Adult	99	16 16.2 0.79	26 26.3 1.0	22 22.2 0.22	10 10.1 0.12	28 28.3 0.12
Male	36	5 13.9 1.0	11 30.6 0.7	4 11.1 0.03	- - 0.17	13 36.1 0.97
Female	59	9 15.3 1.0	11 18.6 0.16	23 39.0 0.03	5 8.5 0.73	23 39.0 0.49

	Total No	11 No Row% Sig	13 No Row% Sig	16 No Row% Sig	Segmented No Row% Sig	Cruciform No Row% Sig
Total	241	52 21.6	17 7.1	33 13.7	101 41.9	73 30.3
SKELETAL GROUP PRESENT:						
Infant	9	2 22.2 1.0	1 11.1 1.0	2 22.2 0.79	3 33.3 0.85	3 33.3 1.0
Child	45	11 24.4 0.75	2 4.4 0.66	4 8.9 0.42	17 37.8 0.65	14 31.1 1.0
Adolescent	24	5 20.8 1.0	1 4.2 1.0	1 4.2 0.26	9 37.5 0.81	7 29.2 1.0
Young adult	48	16 33.3 0.04	4 8.3 0.94	7 14.6 1.0	19 39.6 0.84	21 43.7 0.04
Mature adult	37	6 16.2 0.52	2 5.4 0.94	5 13.5 1.0	19 51.4 0.28	8 21.6 0.29
Old adult	14	4 28.6 0.75	2 14.3 0.58	1 7.1 0.74	6 42.9 1.0	7 50.0 0.18
Adult	99	20 20.2 0.78	6 6.1 0.81	12 12.1 0.69	37 37.4 0.29	27 27.3 0.48
Male	36	8 22.2 1.0	3 8.3 1.0	4 11.1 0.82	15 41.7 1.0	11 30.6 1.0
Female	59	15 25.4 0.52	1 1.7 0.12	9 15.3 0.85	27 45.8 0.59	17 23.3 0.9

Further tests were performed in order to check these results. Now only positive skeletal identifications were included, although this led to such a reduction in the number of cases that problems of low numbers were encountered. Nevertheless, significant details about the use of repeated design stamps (Groups 3-5) did emerge. Firstly, no definite males were buried in vessels decorated with one of these stamps . In the study sample, these stamps were used exclusively for females and children. However, when they were cross-tabulated with vessels containing just a child (i.e. single burials), there was no significant association. It would appear, therefore, that the motif was particularly used to indicate the burial of a mother and child together. Furthermore, if all the mature adults are combined together (i.e. mature adults, old adults and the general adults category), there are no significant links with the design of the stamped decoration. It appears that the stamp designs are used to distinguish the younger age groupings, but do not differentiate older age groupings.

3.432 Arrangement of stamped decoration

As well as the design of the individual stamps, stamped decoration is often arranged in such a way as to create an overall pattern. Sometimes the area available may be delimited by the use of incised or plastic decoration; in other cases the stamps may be used in an open area, although the patterns usually echo those produced within an incised border, such as chevrons and triangles. There are also variations in the number of different stamp dies which may be used on one vessel, and in the number of impressions of each die. Possibly the arrangement of stamped decoration and the number of stamps applied were also meaningful to the Anglo-Saxons.

Detailed information about the layout of stamped decoration was collected for the Phase One pilot sample of Elsham and Spong Hill vessels. The principal ways of arranging stamped decoration were identified as:

    i)   In continuous horizontal bands
    ii) In broken horizontal bands
    iii)In vertical band
    iv) In triangular fields
    v)   In rectangular fields

Those vessels with each of these types of decoration were cross-tabulated against each of the most popular grave-goods at Elsham and Spong Hill. In only one case was there a link significant at the 0.1 level (miniature tweezers being almost twice as likely to be in urns with triangular fields of stamps, significant at 0.01). In all other cases, the grave-goods deposited within an urn were irrelevant to the layout of the stamps. Triangular fields were further subdivided into three sub-categories of chevron, solid triangles and stamps within a triangular frame. In fact, tweezers were still positively linked with each of the sub-categories, indicating that the distinction between the types was not important. The classification which grouped all types of triangular field together was a meaningful

Table 71 Proportion of number of stamp dies per vessel for each grave-good

	NUMBER OF STAMP DIES PER VESSEL (Cumulative frequency %)								SIGNFICANCE LEVEL (Kolmogorov-Smirnov test)
	1	2	3	4	5	6	7	8	
Total	45.6	75.8	90.8	95.2	98.2	98.9	99.6	99.9	
GRAVE-GOOD PRESENT:									
Bone fitting	45.5	63.6	81.8	81.8	90.9	90.9	90.9	100.0	
Bronze fragment	49.4	75.3	96.1	98.7	100.0				
Bronze sheet	50.0	83.3	100.0						
Bronze tweezers	40.5	75.7	83.8	89.2	97.3	100.0			
Brooch	47.2	69.4	88.9	94.4	100.0				
Comb	49.6	77.9	88.5	94.7	98.2	99.1	99.1	100.0	
Crystal	7.7	38.5	92.3	92.3	100.0				0.05
Glass	38.3	68.3	90.0	96.7	100.0				
Glass beads	50.0	80.5	92.4	97.5	99.2	100.0			
Glass vessel	25.9	74.1	85.2	88.9	92.6	96.3	100.0		
Iron fragment	54.2	79.2	95.8	100.0					
Iron rivet	30.8	73.1	88.5	100.0					
Ivory	45.7	73.9	91.3	97.8	100.0				
Miniature iron blade	68.2	90.9	90.9	95.5	95.5	100.0			
Miniature iron shears	51.3	82.1	89.7	94.9	97.4	100.0			
Miniature iron tweezers	52.9	76.5	88.2	94.1	100.0				
Playing piece	43.5	73.9	87.0	91.3	95.7	100.0			
Spindlewhorl	50.0	80.8	100.0						
Worked flint	11.1	77.8	88.9	100.0					0.2

Table 72 Proportion of number of stamp dies per vessel for each skeletal grouping

	NUMBER OF STAMP DIES PER VESSEL (Cumulative frequency %)								SIGNFICANCE LEVEL (Kolmogorov-Smirnov test)
	1	2	3	4	5	6	7	8	
Total	45.6	75.8	90.8	95.2	98.2	98.9	99.6	99.9	
SKELETAL GROUP PRESENT:									
Infant	44.4	66.7	88.9	100.0					
Child	54.3	78.3	95.7	100.0					
Adolescent	48.0	68.0	92.0	92.0	96.0	96.0	96.0	100.0	
Young adult	50.0	75.0	95.8	95.8	97.9	100.0			
Mature adult	51.4	75.7	89.2	100.0					
Old adult	53.3	73.3	86.7	86.7	100.0				
Adult	58.6	81.8	94.9	97.0	98.0	100.0			0.1
Male	52.8	88.9	97.2	100.0					
Female	46.7	71.7	90.0	93.3	98.3	100.0			
Animal bones present:	51.5	75.8	93.9	98.5	98.5	100.0			
Sheep	51.6	74.2	93.5	100.0					
Cow/Ox	50.0	80.0	100.0						
Pig	50.0	62.5	100.0						
Horse	28.6	71.4	85.7	85.7	85.7	100.0			

unit.

Stamped vessels were also categorised according to whether the stamps were enclosed within incised lines or in an open arrangement. The distinction is important for the way in which the vessel is decorated; in the former case, the use of stamps is determined by an incised frame; in the latter, the stamps are used independently. When the two ways of executing a stamped design were cross-tabulated against the Elsham and Spong Hill grave-goods it transpired that miniature iron tweezers and shears were almost twice as likely to be deposited in vessels with unrestricted use of stamps (significant at the 0.01 and 0.05 respectively), but that all other grave-goods were equally likely to be in vessels with either restricted or unrestricted stamping[1]. Again, we may conclude that the use of stamping is sensitive to the inclusion of miniature toilet implements and that there must be a link between the two.

Finally, each of the ways of arranging stamped decoration was also cross-tabulated with each of the skeletal categories, where this information was available, but no significant links were found.

The number of different stamp dies used on each vessel was recorded for all pots in the sample. Table 71 compares the frequency distribution for each of the popular grave-goods, with the overall frequency distribution for all stamped vessels. The Kolmogorov-Smirnov test was used to test the significance of differences from the overall distribution. Vessels containing worked flint and those containing crystal were both significantly different (at 0.2 and 0.05 respectively). Both tended to be deposited in vessels with more than one type of stamp.

The assemblage was broken down into individual sites to check for inter-site variation. With the lower sample sizes only crystal remained significantly different (at Elsham and Spong Hill) at 0.2. However, at Spong Hill, the distribution for glass vessels was significantly different at the 0.01 level. At Spong Hill urns containing glass vessels tend to be decorated with more than one stamp. This underlines the association between glass vessels and stamping identified above (see table 65). Both stamps and glass vessels must relate to similar aspects of social identity.

NOTE

<1> The link between the deposition of miniatures and unrestricted stamped decoration is not just a link with vessels with stamped but with no incised decoration. Only three vessels fall into this category, out of 29 with tweezers and stamped decoration. Therefore, the link is with vessels which have both incised decoration and stamped decoration, but where the incising does not constrain the stamping.

Table 73 Spong Hill: variation in number of stamp dies within stamp
groups

	No. of urns	STANDARD DEVIATION for Number of stamp dies
TOTAL	381	1.301
Stamp group		
1	3	0.577
4	4	1.732
5	3	1.0
7	17	2.152
8	4	0.957
10	2	0.707
11	2	0.707
14	2	0.0
15	2	0.0
17	3	1.155
19	2	0.707
20	3	0.577
22	2	2.828
26	2	0.0
28	2	0.0
31	3	1.0
38	2	0.0
41	2	0.0
42	3	0.0

Table 74 Elsham and Spong Hill - association between number of
impressions per stamp die and grave-goods

| | Number of impressions of one stamp die | | | | |
| | Less than 60 | | 60 or above | | |
	No	Row%	No	Row%	Sig
Total	475	79.7	121	20.3	
GRAVE-GOOD PRESENT:					
Bronze fragment	53	77.9	15	22.1	0.82
Bronze sheet	35	83.3	7	16.7	0.68
Brooch	32	84.2	6	15.8	0.61
Comb	73	76.8	22	23.2	0.54
Crystal	11	64.7	6	35.3	0.21
Glass beads	120	80.5	29	19.5	0.86
Glass vessel	14	58.3	10	41.7	0.02
Iron rivet	15	75.0	5	25.0	0.8
Ivory	38	79.2	10	20.8	1.0
Shears	43	79.6	11	20.4	1.0
Single blade	33	84.6	6	15.4	0.56
Spindlewhorl	16	66.7	8	33.3	0.17
Tweezers	43	69.4	19	30.6	0.05
Worked flint	18	85.7	3	14.3	0.67

Table 75 Spong Hill: variation in number of stamp impressions

	No. of urns	Stamp type	STANDARD DEVIATION for Number of impressions (a)in Group	(b)for Stamp Type
TOTAL	381			
Stamp Group				
1	3	D5	1.16	34.51
		I5	7.07	51.12
4	4	E24	12.73	12.73
5	3	A2	90.51	114.8
		G7	36.77	58.22
		P1	11.31	15.5
6	2	E20	2.12	12.37
7	17	A2	94.76	114.8
		A5	11.53	51.87
		A11	140.98	91.34
		A13	34.71	31.9
		E7	69.98	50.16
		H5	3.51	13.12
		I5	48.91	51.12
		J2	25.15	19.79
		J6	5.85	5.85
		J12	15.56	36.15
		K2	42.1	40.27
		L6	32.79	32.79
8	4	A5	5.66	51.87
		A15	7.07	14.7
		F14	10.91	10.91
10	2	E20	5.66	12.37
11	2	G7	23.34	58.22
14	2	A11	4.95	91.34
		H6	0.71	0.71
15	2	A15	22.63	14.7
17	3	A5	66.01	51.87
19	2	A9	24.75	60.4
		E7	1.41	50.16
		K1	9.19	61.8
20	3	A12	13.44	17.76
		A16	7.07	42.91
22	2	K1	40.31	61.8
26	2	D5	7.07	34.51
28	2	A9	67.18	60.4
31	3	A5	15.56	51.87
		A13	21.5	31.9
		D2	41.01	41.01
38	2	A16	22.63	42.91
		K5	12.02	30.46
41	2	I1	28.28	28.28
42	3	C6	22.72	24.9

The frequency distribution of number of stamp dies per vessel for each of the skeletal groupings was also compared against the overall distribution (table 72). The results indicate that vessels containing adult burials tend to be simply stamped with just one stamp die (significant at 0.1). All other ages appeared to be randomly distributed, and sex seemed irrelevant to the number of stamp dies used. When the sample was split into individual sites the numbers were too small to examine inter-site variation.

In order to confirm that the number of stamp dies used was related to the social identity of the deceased, rather than stylistic preferences of the potter, the variation within stamp groups was compared to overall variation. Table 73 compares the standard deviation for the number of different stamp dies per vessel at Spong Hill. It will be seen that in three cases there is more variation within stamp groups than between stamp groups. Therefore, even though all the pots within a group are stylistically related, they do not show a high level of consistency in the number of different stamps applied. This confirms that this number may, instead, be related to the identity of the deceased.

For Elsham and Spong Hill it was possible to test if the actual number of impressions of each die was also significant. Using the mean value for the number of impressions as a divider the stamped vessels could be split into two groups of those with less than 60 impressions of one die, and those with 60 or more impressions. Where a vessel had stamps with both more and less than 60 impressions then it would be incorporated in both groups, and so would cancel itself out. The chi-square statistic was used to test if urns with particular grave-goods tended to belong to one group rather than another. The results are shown in table 74. Only tweezers (including both bronze and iron examples as they were grouped together at this stage), and possibly glass vessels, show a preference for urns with a large number of impressions per die. When the Elsham skeletal groups were tested no significant results were found.

Finally, by dividing the vessels according to potters' groups it became possible to test if there was less variation in the number of impressions of stamps of the same die, than for all stamps of that type. Table 75 compares the standard deviation for numbers of impressions of stamps of identical dies to the standard deviation for numbers of impressions of all stamps of that type. Generally there is less variation within a potters' group, although there are five exceptions. This implies that the number of impressions used is a stylistic variable, linked to the habits of individual potters, and that it does not relate to the social identity of the deceased.

CHAPTER 4

CONCLUSIONS

In section 1.5 it was suggested that material culture could be understood as a form of language. At one level artefacts may be regarded as functioning tools, but at another level they are used to communicate information. Hodder (1986, 123) has argued that a material culture language may be easier to read than a written language. Since it is less precise and complex there is greater scope for ambiguity, but the message conveyed must be correspondingly simpler. Nevertheless, the language of another society is still alien to us, and the syntax and vocabulary of the Anglo-Saxon potter must be translated, just as much as the Old English of the _Beowulf_ poet.

In order to translate a material culture language one must try to categorise it in a fashion which would have been meaningful to the society responsible. The debate over whether classifications are "real" or "invented", "emic" or "etic", was rehearsed in Chapter One. Hodder has argued that one can recover typologies which approximate to indigenous perceptions by a method he describes as contextual archaeology:

> Success in such endeavours depends on including as much information as is available on the historical contexts and associations of traits, styles and organizational design properties, as well as on a reconstruction of the active use of such traits in social strategies (1986, 133).

I have tried to demonstrate that information about the identity of the occupants of Anglo-Saxon cremation urns, derived from grave-goods and skeletal remains, provides a context, within which it is possible to understand the form and decoration of the funerary pottery. By looking for statistical associations of these traits, according to a method propounded by David Clarke and discussed in Chapter Two, it has been possible to describe Anglo-saxon pottery in a manner which approximates to the way in which Anglo-Saxons would themselves have understood it. Background noise means that the translation must necessarily be imperfect, but the correlations revealed in Chapter Three may nevertheless provide a starting point from which to understand Anglo-Saxon society.

In this final section I shall discuss the implications of the results of this research for understanding variability in material culture in general, and Anglo-Saxon mortuary ritual in particular. Firstly it may be useful to summarise the results.

4.1 Summary of results

The principal results of the research are in four areas:

(i) Description of the range of form, decoration and grave-goods of Early Anglo-Saxon cremations;

(ii) Examination of regional variation in this range;

(iii) Identification of several levels of variability in pottery style;

(iv) Consideration of associations between grave-goods and skeletal groupings.

It has been argued that we have enough information about Anglo-Saxon mortuary behaviour to lead us to examine the funerary pottery in a ritual context. It has been demonstrated that, of nearly 2500 cremation vessels examined, almost 80% are decorated; 75% with incised decoration, 40% with stamped decoration, and 30% with plastic decoration. 48% of the vessels contained grave-goods. The average height of the vessels is c. 19.5cm.

There is variation in proportions of types of decoration, in proportions of grave-goods, and in vessel form. However, the extent of variation is so limited as to suggest that Anglo-Saxon potters were generally working to a tightly-defined cultural type. Such rigid control might be expected if potters were using a symbolic language, but might also be a consequence of a migratory people under social and economic change and stress. Anthropologists and sociologists have described how material culture symbols may be strictly controlled at times of conflict between cultures (Cohen 1974, Watson 1977).

At most sites, there are very similar proportions of vessels with incised decoration and plastic decoration, and vessels belong to an identical range of forms. The similarities are such that all Anglo-Saxon cremation vessels from England may be regarded as one assemblage, with as much variation within sites, as between sites. This suggests a high level of contact and conformity between peoples practicing the new burial rite, indicating its common origin. Only in stamped decoration (including both if it is used, and how it is used) can greater variation be identified. The use of stamped decoration was evidently under less rigorous cultural control, which is what would be expected if it developed locally in England, as has been suggested.

Much of the limited variation which has been identified seems to be between those sites traditionally regarded as Saxon, and those seen as Anglian. Urns from the Saxon cemeteries have a lower average height, and at Mucking, fewer urns are decorated, there is very little stamping, and the use of plastic decoration is idiosyncratic. There is also greater variation of pottery forms within the site, suggesting that this was less tightly controlled. Two other cemeteries are also atypical: Illington and South Elkington. Many of the traits exhibited suggest other influences, perhaps with some links with the Saxon rather than the Anglian area. At Illington, the vessels tend to be shorter; they have more vertical incised lines, more hanging arches, fewer dots and slashes and less plastic decoration. However, they do have lots of stamping, with many pots with more than one die, and the use of unusual stamps as well. At South Elkington, there are more examples of diagonal incised decoration than at other sites, including chevrons, and diagonals sloping to both left and right. There are also more standing arches, and the highest proportion of vessels with dots of all the cemeteries.

Grave-goods survive in roughly half of Anglo-Saxon cremations. They also generally appear in roughly equivalent numbers at most sites, but Elsham and Spong Hill have more than the average, whilst Loveden Hill and South Elkington have less[1]. Most grave-goods occur regularly on most sites, whilst a few are rare, and are only found on one or two sites. Some, such as brooches, are found in consistent proportions, whilst others, such as combs, are common on some sites, but rare on others. It would appear that some items were used by all Anglo-Saxon peoples, but others were more restricted. The cemeteries can be placed in three groupings according to the proportions of grave-goods: (i) Mucking and South Elkington, (ii) Illington, Loveden Hill and Caistor, (iii) Elsham, Newark, Sancton, and Spong Hill.

Finally, if the skeletal assemblages for each site are compared, there are some unexpected aspects of the Anglo-Saxon population structure, including a low proportion of infant and child burials, and apparently an unequal ratio of the sexes at several sites. The latter might be a sampling problem, but could equally well reflect unequal usage of the cemeteries by the respective sexes.

Looking at the assemblage as a whole, we can draw several conclusions about different levels of variability in pottery form and decoration, and what they relate to. These conclusions confirm that the form and design of cremation vessels are making a statement about the occupant.

Size is apparently being used to describe the age and status of the deceased. Size, including overall height, height of maximum diameter, and maximum width, appears to vary independently of shape and decoration. Larger vessels most frequently contain grave-goods, but are not linked with some types in preference to others. The height of a cremation vessel is closely correlated with the age of the occupant,

NOTE

[1] Lackford also has less, but must be excluded because of problems with the sample.

although the relative status of the individual also needs to be taken into account. Adult females, for example, are not generally buried in such tall vessels as adult males. Rim diameter is not linked to age, but does seem to be correlated with the sex of the deceased. Similarly males tend to be buried in wider vessels; females in narrower ones.

The shape of the cremation vessels does have a bearing on the classes of decoration which are used. How constricted the neck of a vessel is appears to have been particularly important to the Anglo-Saxons in distinguishing between vessel forms, perhaps because it has connotations of whether the urn is of domestic cooking type or not. Most grave-goods tend to be more common in narrow-necked urns.

Decoration is very important in describing the identity of the deceased. Over three-quarters of cremation urns are decorated, but where a plain urn is used then this also conveys a message. Some aspects of decoration are richly symbolic and are associated with the presence of a wide variety of grave-goods; others are apparently not reflected in the selection of objects. It is not necessarily the most visible differences that are the most significant; quite fine details can be very important.

The various classes of decoration can be used independently, but their use is generally interlinked, and some classes, such as incised and plastic forms, are likely to occur together. The use of incised decoration is closely tied to the identity of the occupant(s) of the vessel. Every motif, except hanging arches, is significantly correlated with at least one type of grave-good. However, there are fewer links with the age and sex of the deceased, so the incised motifs seem to reflect aspects of social identity other than age and sex. The arrangement of the incised decoration, including both the number of motifs, and their layout, appears to be less important as an indicator of the identity of the deceased. Similarly, the average number of lines used in a motif also appears to be irrelevant in marking the occupant. All these attributes seem to be related to the identity of the potter, rather than that of the deceased. The only possible exceptions identified are the number of chevrons, and the number of lines in a horizontal band. However, the former, at least, is also linked to the size and shape of the vessel, so may not be significant. In the latter, the presence of a broad band of horizontal lines is correlated with the inclusion of a comb.

The use of plastic decoration has an inverse relationship with the use of stamping. The types of boss and cordon are correlated with the grave-goods included in the vessel, but not with the skeletal remains. Again, they must be related to other aspects of social identity. Similarly, the number of bosses employed is related to the identity of the potter, rather than the occupant.

The use of stamped decoration appears to be correlated with the inclusion of some grave-goods, but there are very few links between individual stamp types and particular objects, or with skeletal groups. When the stamps are combined according to overall form or design more links are apparent, especially with age and sex, but less so with grave-goods. This is not in conflict with the "heraldic" interpretation of stamped decoration proposed by C.Arnold (1983). If the combination of particular types of stamp is used to mark the exact kinship position of the deceased, then one would not expect it to be correlated with the grave-goods deposited, as there need be no relationship between one's position in a kinship network and the other aspects of one's social identity. On the other hand, the broader categories of stamp form and design might be expected to show links with the skeletal remains, as they might relate to broader aspects of the heraldic scheme, such as whether an individual was of the male or female line, and how old he or she was. The number of different stamp dies used on a single urn also appears to be related to social identity, but the layout of the stamped decoration, including the number of impressions of each stamp die, appears to be irrelevant to the identity of the deceased. Instead, layout and number of impressions may be determined by the style of the particular potter.

Grave-goods must originally have been included in more than half of cremation burials. Some items, such as brooches, are found in consistent proportions throughout Anglo-Saxon England; others exhibit significant regional variation. They do not appear to be directly related to age and sex groupings, although there are several correlations. These suggest that they relate to other aspects of social identity, which are linked to age and sex, but are not coterminous with them. In section 1.54 several other attributes of social identity were identified which might be marked at death, including ethnic and group affiliation, status, and circumstances of death. Of these, it would intuitively seem more likely that grave-goods would be used to mark the first three aspects. Binford (1971) has suggested that the more complex a society is, then the less likely that age and sex will be represented in the burial rite, and the more likely that other dimensions will be represented instead. These results, with age and sex represented, but other features cross-cutting them, support the picture of a society in an intermediate stage, midway between an anarchistic tribe and hierarchically structured kingdoms. That more women than men should be given grave-goods, but that gender distinctions should not be so heavily emphasised might, at first sight, seem surprising. Nevertheless it is perhaps compatible with Anglo-Saxon women fulfilling a variety of roles, at many different status levels (Fell 1984).

Similarly, the graves of children are marked differently to those of adults, both in terms of vessel size and in aspects of decoration. Yet they are given the same range of grave-goods, which suggests that in many cases status may have been ascribed rather than achieved.

Archaeologically, we cannot precisely define the relationship between grave-goods and social identity, but by examining individual correlations between grave-goods, skeletal attributes, pottery form and pottery decoration for the assemblage as a whole, we may better understand both the grave-goods, and the nature of Anglo-Saxon symbolism.

Brooches are not related to vessel size, nor to the shape of the neck, in contrast to virtually every other object found in the cremations. Nor are they correlated with the age or sex of the deceased. Taken with the fact that they are found in equal proportions at each of the cemeteries, it would appear that they are not generally used to distinguish between groups within Anglo-Saxon society. Instead, it is proposed that they are simply used to mark ethnic identity on a broad level, that is, to define a cremation as Anglo-Saxon. Shouldered urns, and those with impressed dots, are the only pottery attributes with which brooches are correlated.

Bronze tweezers also appear to be unrelated to the age and sex of the deceased. However, they are linked with a wide range of decoration, and may be used to indicate status. They are correlated with the use of both horizontal and vertical lines, dots, upright (but not reversed) chevrons, and vertical bosses (especially where there are more than 7). They are found especially in tall vessels with a narrow neck. They appear to be used differently to iron tweezers.

Bronze fragments are also found especially in tall pots with narrow necks, but are not linked with any type of incised decoration, and are rarely found with round bosses. They are correlated with those vessels which have a deliberate hole, and also with child burials.

Bronze sheet fragments are linked with holed vessels, but they are also correlated with other features, indicating that they represent different objects from the other bronze fragments. They are associated especially with tall wide vessels, and those decorated with round bosses and dots. They tend to be found with children rather than adults.

Miniature toilet implements are often deposited in sets, and consequently show a number of links in common. Shears, tweezers, and single blades are each found most frequently in narrow-necked tall pots decorated with vertical lines and standing arches. They appear to be used to mark the burials of a general category of people of a high status. However, each item also exhibits correlations with other classes of fairly elaborate decoration, and age and sex groups. Miniature shears are linked with the use of dots, round bosses, cordons, and unrestricted stamping. They are slightly more likely to be buried with males than females, although they are found with both, and are correlated with children. Miniature tweezers are linked with the use of diagonal lines sloping to both the left and right, slashes, dots and cordons. They are less common in stamped vessels, unless the stamping is not confined by incised lines. They also tend to be found more with males than females, but are correlated with adults rather than children. Single miniature blades are correlated with diagonal lines sloping to the left (but not to the right); they are less commonly deposited in vessels with a continuous chevron design, or with stamped decoration of any sort. They are linked with the use of vertical bosses, and large numbers of round bosses. They do not exhibit any particular age or sex links.

Iron <u>fragments</u> are also correlated with tall vessels with narrow necks; many may have come from iron miniatures. However, they are also linked with pots decorated with dots, and apparently do not occur often with young adults.

Bone <u>fittings</u> are correlated with tall pots, the use of horizontal lines, and the use of a large number of round bosses. They are linked with mature adults, and are likely to represent the remains of high-status items.

Bone <u>rings</u> are fairly rare, and are not correlated with any particular form or style of decoration. There is the suggestion that they may be age-linked, as they are frequently found with adolescents.

<u>Spindlewhorls,</u> like brooches, do not appear to be used to mark status, or local group affiliation. They are not related to vessel size or shape, and the only decorative link is with vessels with few bosses. Perhaps surprisingly, they exhibit no age or sex link either.

<u>Combs</u> are correlated with tall vessels, and those with narrow necks. They are linked with the use of standing arches, slashes, dots, round bosses, and stamps of design type 1. They rarely accompany infants, but occur equally frequently with all other age and sex groupings. Of all the grave-goods, they are exceptional in being correlated with the usage of particular numbers of incised lines, namely vessels with a large number of incised lines around the neck, especially those with more groups of lines totalling an even number.

<u>Ivory</u> fragments are correlated with tall pots, and decorated vessels, but not really with any particular class of decoration, apart from bands of horizontal lines which are found on most pots, and stamp design type 11. They are linked with adult females, and so it would appear that they may be associated with high-status females.

<u>Crystal</u> beads are also more common in tall pots, and are correlated with swastikas, vertical bosses, and vessels with more than one class of stamp. They are not linked to a particular age or sex.

<u>Glass</u> <u>beads</u> are amongst the most popular grave-goods. Surprisingly, they are not noticeably linked to age or sex. They are correlated with wide vessels, especially with narrow necks, but are not common in very small pots, perhaps suggesting that they are less frequently deposited with infants and children than adults. They are linked with the use of cordons, and slashes and dots, and are rare with stamp forms A and K.

<u>Glass</u> <u>vessels</u> are associated with very tall vessels, and they are the only grave-good to be correlated with the use of stamped decoration, especially with design types 3-5, and, at Spong Hill, with the use of several different stamp dies. Unlike other grave-goods, they are not especially common in urns decorated with incising. They are expensive items to deposit in a grave, and are likely to command a high status.

The unidentified <u>glass</u> fragments may represent beads or vessels, and so may present a confused picture. They are linked with tall narrow-necked vessels, and with decorated vessels, and apparently stamp design type 7. They appear to be more popular with mature adults, and less so with children.

<u>Playing</u> <u>pieces,</u> like glass vessels, are correlated with very tall pots, and are likely to be buried with those of a high status. This is supported by the fact that they are also linked with old adults. They are also associated particularly with pots with a narrow neck, vertical bosses, and incised slashes.

<u>Worked</u> <u>flints,</u> unlike most grave-goods, are not related to size of vessel, but their association with narrow-necked urns, and vessels decorated with more than one class of stamp, does suggest that these are also deliberate grave-goods, rather than accidental inclusions.

Animal bones may also be regarded as grave offerings. The act of cremating an animal and including it with a human burial must be seen as a symbolic statement about that person, and appears to relate principally to their age. Like the grave-goods discussed above, animals are generally linked with tall pots although this is less marked for sheep. They are also correlated with deliberately-holed urns, and vessels decorated with horizontal and vertical incised lines, diagonal lines sloping to the right, crosses, and the use of stamped decoration. Most animals are found especially in male burials, and are more common with mature adults, and less so with infants. The actual choice of animal seems less important. Sheep are the most popular, but horses, cows and pigs exhibit the strongest correlations, especially with adults, and especially with those buried in tall pots.

The results for the PCA identity groups of combined grave-goods really repeat those for the individual items. As one would expect, GROUP ZERO, without grave-goods, shows the opposite relationship to many of the objects described above. Pots of GROUP ZERO tend to be wide-mouthed vessels of below average height. They tend to have less vertical incised lines, fewer diagonals sloping to the left, fewer standing arches, and fewer dots, slashes, swastikas and crosses. They are linked with infants and adolescents, and do not tend to be associated with females and animal offerings. By contrast, GROUP ONE shows a combination of the results obtained for each of the iron miniatures. They are correlated with very tall vessels with restricted necks, and do not tend to have deliberate holes. They are predominantly male, but show no particular age links. They have more vertical incised decoration, more leftwards sloping diagonals, more standing arches, and more slashes and dots. GROUP TWO are also found more in vessels of above average height, but are also correlated with wide vessels. They are linked with vessels decorated with slashes and dots, and are frequently associated with females, and possibly pigs, but are infrequently with infants.

Finally, several of the skeletal groups themselves exhibit particular links with forms of pot and types of decoration. As well as being in the smallest vessels, infants also tend to be in

wide-mouthed urns, perhaps emphasising their low status. The shape of
the urn is less relevant for child burials. However, they are less
likely to be buried in vessels with diagonal lines sloping to the
right, slashes, and plastic decoration, and more likely to be buried
in pots decorated with stamp design types 3-5. Adolescents are linked
with stamp design type 2, and young adults with types 11 and 18. The
latter are also less likely to be buried in pots bearing slashes, and
with stamp form type K. Adult males are correlated with hanging
arches, and adult females with standing arches; here would seem to be
a simple case of binary opposition. Females are also correlated with
the use of chevrons, whether upright or reversed, and with stamp form
E and design 3-5, but are less likely to be buried in vessels
decorated with cordons or bosses. Most adults tend to be placed in
vessels with fairly simple stamping (only one stamp die), and are not
often found with stamp form J.

As has been noted, at most sites, there is a direct correlation
between age at death and size of cremation urn. At Illington, Mucking
and Worthy Park, however, remains of all ages and both sexes are found
spread throughout the size range. Again it appears that at Saxon
sites, or sites with Saxon links, there is less rigid cultural control
of the marking of social identity than at Anglian cemeteries.

In summary, it appears that aspects of the form and decoration of
Anglo-Saxon cremation vessels, can, with a limited degree of
confidence, be used to predict details of the social identity of the
occupant(s), just as a more recent gravestone can tell us about the
person(s) interred beneath.

4.2 Variability in Anglo-Saxon cremation vessels

Anglo-Saxon pottery has conventionally been studied as a spatial
indication of race and culture and as a chronological indication of
historical events. Variability in pottery style has been regarded as
being determined by variations in ethnic origins according to
traditional cultural-history models. It has been seen as providing a
passive reflection of movements of peoples.

The role of prehistoric archaeology, on the other hand, is now seen
much more as a means of studying process and pattern rather than
particular events. Pottery is studied for the light it can throw on
all aspects of human behaviour.

Between the particularist Anglo-Saxonist and the processualist
prehistorian there has opened a great, and ever-widening, gulf of
methods and objectives. It has begun to appear as if there is no
common ground between the two. One reaction has been to deny
completely the relevance of existing work on written sources to early
Anglo-Saxon England in an attempt to reintegrate Anglo-Saxon
archaeology with prehistory (see, for example, Pader 1982). Whilst
this approach has many attractions, in the long run it must be
counter-productive. In general, there are many unknown variables in
the "black box" of archaeology (cf. Leach 1973). In the early
Anglo-Saxon period the written sources provide contextual information

that may eventually allow us to give values to some of these variables, and so gain a better understanding of society as a whole. They may, in fact, illuminate the crucial relationship between material culture and human behaviour which is at the root of many problems in prehistory.

The most productive way forward, therefore, appears to lie in the reintegration of the best of the old archaeology with the best of the new (cf. Rahtz 1983). This research suggests one way in which it may be possible to integrate traditional interpretations of Anglo-Saxon pottery with current explanations of style.

Rival interpretations of the relationship between material culture and social interaction were discussed in Chapter One (see especially Plog 1980). Wobst (1977) assigns stylistic variability a functional role in the transmission of messages about an individual's social position. This function may become particularly important in marking social relationships at times of stress, such as may have existed in early Anglo-Saxon England (cf. Arnold 1982). When social positions are in upheaval then more emphasis may be placed upon marking them. Childe (1945, 17) notes that the deposition of grave-goods tends to increase when the stability of a society is upset by invasion or immigration that requires radical reorganisation. Parker-Pearson (1982, 112) describes the situation thus:

> Social advertisement in death ritual may be expressly overt where changing relations of domination result in status re-ordering and consolidation of new social positions.

Social interaction can occur vertically (between individuals living in the same place) or horizontally (between individuals living in different places). Wobst (ibid) and Hodder (1982) conclude that different artefacts can carry different kinds of messages to different audiences. It is proposed here that the same artefacts can also carry different messages to different audiences. Each artefact consists of a large number of attributes which can vary independently of each other. Some attributes may be used to distinguish sub-types used in particular regions; others may distinguish social groups within that region. Furthermore, even the same attributes may carry different messages according to the context of use.

The style of Anglo-Saxon cremation urns is seen as making a statement about the place of the deceased in Anglo-Saxon society, reinforcing the corporate identity of the group:

> By summarizing an individual's economic and social situation, stylistic messages may play a more active role in the integration of social groups (Wobst 1977, 327).

Thus the form and decoration of a cremation vessel may signify the social role of the individual(s) buried within it on many levels. Some attributes may mark the deceased as an Angle; others may suggest that he is a high-ranking male; others may relate to clan or moiety groupings, and so on. Wobst (1977, 336) has proposed a sliding scale relating message content to stylistic form. The more widely a message is to be broadcast the more visible will be the artefact chosen to convey it.   It is suggested that the more general the message then, broadly speaking, the more visible the attribute used to represent it. Thus the most gross aspects of pottery form and decoration identify a cremation urn as Anglo-Saxon, the finer details transmit finer points of social role.

It is proposed that, running from the general to the particular, the following levels may be differentiated in pottery style[1]:

       'Horizontal' differentiation
           (i)   culture group - Germanic cremation rite
           (ii) ethnic group - Angle, Saxon etc.
           (iii) regional group - East Angle, Middle Angle, and
                 finer regional sub-groupings
       'Vertical' differentiation
           (iv) age, sex, or other social group
       'Motor-habit' differentiation
           (v)   potter's style group

The significance of this hypothesis is that it allows that traditional and more recent approaches to artefact variability may both be valid. It promises a reconciliation between the culture historical view of Myres, and the more recent culture process (including functionalist and structuralist) interpretations, and promotes a reintegration of historical and archaeological material.

(i) Culture group

It has been demonstrated that the size, shape, and general appearance of an Anglo-saxon cremation urn would have served to distinguish it from pottery produced by any other cultural group, and would also distinguish between funerary and domestic assemblages, despite some overlap between them.

(ii) Ethnic group

We have noted, above, that there seem to be distinctions between the Saxon and Anglian sites, mainly in the average size of vessels, but also in the proportions of different classes of decoration, and in variation within a cemetery. However, we have also seen that there are further fine distinctions between sub-groupings within the Anglian area, for example in the different proportions of grave-goods. Stylistic analysis may indicate the presence of distinctions more

NOTE

<1> This is not intended as an exhaustive list, and there may be other levels of stylistic variation, such as chronological variation. However, in the absence of a well-secured chronology for Early Anglo-Saxon pottery, this has to be outside the scope of the present research.

subtle than those of "kingdom" level.

(iii) Regional group

The conclusion from the groupings of grave-good assemblages is that Bede's account ia a gross over-simplification. In the Historia Ecclesiastica (i.15) Bede states that:

> They came from three very powerful Germanic tribes, the Saxons, Angles, and Jutes. The people of Kent and the inhabitants of the Isle of Wight are of Jutish origin and also those opposite the Isle of Wight, that part of the Kingdom of Wessex which is still today called the nation of the Jutes. From the Saxon country, that is, the district now known as Old Saxony, came the East Saxons, the South Saxons, and the West Saxons. Besides this, from the country of the Angles, that is, the land between the kingdoms of the Jutes and the Saxons, which is called Angulus, came the East Angles, the Middle Angles, the Mercians, and all the Northumbrian race (that is those people who dwell north of the river Humber) as well as the other Anglian tribes (Colgrave and Mynors 1969, 51).

At a very general level, the archaeological evidence lends some support to this picture, although it is widely accepted that there was a greater mixing of peoples than allowed for by Bede, and that there is likely to have been a substantial indigenous contribution to the Sub-Roman population. At a finer level of detail, however, it appears that there are other groupings which are not accounted for by the traditional model. There are groupings of cemeteries, for example, comprising sites in widely separated locations such as Elsham, Newark, Sancton and Spong Hill. One explanation might be that several groups of Anglo-Saxon newcomers, each importing their own variation of the cremation burial rite, may each have split into smaller groups, and have settled in different areas of England where they maintained or developed their own customs. Whilst they may have shared the practice of cremation with their neighbours, the use of particular grave-goods may have differentiated them from their immediate neighbours, and united them with related peoples living further afield. These distinctions may have been consciously maintained as a means of reinforcing social ties.

(iv) Age, sex or other social group

The correlations between social identity and the use of particular decorative motifs, and sizes and shapes of vessels, have been fully described above. In summary, it is apparent that within a cemetery, pottery and grave-good attributes, which on a horizontal level mark regional and sub-regional differences, may also mark vertical aspects of social role within one area. Some grave-goods appear to be age and sex linked, but others mark some other aspect of social role, about which we can only speculate, such as totemic or moiety grouping. Even groups of items frequently found together, such as miniature toilet implements, must be split into specific items, each reflecting different aspects of social role. Whilst we have observed that many of the attributes which are used to differentiate groups on a vertical scale seem to be used in common at each cemetery, it is possible that local variations in symbolism might develop, marking differences in social identity within a site. Bunzel (1929) notes that several areas may share a similar style of pottery, but in some areas a particular motif may be symbolic, whilst in another nearby area it may have no significance.

(v) Potter's style group

Finally, it is proposed that there is a level of micro-variation of style which does not relate to horizontal or vertical roles of the deceased, but rather, reflects the style of individual potters. It has been demonstrated that potters appeared to favour the use of specific numbers of fields of lines, and numbers of lines within a field, and it would have been possible to identify the work of particular potters by the details of their pottery. On the other hand, such fine details of style are not generally used to mark any of the broader aspects of vertical and horizontal social differentiation discussed above.

This research has sought to demonstrate that stylistic variability in Anglo-Saxon pottery can operate on several levels. Different attributes are used to mark different aspects of social role. There is a sliding scale of visibility of these attributes, according to the size of the audience that the message is being broadcast to, although there is considerable overlap between levels. The overall picture is extremely complex, with a particular grave-good, for example, representing a particular social role, according to which other attributes (both ceramic and other grave-goods) it is associated with.

The general appearance of a vessel identifies it as Germanic. The proportion of decorated vessels and of different forms allow a cemetery assemblage to be distinguished from a settlement assemblage. Differences in the proportions of vessels with particular classes of incised decoration mark an assemblage as Anglian or Saxon, whilst finer differences distinguish between regional sub-groupings. Within a single site, specific decorative motifs appear to mark age, sex, and also other social groupings. The use of incised arches, for example, signifies a group who are also represented by the inclusion of miniature iron blades and shears on the pyre. Some of these miniatures may be marking the burial as that of a child, but others may be representing other aspects of identity, and not all children will be accompanied by blades and shears. The actual number of arches, however, and the number of lines per arch may be used to distinguish vessels produced by particular potters, and would have no significance to a wider audience. In conclusion, one cannot fully explain the stylistic variability in Anglo-Saxon ceramics by examining one level alone. A composite model is needed, incorporating several levels of differentiation, and offering reconciliation between cultural history and more recent schools of archaeological thought. The overall impression is of a society with a highly complex iconography and finely divided but well-defined social roles.

4.3 Implications for Anglo-Saxon mortuary ritual

We have now established that on one level the form and decoration of an Early Anglo-Saxon cremation vessel communicates information about the occupant(s). This has several implications, both for the nature of the production of Anglo-Saxon pottery, and for the nature of Anglo-Saxon funerary ritual.

Firstly, we can no longer see the designs inscribed and impressed upon the pottery as purely "decorative". To the Anglo-Saxons, they had meaning in a funerary context. This confirms the view that the pots are not generally re-used domestic vessels, but are specifically produced for a funerary role. Some, especially the plain vessels, may have been taken from a domestic context and re-used for those who were not considered deserving of a decorated vessel. It might be possible too, that some of the decorated urns may originally have served a domestic function, (and were decorated according to the social identity of their owner perhaps). Once utilised as a cremation vessel, however, the form and decoration gain a new role, symbolising the identity of the deceased. Wilson (1939) reports that, amongst the Nyakyusa, the pots of a dead woman are broken at her burial so as not to remind her relatives of her. Perhaps these personalised Anglo-Saxon vessels were buried for similar reasons.

The corollary of this is that any vessel is appropriate to a particular individual, or sometimes two, and rarely three, individuals. This explains the unique character of every cremation urn. In a small community, therefore, it would appear that urns were carefully manufactured with a particular "client" in mind, according to a culturally controlled set of symbolic rules. This may also be supported by the fact that vessels which had warped and been damaged during firing were still used. If they were intended for a particular individual then another vessel could not have been substituted. Manufacture may have been by a specialist potter, or by someone within the family group. If professional potters were involved, then alternatively, they may have had a range of vessels available, from which an appropriate vessel was selected according to the same rules. This is perhaps less likely, as it would entail maintaining a considerable stock of cremation urns. Either way, we cannot know whether the Anglo-Saxons were consciously aware of these rules, or whether they were just culturally accepted. We cannot even be sure if this is a valid distinction anyway. The form and decoration of the cremation vessels may have been a simple "mirror" reflection of the social identity of the deceased, or, according to the archaeological thinking described in section 1.51, they may have been deliberately controlled and manipulated, both in the working out of social tensions, and in the reinforcement of social solidarity and group cohesion.

In those cases where two or more individuals are buried in the same vessel, we must presume that the form and decoration of the vessel represents each of them. In cases where one individual died first, but it was intended to bury several people together, the first to die must have been cremated, and the ashes saved, perhaps in the cremation vessel. The respective cremated bones are often separated within the urn (Putnam <u>pers</u> <u>comm</u>) and must originally have been contained in textile or leather pouches, possibly the source of the ivory "bag handles". These multiple burials, therefore, are unlikely to have been the result of accidental collection of bone from shared pyres.

The people who made the pottery, whether itinerant professionals, or local amateurs, must have held an important role in Anglo-Saxon society. They were responsible for recording the identity of the deceased; in a sense, their job overlapped with that of "funeral director". They must also have been the keepers of the knowledge about the funerary symbolism; through their work they maintained and transformed social allegiances and status differences. The authority vested in their position gives them, perhaps, a mystical role, possibly related to that of the "runemaster", whose act of inscribing a rune upon an object gives it its power.

In the recording of the social identity of an individual in his or her burial, we also observe the significance attached to the treatment of the dead in Anglo-Saxon society. We may note the labour invested in the cremation, both in the quantity of fuel required for the pyre, and the precious objects and animals sacrificed to accompany the deceased. We can see here a scaled down version of the ceremony witnessed in <u>Beowulf</u> and at Sutton Hoo, in which context we should consider the majority of Anglo-Saxon burials. At Sutton Hoo, the grave-goods combine to tell us much about the social identity of the deceased. For the mass of the population too, burial was used to record and manipulate social relations. We can be less certain whether this was for the benefit of the deceased in the "afterlife", or for the good of the surviving community on earth. To them, it was perhaps of more immediate interest that the status of their deceased kinsfolk and neighbours should be recorded.

4.4 Problems and potential for future work

Any research inevitably provokes more questions than it provides answers, and this project has been no exception. Some of these questions may be clarified by further work, beyond the scope of the current research. However, it may be useful to provide some guidelines as to where the main difficulties are seen to lie, and how the present writer envisages future work might proceed.

The research has established that there are real correlations between the form and decoration of Anglo-Saxon cremation vessels, and the social identity of the occupant(s). It has been argued that these represent a symbolic function of pottery style. Two kinds of difficulty are outstanding. Firstly, few of the correlations identified are clear-cut. Some links are ambiguous; others are apparently contradictory. Secondly, having identified and described correlations, it could still be argued that we have not explained them. We cannot say, for example, <u>why</u> females tend to be buried in pots decorated with standing arches.

The first problem is really one of quality of the data. We have outlined (section 1.5) several reasons which may explain why correlations are not 100%. Most of these factors are inevitable, and stem from having to rely upon material from old excavations which has not been recorded to today's standards. Other factors are also out of the control of the researcher, but could be resolved, such as the inconsistent categorisation of human skeletal remains. Some factors, however, may be a result of the coding system adopted at the start of the research.

Once finalised, any classification scheme will tend to constrain the questions that might be asked. In an effort to be as objective as possible and to get away from the descriptive terms of Myres, the form and decoration of the pottery was described in a rigorous, but somewhat "clinical" fashion. Decoration, in particular, was categorised according to the presence or absence of a limited number of motifs. The fact that some significant correlations were identified with pottery attributes suggests that the classification was not completely wrong. Form and decoration were being described in a manner approximating to that in which the Anglo-Saxons also conceived them. It is unlikely, however, that the scheme adopted completely matched the Anglo-Saxon conception. With the benefit of hindsight, a more appropriate classification might have paid more attention to how different motifs may be combined, and less to individual items. It is frequently the combination of motifs that produces the overall visual effect, rather than whether a pot has lines sloping downwards to the left or right. PCA was used to try to identify groups of commonly co-occurring decorative attributes, but did not produce sensible results. This was probably because the PCA was combining so many attributes, at such a low level, that groups which seemed intuitively obvious to the experienced eye did not emerge above the background noise. The current work attempted to be rigorously analytical; a future researcher might be recommended to proceed more intuitively, at least in the definition of styles of Anglo-Saxon pottery.

The second problem is more difficult to resolve. Symbolic interpretations are frequently criticised for describing rather than explaining. Symbolism is notoriously difficult to comprehend. Even to anthropologists, studying living peoples, there frequently appears to be no logical or rational explanation why one symbol is chosen in preference to another. When asked, informants will simply reply that that is the way it is done. In the work of Levi-Strauss no logic is looked for; symbols do not have to be particularly appropriate to what they symbolise; they are purely tools for thinking about and describing the real world. I have already noted (Chapter One) that according to Saussure symbols may be purely arbitrary and there need be no necessary relationship between the sign and the thing signified. If this is so then the important thing is to identify the pattern, for the choice of symbol may be beyond explanation. Hodder has suggested that:

> To note a pattern is simultaneously to give it meaning, as one describes dimensions of variance as being related to dress, colour, sex and so on (1986, 138).

By describing the associations between aspects of funerary design and Anglo-Saxon social identity we are, therefore, simultaneously explaining that design:

> The symbolic meaning given to an object is simply a description of aspects of its control and use (Hodder 1986, 143).

Some designs, such as the wyrm, do suggest that the symbols may be partly representational, but in the absence of contemporary literature on Anglo-Saxon iconography any interpretation must be purely speculative. In other cases, the choice of one geometric pattern in preference to another, may just be a "tool for thinking" and it would be futile to try to pursue the reasoning further. Certainly, the situation could perhaps be clarified if the first problem were resolved, and the nature of the links was defined more clearly. We need to establish, for instance, if the link between standing arches and females is with all classes of female, or just with females who also have another role in society, perhaps indicated by a particular grave-good. To do this would require more work, with more cremations.

If extra material were to become available, further work should be conducted to establish if the correlations identified here hold good for other samples. In particular, it would be useful to analyse complete cemetery assemblages, where the archaeologist may be confident that all of the burials have been recovered, in order to avoid any suspicion of unrepresentative samples. Furthermore, such analyses should be conducted for cemeteries where the skeletal material has been fully worked, in order to try to pin down the nature of some of groups loosely described here as "social identity". Accessory vessels should also be examined, to determine if the symbolic role of pottery extends to the inhumation rite. A study should also be made of the extensive continental material, to trace the development of the variability, and to check if cremation vessels also had a symbolic role on the continental mainland, or whether this was something that developed under the stressful conditions of the migration. Finally, it should be a high priority to look at the problem spatially, within a single site. Intra-site variability may hold the key to looking at stylistic variability chronologically. If the development of a cemetery can be studied from archaeological rather than typological grounds through the use of horizontal stratigraphy, then we shall be able to provide independent dating for the cremations. Only then can we begin to determine if we should add a chronological dimension to the levels of variability described above.

Finally, verification of our understanding of Anglo-Saxon symbolism should be sought in other classes of data. The aim of this research has been to read Anglo-Saxon cremation urns as if they were a language from which information about the structuring of Anglo-Saxon society can be extracted. The message has become faint through time; whole sentences may have been lost; and the translation may have been a poor one. Nevertheless, if the theory is correct then the message will have been transformed and repeated many times, and should underlie other aspects of material culture, art and literature. It should be possible to read these as well, in order to refine and eventually to complete the translation.

BIBLIOGRAPHY

Adalbjarnarson,B. 1941. Heimskringla. Islenzk fornit, vols 26-28, Reykjavik.

Adams,M.J. 1973. "Structural aspects of a village art", American Anthropologist, 75(1), 265-79.

Alcock,L. 1981. "Quantity or quality: the Anglian graves of Bernicia", in Evison,V.I. (ed.), 1981, 168-83.

Alekshin,V.A. 1983. "Burial customs as an archaeological source", Current Anthropology, 24, 137-50.

Arnold,C.J. 1980. "Wealth and social structure: a matter of life and death", in Rahtz,P., Dickinson,T. and Watts,L. (eds.), 1980, 81-142.

- 1981. "Early Anglo-Saxon pottery: production and distribution", in Howard,H. and Morris,E.L. (eds.), 1981, 243-55.

- 1982. "Stress as a stimulus for socio-economic change: Anglo-Saxon England in the seventh century", in Renfrew,A.C. and Shennan,S. (eds.), 1982, 124-31.

- 1983. "The Sancton Baston Potter", Scottish Archaeological Review, 2(1), 17-30.

Arnold,D.E. 1983. "Design structure and community organisation in Quinua, Peru", in Washburn,D.K. (ed.), 1983, 56-73.

Arthur,B.V. and Jope,E.M. 1961-3. "Early Anglo-Saxon pottery kilns at Purwell Farm, Cassington, Oxon.", Medieval Archaeology, 6-7, 1-14.

Avent,R. 1975. Anglo-Saxon disc and composite brooches. British Archaeological Reports British Series 11, Oxford.

Barley,N. 1974. Anthropological aspects of Anglo-Saxon symbolism. Unpublished DPhil thesis. University of Oxford.

- 1981. "The Dowayo dance of death", in Humphreys,S.C. and King,H. (eds.), 1981, 149-59.

- 1983. Symbolic structures: An exploration of the culture of the Dowayos. Cambridge University Press, Cambridge.

Barrett,J.C. 1981. "Aspects of the Iron Age in Atlantic Scotland. A case study in the problems of archaeological interpretation", Proceedings of the Society of Antiquaries of Scotland, 111, 205-19.

Bartel,B. 1982. "A historical review of ethnological and archaeological analyses of mortuary practice", Journal of Anthropological Archaeology, 1, 32-58.

Bastian,A.   1860.   Der mensch in der geschichte.   Otto Wigand, Leipzig.

Battaglia,D.   1983.   "Projecting personhood in Melanesia: the dialectics of artefact symbolism on Sabarl Island", Man, 18, 289-304

Bendann,E. 1930. Death customs: an analytical study of burial rites. Kegan Paul, Trench, Trubner and Co, London.

Binford,L.R.   1962.   "Archaeology as anthropology", American Antiquity, 28, 217-25.

- 1965.   "Archaeological systematics and the study of culture process", American Antiquity, 31, 203-10.

- 1971.   "Mortuary practices: their study and potential",   in Brown,J.A. (ed.), 1971, 6-29.

- 1972. An archaeological perspective. Seminar Press, New York.

Birkhoff,G.D. 1933. Aesthetic measure. Cambridge.

Birmingham,J. 1975. "Traditional potters of the Kathmandu Valley: an ethno-archaeological study", Man, 10 (New Series), 370-86.

Bloch,M. 1971. Placing the dead. Seminar Press, London.

Boas,F. 1927. Primitive art. Capitol, New York.

Bourdieu,P. 1979. "Symbolic power", Critique of Anthropology, 13-4, 77-85.

Bradley,R. 1980.   "Anglo-Saxon cemeteries: some suggestions for future research", in Rahtz,P., Dickinson,T. and Watts,L. (eds.), 1980, 171-6.

Bradley,S.A.J. (ed.) 1982. Anglo-Saxon Poetry Everyman's Library. J.M.Dent and Sons Ltd, London.

Braithwaite,M. 1982. "Decoration as ritual symbol: a theoretical proposal and an ethnographic study in southern Sudan", in Hodder,I. (ed.), 1982b, 80-8.

Brisbane,M. 1980. "Anglo-Saxon burials: pottery, production and social status", in Rahtz,P., Dickinson,T. and Watts,L. (eds.), 1980, 209-16.

- 1981.   "Incipient markets for early Anglo-Saxon ceramics: variations in levels and modes of production", in Howard,H. and Morris,E.L. (eds.), 1981, 229-42.

Briscoe,T. 1981. "Anglo-Saxon pot stamps", in Brown,D., Campbell,J. and Hawkes,S.C. (eds.), 1981, 1-36.

- 1983. "A classification of Anglo-Saxon pot stamp motifs and proposed terminology", Studien zur Sachsenforschung, 4, 57-71.

Brown,D. 1977. "Firesteels and pursemounts again", Bonner JahrBücher, 177, 451-77.

- 1981. "Swastika patterns", in Evison,V.I. (ed.), 1981, 227-40.

Brown,D., Campbell,J. and Hawkes,S.C. (eds.) 1981. Anglo-Saxon Studies in Archaeology and History 2. British Archaeological Reports British Series 92, Oxford.

Brown,J.A. (ed.) 1971. Approaches to the social dimensions of mortuary practices. Memoirs of the Society for American Archaeology, No.25.

Bruce-Mitford,R. 1972. The Sutton Hoo ship-burial: a handbook. Second edition. British Museum, London.

- 1975. The Sutton Hoo ship-burial. Volume I. British Museum, London.

Bunzel,R.L. 1929. The Pueblo potter: a study of creative imagination in primitive art. Dover Publications Inc, New York.

Burnham,B.C. and Kingsbury,J. (eds.) 1979. Space, hierarchy and society: interdisciplinary studies in social area analysis. British Archaeological Reports International Series 59, Oxford.

Butler,L.A.S. 1964. "Minor Medieval monumental sculpture in the East Midlands", Archaeological Journal, 121, 111-53.

Carver,M.O.H. 1986. "Anglo-Saxon objectives at Sutton Hoo, 1985", Anglo-Saxon England 15, 139-52.

Chantrey,D.F., Wilcock,J.D. and Celoria,F.S.C. 1975. "The sorting of archaeological materials by computer and by man: an interdisciplinary study in pottery classification", Science and Archaeology, 14, 5-31.

Chapman,R.W. 1977. "Burial practices: an area of mutual interest", in Spriggs,M. (ed.), 1977, 19-33.

Chapman,R.W., Kinnes,I. and Randsborg,K. (eds.) 1981 The archaeology of death. Cambridge University Press, Cambridge.

Chapman,R.W. and Randsborg,K. 1981. "Approaches to the archaeology of death", in Chapman,R.W., Kinnes,I. and Randsborg,K. (eds.), 1981, 1-24.

Childe,V.G. 1929. The Danube in prehistory. Clarendon, Oxford.

- 1945. "Directional changes in funerary practices during 50,000 years", Man, 45, 13-9.

- 1956. Piecing together the past. Routledge and Kegan Paul, London.

- 1957. The dawn of European civilisation. Sixth edition. Routledge and Kegan Paul, London.

Chomsky,N. 1957. Syntactic structures. Mouton and Co, The Hague.

Clark,J.G.D. 1966. "The invasion hypothesis in British archaeology", Antiquity, 40, 172-89.

Clarke,D.L. 1962. "Matrix analysis and archaeology with particular reference to British Beaker pottery", Proceedings of the Prehistoric Society, 28, 371-82.

- 1968. Analytical Archaeology. Methuen and Co Ltd, London.

- 1970. Beaker Pottery of Great Britain and Ireland. Cambridge University Press, Cambridge.

- (ed.) 1972. Models in Archaeology. Methuen and Co Ltd, London.

- 1973. "Archaeology: the loss of innocence", Antiquity, 47, 6-18.

Clelland,C.E. (ed.) 1977. For the director: essays in honor of James B. Griffin. Museum of Anthropology, University of Michigan, Anthropological Papers 61.

Cogbill,S. 1982. "The Bronze Age exhumed", Scottish Archaeological Review, 1, 78-90.

Cohen,A. 1974. Two-dimensional man. Routledge and Kegan Paul Ltd, London.

Colgrave,B. and Mynors,R.A.B. (eds.) 1969. Bede's ecclesiastical history of the English people. Clarendon Press, Oxford.

De Coppett,D. 1981. "The life-giving death", in Humphreys,S.C. and King,H. yeds.), 1981, 175-204.

Cosack,E. 1982. Das sächische Gräberfeld bei Liebenau, Kr. Nienburg (Weser). Teil 1. Germanische Denkmäler der Völkerwanderungzeit, Serie A, Band XV, Berlin.

Cowgill,G.L. 1977. "The trouble with significance tests and what we can do about it", American Antiquity, 42, 350-68.

Deetz,J. 1967. Invitation to archaeology. The Natural History Press, New York.

- 1977. In small things forgotten: the archaeology of Early American life. Anchor Press/Doubleday, New York.

Dickinson,T. 1978. "British antiquity: Post-Roman and Pagan Anglo-Saxon", Archaeological Journal, 135, 332-44.

- 1980. "The present state of Anglo-Saxon cemetery studies", in Rahtz,P., Dickinson,T. and Watts,L. (eds.), 1980, 11-34.

Doran,J.E. and Hodson,F.R. 1975. Mathematics and computers in archaeology. Edinburgh University Press, Edinburgh.

Douglas,M. 1973. Natural symbols: explorations in cosmology. Penguin Books Ltd, Harmondsworth.

Durkheim,E. 1915. The elementary forms of the religious life. Allen and Unwin, London.

Eggert,M.K.H. 1977. "Prehistoric archaeology and the problem of ethno- cognition", Anthropos, 72, 242-55.

Elliott,R.W.V. 1959. Runes. Manchester University Press.

Elsdon,S.M. 1975. Stamped Iron Age pottery. British Archaeological Reports British Series 10, Oxford.

Ericson,J.E. and Stickel,E.G. 1973. "A proposed classification system for ceramics", World Archaeology, 4, 357-67.

Evison,V.I. 1963. "Sugar-loaf shield bosses", Antiquaries Journal, 43, 38-96.

- 1965. The fifth century invasions south of the Thames. The Athlone Press, University of London.

- 1979. A corpus of wheel-thrown pottery in Anglo-Saxon graves. Royal Archaeological Institute Monograph Series.

- (ed.) 1981. Angles, Saxons, and Jutes: essays presented to J.N.L.Myres. Clarendon Press, Oxford.

Faull,M. 1976. "The location and relationship of the Sancton Anglo-Saxon cemeteries", Antiquaries Journal, 56, 227-33.

- 1977. "British survival in Anglo-Saxon Northumbria", in Laing,L. (ed.), 1977, 1-55.

Fell,C. 1984. Women in Anglo-Saxon England. British Museum, London.

Fennell,K.R. 1964. The Anglo-Saxon cemetery at Loveden Hill, Lincs., and its significance in relation to the Dark Age settlement of the East Midlands. Unpublished doctoral thesis. University of Nottingham.

- 1974. "Pagan Saxon Lincolnshire", Archaeological Journal, 131, 283-93.

Ford,J.A. 1954. "On the concept of types", American Anthropologist, 56 ,42-54.

Friedman,J. and Rowlands,M.J. (eds.) 1977. The evolution of social systems. Duckworth, London.

Gaines,S.W. 1970. "Computer ceramics", Newsletter of Computer Archaeology, 5, 2-4.

Geertz,C. 1973. The interpretation of cultures. Basic Books, New York.

Giddens,A. 1979. Central problems in social theory: action, structure and contradiction in social analysis. Macmillan, London.

Goody,J. 1962. Death, property and the ancestors: a study of the mortuary customs of the LoDagaa of West Africa. Stanford University Press, Stanford.

Graham,I. and Webb,E. (eds.) 1982. Computer applications in Archaeology 1981. Institute of Archaeology, University of London.

Green,B., Milligan,W.F. and West,S.E. 1981. "The Illington/Lackford workshop", in Evison,V.I. (ed.), 1981, 187-226.

Harden,D.B. (ed.) 1956. Dark Age Britain. Methuen, London.

Hardin,M.A. 1979. "The cognitive basis of productivity in a decorative art style: implications of an ethnographic study for archaeologist's taxonomies", in Kramer,C. (ed.) 1979, 75-101.

- 1983. "The structure of Tarascan pottery painting", in Washburn,D.K. (ed.), 8-24.

Hardy-Smith,A. 1974. "Post-Medieval pot shapes: A quantitative analysis", Science and Archaeology, 11, 4-15.

Hässler,H.-J. 1983. "Das sächsische Gräberfeld bei Liebenau, Kr. Nienburg (Weser)". Teil 2, Studien zur Sachsenforschung, 5(1), Hildesheim.

Hawkes,C.F.C. 1954. "Archaeological theory and method: some suggestions from the Old World", American Anthropologist, 56, 155-68.

- 1956. "The Jutes of Kent", in Harden,D.B. (ed.), 1956, 91-111.

Hawkes,S.C. 1977. "Orientation at Finglesham: sunrise dating of death and burial in an Anglo-Saxon cemetery in East Kent", Archaeologia Cantiana, 92, 33-51.

Hawkes,S.C., Brown,D. and Campbell,J. (eds.) 1979. Anglo-Saxon Studies in Archaeology and History I. British Archaeological Reports British Series 72, Oxford.

Hawkes,S.C. and Wells,C. 1975. "Crime and punishment in an Anglo-Saxon cemetery?", Antiquity, 49, 118-22.

Hertz,R. 1907. "Contribution à une étude sur la représentation collective de la mort", Année sociologique, 10, 48-137.

Hill,J.H. and Evans,R.K. 1972. "A model for classification and typology", in Clarke,D.L. (ed.) 1972, 231-73.

Hills,C.M. 1974. "A runic pot from Spong Hill, North Elmham, Norfolk", Antiquaries Journal, 54, 87-91.

- 1976. The results of the excavations at the Anglo-Saxon Cremation cemetery at Spong Hill, Norfolk. Unpublished doctoral thesis. Birkbeck College, University of London.

- 1977a. "A chamber grave at Spong Hill", Medieval Archaeology, 21, 167-76.

- 1977b. The Anglo-Saxon cemetery at Spong Hill, North Elmham, Part I. East Anglian Archaeology Report No. 6.

- 1979a. "The archaeology of Anglo-Saxon England in the pagan period: a review", Anglo-Saxon England, 8, 297-329.

- 1979b. Review of Myres (1978), Antiquity, 53, 65-7.

- 1980. "Anglo-Saxon cremation cemeteries, with particular reference to Spong Hill, Norfolk", in Rahtz,P., Dickinson,T. and Watts,L. (eds.), 1980, 197-207.

- 1981. "Barred zoomorphic combs of the migration period", in Evison,V.I. (ed.), 1981, 96-125.

- 1983. "Animal stamps on Anglo-Saxon pottery in East Anglia", Studien zur Sachsenforschung, 4, 93-110.

Hills,C.M. and Penn,K. 1981. The Anglo-Saxon cemetery at Spong Hill, North Elmham, Part II. East Anglian Archaeology Report No. 11.

Hills,C.M., Penn,K. and Rickett,R. 1984. The Anglo-Saxon cemetery at Spong Hill, North Elmham, Part III. East Anglian Archaeology No. 21.

Hinton,D.A. (ed.) 1983. 25 years of Medieval Archaeology. Department of Prehistory and Archaeology, University of Sheffield.

Hirst,S.M. 1985. An Anglo-Saxon inhumation cemetery at Sewerby, East Yorkshire. York University Archaeological Publications 4.

Hodder,I. 1977. "The distribution of material culture items in the Baringo district, Western Kenya", Man, 12, 239-69.

- (ed.) 1978a. The spatial organisation of culture. Duckworth, London.

- 1978b. "Social organisation and human interaction: the development of some tentative hypotheses in terms of material culture", in Hodder,I. (ed.), 1978a, 199-269.

- 1980. "Social structure and cemeteries: a critical appraisal", in Rahtz,P., Dickinson,T. and Watts,L. (eds.), 1980, 161-70.

- 1982a. Symbols in action. Cambridge University Press, Cambridge.

- (ed.) 1982b. Symbolic and structural archaeology. Cambridge University Press, Cambridge.

- 1982c. "Theoretical archaeology: a reactionary view", in Hodder,I. (ed.), 1982b, 1-16.

- 1982d. "Sequences of structural change in the Dutch Neolithic", in Hodder,I. (ed.), 1982b, 162-77.

- 1982e. The present past. B.T.Batsford Ltd, London.

- 1986. Reading the past: current approaches to interpretation in archaeology. Cambridge University Press, Cambridge.

Hogarth,A.C. 1973. "Structural features in Anglo-Saxon graves", Archaeological Journal, 130, 104-19.

Hole,F. 1984. "Analysis of structure and design in prehistoric ceramics", World Archaeology, 15, 326-47.

Hope-Taylor,B. 1977. Yeavering: an Anglo-British centre in early Northumbria. DOE Archaeological Report No.7, HMSO, London.

Howard,H. and Morris,E.L. (eds.) 1981. Production and distribution: a ceramic viewpoint. British Archaeological Reports International Series 120, Oxford.

Humphreys,S.C. and King,H. (eds.) 1981. Mortality and immortality: the anthropology and archaeology of death. Academic Press, London.

Hurst,J.G. 1976. "The pottery", in Wilson,D.M. (ed.) 1976, 283-348.

- 1977. "Annotations on Anglo-Saxon pottery", Medieval Ceramics, 1, 15-8.

James,E.O. 1928. "Cremation and the preservation of the dead in North America", American Anthropologist, 30, 214-42.

Janssen,W. 1972. Issendorf, ein Urnenfriedhof der späten Kaiserzeit und der Völkerwanderungzeit. Vol 1 (Materialhefte zur Ur- und Frühgesch. Niedersachsens, 6), Hildesheim.

Jessup,R. 1975. Man of many talents: an informal biography of James Douglas, 1753-1819. London/Chichester.

Jones,M.U. 1969. "Saxon pottery from a hut at Mucking, Essex", Berichten van de Rijksdienst voor het Oudheidkundig Bodemonderzoek, 19, 145-56.

- 1979. "Saxon Mucking - a post-excavation note", in Hawkes,S.C., Brown,D. and Campbell,J. (eds.), 1979, 21-37.

Jones,R. 1980. "Computers and cemeteries: opportunities and limitations", in Rahtz,P., Dickinson,T. and Watts,L. (eds.), 1980, 179-95.

Jones,W.T. 1980. "Early Saxon cemeteries in Essex" in Buckley,D.G. (ed.), Archaeology in Essex to AD 1500, 87-95, CBA Research Report 34, Council for British Archaeology, London.

Kemble,J.M. 1855. "Burial and cremation", Archaeological Journal, 12, 309-37.

Kempton,W. 1981. The folk classification of ceramics: a study of cognitive prototypes. Academic Press, New York.

Kendall,G. 1982. "A study of grave orientation in several Roman and post-Roman cemeteries from southern Britain", Archaeological Journal, 139, 101-23.

Kennett,D.H. 1978. Anglo-Saxon pottery. Shire Publications Ltd, Aylesbury.

Kidd,D.S.W. 1976. Review of Myres and Southern (1973), Medieval Archaeology, 20, 202-4.

- 1977. "Some questions of method in the study of Migration Period Pottery", in Kossack,G. and Reichstein,J. (eds.) 1977, 93-102.

Kirk,J.R. 1956. "Anglo-Saxon cremation and inhumation in the Upper Thames Valley in pagan times", in Harden,D.B. (ed.), 1956, 123-31.

Kossack,G. and Reichstein,J. (eds.) 1977. Archäeologische Beitrage zur Chronologie der Völkerwanderungszeit Antiquitas, Reihe 3, Serie 4, Bd. 20, Bonn.

Kossinna,G. 1911. Die herkunft der Germanen. Kurt Kabitsch, Leipzig.

- 1926. Ursprung und verbreitung der germanen in vorund fruhgeschichtlicher zeit. Germanen-Verlag, Berlin.

Kramer,C. (ed.) 1979. Ethnoarchaeology. Columbia University Press, New York.

Krieger,A.D. 1944. "The typological concept", American Antiquity , 9, 271-88.

Kristiansen,K. and Poludan-Müller,C. (eds.) 1978. Studies in Scandinavian Prehistory and Early History Volume I. National Museum of Denmark.

Kroeber,A.L. 1927. "Disposal of the dead", American Anthropologist, 29, 308-15.

Kuhn,T.S. 1962. The structure of scientific revolutions. University of Chicago Press, Chicago.

Laing,L. (ed.) 1977. Studies in Celtic survival. British Archaeological Reports British Series 37, Oxford.

Laing,L. and J. 1979. Anglo-Saxon England. Routledge and Kegan Paul Ltd, London.

Lathrap,D.W. 1983. "Recent Shipibo-Conibo ceramics and their implications for archaeological interpretation", in Washburn,D.K. (ed.), 1983, 25-39.

Leach,E. 1958. "Magical hair", Journal of the Royal Anthropological Institute, 88 ,147-64.

- 1973. "Concluding address", in Renfrew,A.C. (ed.), 1973, 761-71.

- 1976. Culture and communication: the logic by which symbols are connected. Cambridge University Press, Cambridge.

- 1977. "A view from the bridge", in Spriggs,M. (ed.), 1977, 161-76.

- 1979. Discussion in Burnham,B.C. and Kingsbury,J. (eds.), 1979, 119-24.

Leeds,E.T. 1912. "The distribution of the Anglo-Saxon saucer brooch in relation to the Battle of Bedford AD 571", Archaeologia, 43, 159-202.

- 1913. The Archaeology of the Anglo-Saxon Settlements. Clarendon Press, Oxford.

- 1933. "The early Saxon penetration of the Upper Thames area", Antiquaries Journal, 13, 229-51.

- 1945. "The distribution of the Angles and Saxons archaeologically considered", Archaeologia, 91, 1-106.

- 1947. "A Saxon village at Sutton Courtenay, Berkshire, Third Report", Archaeologia, 92, 79-93.

- 1949. A corpus of early Anglo-Saxon great square-headed brooches.

Leeds,E.T. and Harden,D.B. 1936. The Anglo-Saxon Cemetery at Abingdon, Berkshire. Ashmolean Museum, University of Oxford.

Leeds,E.T. and Pocock,M. 1971. "A survey of the Anglo-Saxon cruciform brooches of florid type", Medieval Archaeology, 15, 13-30.

Leone,M.P. 1982. "Some opinions about recovering mind", American Antiquity, 47, 742-60.

Lethbridge,T.C. 1951. A cemetery at Lackford, Suffolk: report of the excavation of a cemetery of the Pagan Anglo-Saxon period in 1947. Cambridge Antiquarian Society. Quarto Publications. New Series, No. VI.

Levi-Strauss,C. 1958. Anthropologie structurale. Paris.

- 1962. La pensée sauvage. Paris.

Llanos,A. and Vegas,J.I. 1974. "Ensayo de un metodo para el estudio y clasificacion tipologica de la ceramica", Diputación Foral de Alawa, Consejo de Cultura, Vitoria.

Longacre,W. 1964. "Sociological implications of the ceramic analysis", in Martin,P.S. and others, Chapters in the prehistory of eastern Arizona II, 155-67, Fieldiana: Anthropology 55.

Lubbock,J. 1865. Prehistoric times as illustrated by ancient remains and the manners and customs of modern savages. Williams and Norgate, London.

McGhee,R. 1977. "Ivory for the sea woman: the symbolic attributes of a prehistoric typology", Canadian Journal of Archaeology, 1, 141-9.

Main,P.L. 1981. A method for the computer storage and comparison of the outline shapes of archaeological artefacts. Unpublished doctoral thesis. North Staffordshire Polytechnic.

- 1982. "SHU - an interactive graphics program for the storage, retrieval and analysis of artefact shapes", in Graham,I. and Webb,E. (eds.), 1982, 75-82.

Mather,P.M. 1976. Computational methods of multivariate analysis in physical geography. John Wiley and Sons, London.

Mayes,P. and Dean,M.J. 1976. An Anglo-Saxon cemetery at Baston, Lincolnshire. With a report on the pottery by J.N.L.Myres. Occasional Papers in Lincolnshire History and Archaeology No. 3.

Meaney,A.L. 1964. A gazetteer of Early Anglo-Saxon burial sites. London.

- 1981. Anglo-Saxon amulets and curing stones. British Archaeological Reports British Series 96, Oxford.

Miller,D. 1982. "Artefacts as products of human categorisation processes", in Hodder,I. (ed.), 1982b, 17-25.

Miller,D. and Tilley,C. (eds.), 1984. Ideology, power and prehistory. Cambridge University Press, Cambridge.

Molleson,T. 1981. "The archaeology and anthropology of death: what the bones tell us", in Humphreys,S.C. and King,H. (eds.), 1981, 15-32.

Morris,G. and Scarre,C.R. 1982. "Computerised analysis of the shapes of a class of prehistoric stone tools from west central France", in Graham,I. and Webb,E. (eds.), 1982, 83-94.

Morris,J. 1973. The age of Arthur: A history of the British Isles from 350 to 650. Weidenfeld and Nicolson, London.

- 1974. Review of Myres and Green (1973), Medieval Archaeology, 18, 225-32.

Myres,J.L. (ed.) 1906. The evolution of culture and other essays by the late Lt.Gen. A.Lane-Fox Pitt-Rivers. Clarendon Press, Oxford.

Myres,J.N.L. 1937a. "Three styles of decoration on Anglo-Saxon pottery", Antiquaries Journal, 17, 424-37.

- 1937b. "Some Anglo-Saxon potters", Antiquity, 11, 389-99.

- 1941. "The Anglo-Saxon pottery of Norfolk", Norfolk Archaeology, 27, 185-214.

- 1947. "Anglo-Saxon urns from North Elmham, Norfolk", Antiquaries Journal, 27, 47-50.

- 1948. "Some English parallels to the Anglo-Saxon pottery of Holland and Belgium in the migration period", L'Antiquité Classique, 17, 453-72.

- 1951. "The Anglo-Saxon pottery of Lincolnshire", The Archaeological Journal, 108, 65-99.

- 1954. "Two Saxon urns from Ickwell Bury, Beds.", Antiquaries Journal, 34, 201-8.

- 1968. "The Anglo-Saxon pottery from Mucking", Antiquaries Journal, 48, 222-8.

- 1969 Anglo-Saxon Pottery and the Settlement of England. Clarendon Press, Oxford.

- 1970. "The Angles, the Saxons, and the Jutes", Proceedings of the British Academy, 56, 1-32.

- 1973a. "An Anglo-Saxon Buckelurne from Mucking, Essex, cemetery", Antiquaries Journal, 53, 271.

- 1973b. "A fifth century Anglo-Saxon pot from Canterbury", Antiquaries Journal, 53, 77-8.

- 1974. "The Anglo-Saxon Pottery", in "The Roman fortress at Longthorpe" , Frere,S.S. and St.Joseph,J.K. (eds.), Britannia, 5, 112-21.

- 1977a. A corpus of Anglo-Saxon pottery of the Pagan period. Cambridge University Press, Cambridge.

- 1977b. "Zoomorphic bosses on Anglo-Saxon pottery", Studien zur Sachsenforschung, 281-93.

Myres,J.N.L. and Green,B. 1973. The Anglo-Saxon Cemeteries of Caistor-by-Norwich and Markshall, Norfolk. Report of the Research Committee of the Society of Antiquaries of London Number 30.

Myres,J.N.L. and Southern,W.H. 1973. The Anglo-Saxon cremation cemetery at Sancton, East Yorkshire. Hull Museums Publication No. 218.

Nie,N.H., Hadlai Hull,C., Jenkins,J.G., Steinbrenner,K. and Bent,D.H. 1975. Statistical package for the social sciences. McGraw-Hill Book Company, New York.

Nie,N.H. and Hadlai Hull,C. 1981. SPSS update 7-9: new procedures and facilities for releases 7-9. McGraw-Hill Book Company, New York.

Nordbladh,J. 1978. "Images as messages in society. Prolegomena to the study of Scandinavian petroglyphs and semiotics", in Kristiansen,K. and Poludan-Müller,C. (eds.), 1978, 63-78.

Orton,C.R. and Hodson,F.R. 1981. "Rank and class: interpreting the evidence from prehistoric cemeteries", in Humphreys,S.C. and King,H. (eds.), 1981, 103-15.

Owen,G.R. 1981. Rites and religions of the Anglo-Saxons. David and Charles, Newton Abbot.

Ozanne,A. 1962-3. "The Peak dwellers", Medieval Archaeology, 6-7, 15-52.

Pader,E.-J. 1980. "Material symbolism and social relations in mortuary Studies", in Rahtz,P., Dickinson,T. and Watts,L. (eds.), 1980, 143-59.

- 1982. Symbolism, social relations and the interpretation of mortuary remains. British Archaeological Reports International Series 130, Oxford.

Page,R.I. 1973. An introduction to English runes. Methuen and Co Ltd, London.

Palmgren,N. 1934. <u>Kansu mortuary urns of the Pan Shan and Ma Chang groups.</u> Palaeontologia Sinica Series D, III(1), Geological Survey of China, Peking.

Parker-Pearson,M. 1982. "Mortuary practices, society and ideology: an ethno-archaeological study", in Hodder,I. (ed.), 1982b, 99-113.

Petersen,J. 1919. <u>De norske vikingesverd.</u> Vid. selsk. Skrifter. II. Hist.-filos. Klasse, Kristiania.

Plettke,A. 1921. <u>Ursprung und Ausbreitung der Angeln und Sachsen.</u> Urnenfriedhöfe in Niedersachsen, Bd.3, Hildesheim.

Plog,S. 1980. <u>Stylistic variation in prehistoric ceramics.</u> Cambridge University Press, Cambridge.

Pollock,S. 1983. "Style and information: an analysis of Susiana ceramics", <u>Journal of Anthropological Archaeology,</u> 2, 354-90.

Putnam,G. 1980. "Spong Hill cremations", in Rahtz,P., Dickinson,T. and Watts,L. (eds.), 1980, 217-9.

- 1981a. "Analysis of cremated bones", appendix to Hills (1981).

- 1981b. "Demography of early Anglo-Saxon East Anglia". Paper delivered to Sachsensymposium, Cambridge, 8/9/1981.

Radcliffe-Brown,A.R. 1922. <u>The Andaman islanders: a study in social anthropology.</u> Cambridge University Press, Cambridge.

Rahtz,P.A. 1976. "Gazetteer of Anglo-Saxon domestic settlement sites", in Wilson, D.M. (ed.), 1976, 405-52.

- 1978. "Grave orientation", <u>Archaeological Journal,</u> 135, 1-14.

- 1983. "New approaches to Medieval Archaeology, Part 1", in Hinton,D.A. (ed.), 1983, 12-23.

Rahtz,P., Dickinson,T. and Watts,L. (eds.) 1980. <u>Anglo-Saxon cemeteries 1979.</u> British Archaeological Reports British Series 82, Oxford.

Randsborg,K. 1974. "Social stratification in Early Bronze Age Denmark", <u>Prähistorische Zeitschrift,</u> 49, 38-61.

Renfrew,A.C. (ed.) 1973. <u>The explanation of culture change: models in prehistory.</u> Duckworth, London.

- 1977. "Space, time and polity", in Friedman,J. and Rowlands,M.J. (eds.), 1977, 89-112.

Renfrew,A.C. and Shennan,S. (eds.) 1982. <u>Ranking, resource and exchange.</u> Cambridge University Press, Cambridge.

Reynolds,N. 1976. "The structure of Anglo-Saxon graves", Antiquity,
50, 140-3.

- 1980. "The King's whetstone: a footnote", Antiquity , 54, 232-7.

Richards,J.D.   1982.   "Anglo-Saxon   pot   shapes: cognitive
investigations", Science and Archaeology, 24, 33-46.

- 1984. "Funerary symbolism in Anglo-Saxon England: further social
dimensions of mortuary practices", Scottish Archaeological Review, 3,
42-55.

Richards,J.D. and Ryan,N.S. 1985. Data processing in Archaeology.
Cambridge University Press, Cambridge.

Rosch,E.   1973.   "Natural categories", Cognitive Psychology,   4,
328-50.

- 1975.   "Cognitive reference points", Cognitive Psychology, 7,
532-47.

Russel,A.D. 1984. Anglo-Saxon ceramics in East Anglia: a
microprovenance viewpoint. Unpublished doctoral thesis. University
of Southampton.

Rydh,H. 1929. "On symbolism in mortuary ceramics", Bulletin of the
Museum of Far Eastern Antiquities, 1.

Saussure,F. de 1959. A course in general linguistics. Philosophical
Society, New York.

Saxe,A.A.   1970.   Social   dimensions   of   mortuary   practices.
Unpublished doctoral thesis. University of Michigan.

Schiffer,M.B. (ed.) 1978. Advances in archaeological method and
theory. Volume I. Academic Press, New York.

Shanks,M. and Tilley,C. 1982. "Ideology, symbolic power and ritual
communication: a reinterpretation of Neolithic mortuary practices",
in Hodder,I. (ed.), 1982b, 129-54.

Shennan,S. 1975. "The social organisation at Branc", Antiquity, 49,
279-88.

Shennan,S.J. and Wilcock,J.D. 1975. "Shape and style variation in
Central German Bell Beakers: a computer assisted study", Science and
Archaeology, 15, 17-31.

Shepard,A.O. 1957. Ceramics for the archaeologist.   Carnegie
Institution of Washington Publication 609, Washington, D.C.

Shephard,J.F. 1979. "The social identity of the individual in
isolated barrows and barrow cemeteries in Anglo-Saxon England", in
Burnham,B.C. and Kingsbury,J. (eds.), 1979, 47-79.

Shorter,E. 1971. The historian and the computer: a practical guide. Prentice Hall Inc, New Jersey.

Siegel,S. 1956. Nonparametric statistics for the behavioral sciences. McGraw-Hill Book Company, New York.

Simpson,J. 1979. "The King's whetstone", Antiquity, 53, 96-101.

Sjövold,T. 1974. Iron Age settlement of Arctic Norway: a study in the expansion of European Iron Age culture within the Arctic circle. Tromsö Museums Skrifter Vol X,(2), Norwegian Universities Press, Tromsö.

Spaulding,A.C. 1953. "Statistical techniques for the discovery of artifact types", American Antiquity, 18, 305-13.

Spriggs,M. (ed.) 1977. Archaeology and Anthropology: areas of mutual interest. British Archaeological Reports International Series 19, Oxford.

Stead,I.M. 1958. "An Anglian cemetery on the Mount, York", Yorkshire Archaeological Journal, 39, 427-35.

Storms,G. 1978. "The Sutton Hoo ship burial: an interpretation", Berichten van de Rijksdienst voor het Oudheidkundig Bodemonderzoek, 28, 309-44.

Swanton,M.J. 1973. The spearheads of the Anglo-Saxon settlements.

- 1974. A corpus of Pagan Anglo-Saxon spear-types. British Archaeological Reports British Series 7, Oxford.

Tainter,J.A. 1975. "Social inference and mortuary practices: an experiment in numerical classification", World Archaeology, 7, 1-15.

- 1978. "Mortuary practices and the study of prehistoric social systems", in Schiffer,M.B. (ed.) 1978, 105-41.

Tilley,C. 1982. Review of Chapman, Kinnes and Randsborg (1981), Scottish Archaeological Review, 1, 133-9.

- 1984. "Ideology and the legitimation of power in the middle neolithic of southern Sweden", in Miller,D. and Tilley,C. (eds.), 1984, 111-46.

Tylor,E.B. 1865. Researches into the early history of mankind and the development of civilisation. John Murray, London.

- 1871. Primitive culture. John Murray, London.

Ucko,P.J. 1969. "Ethnography and the archaeological interpretation of funerary remains", World Archaeology, 1, 262-77.

van Gennep,A. 1909. Les rites de passage. Emile Nourry, Paris.

van de Velde,P. 1979a. On Bandkeramik social structure: an analysis of pot decoration and hut distributions from the Central European Neolithic communities of Elsloo and Hienheim. Analecta Praehistorica Leidensia XII, Leiden University Press, The Hague.

- 1979b. "The social anthropology of a Neolithic cemetery in the Netherlands", Current Anthropology, 20, 37-58.

Walker,J. 1978. "Anglo-Saxon traded pottery", in Todd,M. (ed.), Studies in the Romano-British villa, 224-8, Leicester.

Washburn,D.K. (ed.) 1983a. Structure and cognition in art. Cambridge University Press, Cambridge.

- 1983b. "Toward a theory of structural style in art", in Washburn,D.K. (ed.), 1983a, 1-7.

- 1983c. "Symmetry analysis of ceramic design: two tests of the method on Neolithic material from Greece and the Aegean", in Washburn,D.K. (ed.), 1983a, 138-64.

Watson,J.L. (ed.) 1977. Between two cultures. Basil Blackwell, Oxford.

Webster,G. 1951. "An Anglo-Saxon urnfield at South Elkington, Louth, Lincolnshire", Archaeological Journal, 108, 25-59.

Welbourn,A. 1984. "Endo ceramics and power strategies", in Miller,D. and Tilley,C. (eds.), 1984, 17-24.

Welch,M. 1980. "The Saxon cemeteries of Sussex", in Rahtz,P., Dickinson,T. and Watts,L. (eds.), 1980, 255-83.

Wells,C. 1960. "A study of cremation", Antiquity, 34, 29-37.

Wells,C. and Green,C. 1970. "Sunrise dating of death and burial", Norfolk Archaeology, 35, 435-42.

West,S.E. 1969a. "The Anglo-Saxon village of West Stow", Medieval Archaeology, 13, 1-20.

- 1969b. "Pagan Saxon pottery from West Stow, Suffolk", Berichten van de Rijksdienst voor het Oudheidkundig Bodemonderzoek, 19, 175-81.

West,S.E. and Owles,E. 1973. "Anglo-Saxon cremation burials from Snape", Proceedings of the Suffolk Institute of Archaeology, 33, 47-57.

Whallon,R. 1968. "Investigations of late prehistoric social organization in New York State", in Binford,S.R. and Binford,L.R. (eds.), 1968, 223-44.

- 1972. "A new approach to pottery typology", <u>American Antiquity</u>, 37, 13-33.

Wheeler,R.E.M. 1954. <u>Archaeology from the earth.</u> Clarendon Press, Oxford.

Wiessner,P. 1984. "Reconsidering the behavioral basis for style: a case study among the Kalahari San", <u>Journal of Anthropological Archaeology</u>, 3, 190-234.

Wilkinson,L. 1980. "Problems of analysis and interpretation of skeletal remains", in Rahtz,P., Dickinson,T. and Watts,L. (eds.), 1980, 221-31.

Williams,P.W. 1983. <u>An Anglo-Saxon cemetery at Thurmaston, Leicestershire.</u> Leicestershire Museums Archaeological Reports Series No.8.

Wilson,D.M. 1959. "Almgren and chronology, a summary and some comments", <u>Medieval Archaeology</u>, 3, 112-9.

- (ed.) 1976. <u>The archaeology of Anglo-Saxon England.</u> Cambridge University Press, Cambridge.

Wilson,G. 1939. "Nyakyusa conventions of burial", <u>Bantu Studies</u>, 13, 1-31.

Wilson,M. 1957. <u>Rituals of kinship among the Nyakyusa.</u> Oxford Univerity Press.

Wilson,M.E. 1972. <u>The archaeological evidence of the Hwiccian area.</u> Unpublished doctoral thesis. Durham University.

Wobst,H.M. 1977. "Stylistic behavior and information exchange", in Clelland,C. (ed.), 1977, 317-42.

Wylie,M.A. 1982. "Epistemological issues in structuralist archaeology", in Hodder,I. (ed.), 1982b, 39-46.

Zimmer-Linnfeld,K., Gummel,H. and Waller,K. 1960. <u>Westerwanna I.</u> 9. Beiheft zum Atlas der Urgeschichte.

APPENDIX A

CHI SQUARE CROSS-TABULATION SPECIMEN

(As produced by SPSS Release 8)

MINIATURE IRON TWEEZERS BY STANDING ARCH

	STANDING ARCH		
COUNT ROW % COL % TOT %	ABSENCE 0	PRESENCE 1	ROW TOTAL
TWEEZERS			
ABSENCE 0	2172 93.7 95.4 89.0	147 6.3 89.6 6.0	2319 95.0
PRESENCE 1	104 86.0 4.6 4.3	17 14.0 10.4 0.7	121 5.0
COLUMN TOTAL	2276 93.3	164 6.7	2440 100.0

CHI SQUARE = 9.71021 WITH 1 DEGREE OF FREEDOM.
SIGNIFICANCE = 0.0018

APPENDIX B

KOLMOGOROV-SMIRNOV TEST SPECIMEN

(As produced by SPSS Release 8 FREQUENCIES procedure)

URN HEIGHT (cm)	TOTAL SAMPLE absolute freq	TOTAL SAMPLE cum freq % (A)	URNS WITH MIN FE TWEEZERS absolute freq	URNS WITH MIN FE TWEEZERS cum freq % (B)	$\frac{(A-B)}{100}$
8.5	5	0.2	–		.002
9.5	9	0.6	–		.006
10.5	19	1.4	1	0.8	.006
11.5	22	2.3	1	1.7	.006
12.5	47	4.2	2	3.3	.009
13.5	81	7.5	2	5.0	.025
14.5	105	11.8	4	8.3	.035
15.5	105	16.1	1	9.1	.07
16.5	145	22.0	6	14.0	.08
17.5	164	28.8	5	18.2	.106
18.5	188	36.5	5	22.3	.142
19.5	198	44.6	7	28.1	.165
20.5	224	53.8	11	37.2	<u>.166</u>
21.5	226	63.0	14	48.8	.142
22.5	250	73.3	15	61.2	.121
23.5	199	81.4	12	71.1	.103
24.5	166	88.2	16	84.3	.039
25.5	119	93.1	7	90.1	.03
26.5	69	95.9	4	93.4	.025
27.5	41	97.6	3	95.9	.017
28.5	33	99.0	3	98.3	.007
29.5	5	99.2	–	98.3	.009
30.5	12	99.7	1	99.2	.005
31.5	–	99.7	–	99.2	.005
32.5	5	99.9	1	100.0	.001
33.5	3	100.0	–		
TOTAL	2440		121		

D = 0.166

Critical value at 0.01 significance level for 120 degrees of freedom = 0.149

Therefore, reject null hypothesis.

Frequency distribution of urn heights for urns containing miniature iron tweezers is different to that for the total population, significant at 0.01 level.

APPENDIX C

PHASE ONE CODING SYSTEM

Grid co-ordinates:
  Easting
  Northing

Reconstruction of urn profile

Urn dimensions:
  Height
  Maximum diameter
  Height of maximum diameter
  Base diameter
  Rim diameter

P/A of pedestal base or footring
  Pedestal diameter

P/A of lid
  Lid height
  Lid diameter

P/A of deliberate hole

P/A of decoration

  Incised decoration
    Horizontal continuous linear grooves
      Number of fields
        Number of lines in each field
    Horizontal discontinuous linear grooves
      Number of fields
        Number of sections in each field
          Number of lines in each section
    Vertical linear grooves
      Number of fields
        Number of lines in each field
        Field imposed on plastic decoration
    Diagonal linear grooves
      Continuous chevron pattern

Number of rows
  Number of left arms in each row
    Number of lines in each left arm
  Number of right arms in each row
    Number of lines in each right arm
Broken chevron pattern
  Number of rows
    Number of fields in each row
      Number of left arms in each field
        Number of lines in each left arm
      Number of right arms in each field
        Number of lines in each right arm
Single upright chevron
  Number of rows
    Number of chevrons in each row
      Number of lines in each left arm
      Number of lines in each right arm
Single inverted chevron
  Number of rows
    Number of chevrons in each row
      Number of lines in each left arm
      Number of lines in each right arm
Single groups of diagonal lines sloping down to left
  Number of rows
    Number of groups in each row
      Number of lines in each group
Single groups of diagonal lines sloping down to right
  Number of rows
    Number of groups in each row
      Number of lines in each group
Curvilinear grooves
  Continuous waves
    Number of fields
      Number of lines in each field
  Discontinuous waves
    Number of fields
      Number of sections in each field
      Number of lines in each field
  Single upright arch
    Number of arches
      Number of lines in each arch
      Imposed on plastic decoration
  Single inverted arch
    Number of arches
      Number of lines in each arch
      Imposed on plastic decoration
  Complex pattern of interlocking arches and waves
  Circular/ sub-rectangular grooves
    Number of fields
      Number of lines in each field
      Imposed on plastic decoration
Slashes
  Enclosed by linear grooves
  In open format
    In horizontal continuous linear band

   In horizontal broken linear band
   In horizontal band with another motif
   In vertical linear band
   In diagonal linear band
   In chevron
   In triangle
   In circle
   In rosette
   In arch
   In triangular field
   In arched field
   In rectangular field
   At random
  Dots
   Enclosed by linear grooves
   In open format
    In horizontal continuous linear band
    In horizontal broken linear band
    In horizontal band with another motif
    In vertical linear band
    In diagonal linear band
    In chevron
    In triangle
    In circle
    In rosette
    In arch
    In triangular field
    In arched field
    In rectangular field
    At random
  Swastikas
   Number of swastikas
    Number of lines in each swastika
  Crosses
   Number of single crosses
    Number of lines in each cross
   Number of crosses in continuous criss-cross
    Number of lines in each cross
  Stars
   Number of stars
  Runes
   Number of runes
  Animals
   Number of animals

 Incised decoration on the base
  Crosses
  Swastikas
  Stars
  Dots
  Continuous lines forming concentric circles
  Diagonal chevrons etc
  Radiating lines

 Incised decoration on the lid

        Crosses
        Swastikas
        Stars
        Dots
        Continuous lines forming concentric circles
        Diagional chevrons etc
        Radiating lines

    Stamped decoration
      Number of different stamp motifs
        Urns with same die employed
        Shape type of each motif
          Circular
          Multiple overlapping circles
          Oval
          Crescent, or "horseshoe" shape
          Rectangular
          Incurving rectangle
          Diamond
          Triangular
          Chevron
          Cruciform
          "S" shape
          "T" shape
          Swastika
          Runic shape
          Animal
          Human
          Miscellaneous
        Design type of each motif
          Solid figure
          Outline figure
          Outline figure with dotted centre
          Repeated figure
          Multiple figure
          Barred figure
          Gridded / Lattice figure
          Outlined gridded figure
          Segmented outline
          Complex segmented figure
          Simple cross
          Complex cross
          Outlined cross
          Pelleted cross
          Pelleted cross in outline
          Radiate figure
          Radiate figure in outline
          Complex radiate figure
          Textile impression
          Swastika
          Rune
          Animal
          Human
          Miscellaneous
        Number of fields each motif is in

        Enclosed by linear grooves
        In open format
          In horizontal continuous linear band
          In horizontal broken linear band
          In horizontal band with another motif
          In vertical linear band
          In diagonal linear band
          In chevron
          In triangle
          In circle
          In rosette
          In arch
          In triangular field
          In arched field
          In rectangular field
          At random
          On lid
            Number of impressions in each field

Plastic decoration
  Bosses
    Vertical
      Number of vertical bosses
    Diagonal
      Number of diagonal bosses
    Horizontal
      Number of horizontal bosses
    Rounded
      Number of rounded bosses
    Horned
      Number of horned bosses
  Lugs
    Number of lugs
  Handles
    Number of handles
  Cordons
    Linear - horizontal
      Number of linear - horizontal cordons
    Linear - vertical
      Number of linear - vertical cordons
    Linear - diagonal
      Number of linear - diagonal cordons
    Hanging arch
      Number of hanging arch cordons
    Standing arch
      Number of standing arch cordons
    Circular
      Number of circular cordons
  Fluting
    Number of individual flutes
  Negative bosses
    Number of negative bosses
  Facets
    Number of facets
  Channels

        Linear - horizontal
          Number of linear - horizontal channels
        Linear - vertical
          Number of linear - vertical channels
        Linear - diagonal
          Number of linear - diagonal channels
        Hanging arch
          Number of hanging arches
        Standing arch
          Number of standing arches
        Circular
          Number of circular channels

Grave-goods
  Brooch(es)
  Miniature iron tweezers
  Miniature bronze tweezers
  Miniature iron shears
  Miniature bronze tweezers
  Miniature iron blade(s)
  Iron shears
  Iron knife
  Razor
  Earscoop
  Coin(s)
  Wristclasp
  Bronze fitting(s)
  Girdle hanger
  Needle(s)
  Pin(s)
  Buckle(s)
  Silver ring(s)
  Bronze ring(s)
  Bronze sheet
  Bronze fragment(s)
  Arrow head
  Spear ferrule
  Iron fragment(s)
  Iron rivet(s)/bar
  Iron nail(s)
  Iron fitting(s)
  Iron ring(s)
  Honestone
  Worked flint(s)
  Crystal
  Glass (unidentified)
  Glass vessel
  Glass bead(s)
  Large bead(s)
  Spindlewhorl(s)
  Ivory
  Coral
  Cowrie shell(s)
  Bone ring(s)
  Playing piece(s)

Bone bead(s)
Comb(s)
Bone fitting(s)
Potsherd(s)

Skeletal evidence
  Number of individuals
    Male / Female
    Neonate
    Infant
    Child
    Adolescent
    Young adult
    Mature adult
    Old adult
    Adult (unknown)
  Animal bones
    Lamb
    Sheep
    Cow / Ox
    Pig
    Horse
    Deer
    Bird
    Fowl
    Dog
      All coded according to whether skeletal identification is
      1 Confident (90 - 100 % chance)
      2 Probable (75 - 90 % chance)
      3 Possible (50 - 75 % chance)

APPENDIX D

CODING SYSTEM

Specimen urn (Spong Hill urn number 1808)

4 1808 1903 4613 0 22.0 24.5 10.5 12.0 13.5 0 0 0 1 1 4 1 4 5 7 2 4 2
1 1 1 6 3 3 3 3 3 3 6 3 3 3 3 3 3 1 3 9 2 2 2 2 2 2 2 2 2 12 11 11 11
11 11 11 11 11 11 11 11 11 0 2 A 15 8 11 11 11 11 11 11 11 11 2 1841A
2250 G 8 10 10 10 10 10 10 10 10 0 0 2 3 5 0 0

4	(code)	Site number
1808		Urn number
1903		Easting
4613		Northing
0	(p/a)	Profile not reconstructed
22.0		Height (cm)
24.5		Maximum diameter (cm)
10.5		Height of maximum diameter (cm)
12.0		Base diameter (cm)
13.5		Rim diameter (cm)
0	(p/a)	No footring / pedestal base
0	(p/a)	No lid
0	(p/a)	No deliberate hole
1	(p/a)	Decoration present
4	(flag)	Number of classes of incised decoration
1	(code)	Horizontal continuous linear grooves
4	(code)	Diagonal linear grooves
5	(code)	Curvilinear grooves
7	(code)	Dots
2		Number of fields of horizontal continuous linear grooves
4		Number of lines in field 1
2		Number of lines in field 2
1	(flag)	Number of classes of diagonal linear grooves
1	(code)	Continuous chevron pattern
1		Number of rows
6		Number of chevron left arms in row 1
3	(x6)	Number of lines in arm 1-6
6		Number of chevron right arms in row 1
3	(x6)	Number of lines in arm 1-6
1		Number of classes of curvilinear grooves
3	(code)	Discontinuous hanging arch
9		Number of arches

2	(x9)	Humber of lines in arch 1-9
12		Number of fields of dots
11	(x12)	Code for triangular enclosed fields of dots
0	(p/a)	No incised decoration on base
2		Number of different stamp motifs
A	(code)	Shape type of stamp 1
15	(code)	Design type of stamp 1
8		Number of fields of decoration of stamp 1
11	(x8)	Code for triangular enclosed fields
2		Number of urns with identical stamps
1841A		Urn number (1)
2250		Urn number (2)
G	(code)	Shape type of stamp 2
8	(code)	Design type of stamp 2
10	(x8)	Code for arched enclosed fields
0		No urns with identical stamp
0	(p/a)	No plastic decoration
2		Number of grave-goods
3	(code)	Shears
5	(code)	Single blade
0		No associated urns
0		No skeletal report

APPENDIX E

PRO-FORMA URN RECORDING FORM

SITE ☐☐☐☐☐☐☐☐☐☐☐☐☐☐ URN NUMBER ☐☐☐☐ GRID: East ☐☐☐☐ North ☐☐☐☐

RECONSTRUCTED Y/N ☐   DELIB. HOLED Y/N ☐   SHAPE ☐☐☐☐☐☐☐☐☐☐☐

DIMENSIONS:

Height ☐☐·☐   Max.Diam. ☐☐☐·☐   H.of Max.Diam. ☐☐☐·☐   Base Diam. ☐☐☐·☐

Rim Diam. ☐☐·☐   Pedestal Diam. ☐☐·☐

INCISED DECORATION:

Field

Horiz.cont. 1☐☐ 2☐☐ 3☐☐ 4☐☐ 5☐☐ 6☐☐ 7☐☐ 8☐☐ 9☐☐ 10☐☐

Vertical 1☐☐ 2☐☐ 3☐☐ 4☐☐ 5☐☐ 6☐☐ 7☐☐ 8☐☐ 9☐☐ 10☐☐

Diagonal

Curvilinear

Other

STAMPED DECORATION:

Form Design   Urns with identical stamps :

1 ☐ ☐☐

2 ☐ ☐☐

3 ☐ ☐☐

4 ☐ ☐☐

PLASTIC DECORATION:

Bosses 1☐☐ 2☐☐ 3☐☐ 4☐☐ 5☐☐   Cordons 1☐☐ 2☐☐ 3☐☐ 4☐☐ 5☐☐

6 ☐☐ Other

GRAVEGOODS:

ASSOCIATED URNS:

COMMENTS:

J.D.R.
20/3/8.

APPENDIX F

STAMPED DECORATION CLASSIFICATION

<u>Shape Groups</u>

A Circular

B Multiple overlapping circles

C Oval

D Crescent, or "horseshoe" shape

E Rectangular

   Virtually straight sides at right angles to each
other, and sharp or nearly sharp corners.

F Incurving rectangles

   Sides at right angles to each other which bow
inwards at centre.

G Diamond

   Virtually straight sides, with two acute and two
obtuse angles, distinguishing it from sideways
impression of Type E.

H Triangular

I Chevron

   Only two sides of the triangle; when the design
is repeated it may give a triangular impression,
but only two sides are outlined.

J Cruciform

K "S" shape

   Often termed the "wyrm" motif.

L "T" shape

   Sides commonly incurving.

M Swastika

N Runic shape

O Animal

P Human

Includes "planta pedis" motif.

Q Miscellaneous

Design Groups

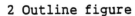

1 Solid figure

No internal elaboration; a simple negative impression of the die is produced.

2 Outline figure

The external die shape is repeated within the head, producing a negative outline around a positive figure.

3 Outline figure with dotted centre

As Type 2 but within the hollowed out interior of the head a dotted line parallel to the external shape is left in relief, producing a dotted negative figure within the positive outline.

4 Repeated figure

As Type 2 but within the interior of the die the external head shape is left in relief, producing a negative internal repetition of the figure, and giving a positive outline.

5 Multiple figure

As Type 2 but the external die shape may be repeated any number of times within the impression.

6 Barred figure

The die is grooved horizontally or vertically to produce a barred figure.

7 Gridded / Lattice figure

The die is grooved regularly horizontally and vertically, producing a design consisting of small negative squares.

8 Outlined gridded figure

As Type 7 but the gridded interior is enclosed within a negative outline of the external die shape.

9 Segmented outline

A negative outline is grooved at right angles to the edge, producing a segmented or gridded outline.

10 Complex segmented figure

A complex design, often combining elements of Types 7 and 9.

11 Simple Cross

A cruciform shape is cut away within the die (not parallel to the edge as in J2), producing a positive cross.

12 Complex Cross

As Type 11 but further elements parallel to the cross are cut away producing a cross whose arms consist of more than a single line.

13 Outlined Cross

Type 11 or 12 contained within a negative outline

14 Pelleted Cross

As Type 11 but the negative areas around the cross have small circles cut away, producing positive pellets around a positive cross.

15 Pelleted Cross in Outline

As Type 14 but enclosed within outline as Type 13.

16 Radiate figure

Sections radiating from a central point are cut away, producing a negative or positive radiating figure.

17 Radiate figure in outline

As Type 16 but enclosed within negative outline as Type 13 and 15.

18 Complex radiate figure

As Type 16 but including an internal outline.

19 Textile figure

Impression of textile on the stamp.

20 Swastika

The dominant design is a swastika, which may be positive or negative.

21 Rune

The dominant design consists of a series of incised lines resembling letters of the runic alphabet.

22 Animal

The dominant design consists of an animal figure, which may be positive or negative.

23 Human

The dominant design consists of a human figure, or part of one, which may be positive or negative.

24 Miscellaneous

APPENDIX G

PHASE TWO CODING SYSTEM

Card 1	column	1-2	Site number	
		4-8	Myres corpus number	
		10-19	Urn number	
		21	Reconstructed profile	(1/0)
		23	Lid	(1/0)
		25	Deliberate hole	(1/0)
		27-30	Height (cm)	
		32-35	Maximum diameter (cm)	
		37-40	Height of maximum diameter (cm)	
		42-45	Rim diameter (cm)	
Card 2	column	1	Decoration	(1/0)
		3	Incised decoration	(1/0)
		5	Number of horizontal fields	
		6-10	Number of lines in each field	
		12	Vertical	(1/0)
		14	Continuous chevron	(1/0)
		15	Discontinuous chevron	(1/0)
		16	Upright chevron	(1/0)
		17	Reversed chevron	(1/0)
		18	Diagonals sloping to left	(1/0)
		19	Diagonals sloping to right	(1/0)
		21	Continuous curvilinear	(1/0)
		22	Hanging arch	(1/0)
		23	Standing arch	(1/0)
		24	Circle	(1/0)
		26	Slashes	(1/0)
		28	Dots	(1/0)
		30	Swastikas	(1/0)
		32	Crosses	(1/0)
		34	Cross on base	(1/0)
		40	Plastic decoration	(1/0)
		42-43	Number of vertical bosses	
		45-46	Number of round bosses	
		48	Cordons	(1/0)
		60	Number of different stamp dies	
		62-63	Stamp group number	
		65	A6	(1/0)

		66	L1	(1/0)
		67	F11	(1/0)
		68	E5	(1/0)
		69	I10	(1/0)
		70	O2	(1/0)
		71	E1	(1/0)
		72	E6	(1/0)
		73	F5	(1/0)
		74	K10	(1/0)
		75	G2	(1/0)
		76	M2	(1/0)
		77	J9	(1/0)
		78	K9	(1/0)
		79	H3	(1/0)
		80	E10	(1/0)
Card 3	column	1	A1	(1/0)
		2	A2	(1/0)
		3	A3	(1/0)
		4	A4	(1/0)
		5	A5	(1/0)
		6	A7	(1/0)
		7	A9	(1/0)
		8	A10	(1/0)
		9	A11	(1/0)
		10	A12	(1/0)
		11	A13	(1/0)
		12	A14	(1/0)
		13	A15	(1/0)
		14	A16	(1/0)
		15	A17	(1/0)
		16	A18	(1/0)
		17	A20	(1/0)
		18	A24	(1/0)
		19	B2	(1/0)
		20	C1	(1/0)
		21	C6	(1/0)
		22	C7	(1/0)
		23	C23	(1/0)
		24	D1	(1/0)
		25	D2	(1/0)
		26	D3	(1/0)
		27	D5	(1/0)
		28	D6	(1/0)
		29	D9	(1/0)
		30	D10	(1/0)
		31	E7	(1/0)
		32	E8	(1/0)
		33	E11	(1/0)
		34	E12	(1/0)
		35	E13	(1/0)
		36	E16	(1/0)
		37	E20	(1/0)
		38	E21	(1/0)
		39	E22	(1/0)

				E24	(1/0)

40	E24	(1/0)
41	F8	(1/0)
42	F14	(1/0)
43	F24	(1/0)
44	G1	(1/0)
45	G5	(1/0)
46	G6	(1/0)
47	G7	(1/0)
48	G8	(1/0)
49	G11	(1/0)
50	G13	(1/0)
51	H1	(1/0)
52	H2	(1/0)
53	H4	(1/0)
54	H5	(1/0)
55	H6	(1/0)
56	H7	(1/0)
57	H8	(1/0)
58	I1	(1/0)
59	I2	(1/0)
60	I5	(1/0)
61	J1	(1/0)
62	J2	(1/0)
63	J6	(1/0)
64	J12	(1/0)
65	K1	(1/0)
66	K2	(1/0)
67	K3	(1/0)
68	K4	(1/0)
69	K5	(1/0)
70	K6	(1/0)
71	K22	(1/0)
72	K24	(1/0)
73	L6	(1/0)
74	M1	(1/0)
75	P1	(1/0)
76	Q1	(1/0)
77	Q2	(1/0)
78	Q4	(1/0)
79	Q7	(1/0)
80	Q24	(1/0)

Card 4   column

1	Brooch(es)	(1/0)
2	Miniature iron tweezers	(1/0)
3	Miniature iron shears	(1/0)
4	Razor	(1/0)
5	Miniature iron blade(s)	(1/0)
6	Earscoop	(1/0)
7	Coin(s)	(1/0)
8	Wristclasp(s)	(1/0)
9	Bronze fitting(s)	(1/0)
10	Needle(s)	(1/0)
11	Buckle(s)	(1/0)
12	Bronze ring(s)	(1/0)
13	Bronze sheet	(1/0)

14	Bronze fragment(s)	(1/0)
15	Arrowhead(s)	(1/0)
16	Spear ferrule	(1/0)
17	Iron fragment(s)	(1/0)
18	Iron rivet/bar(s)	(1/0)
19	Iron ring(s)	(1/0)
20	Iron fitting(s)	(1/0)
21	Honestone	(1/0)
22	Worked flint(s)	(1/0)
23	Crystal	(1/0)
24	Glass (unidentified)	(1/0)
25	Glass vessel	(1/0)
26	Glass bead(s)	(1/0)
27	Large bead(s)	(1/0)
28	Spindlewhorl(s)	(1/0)
29	Ivory	(1/0)
30	Coral	(1/0)
31	Cowrie shell(s)	(1/0)
32	Bone ring(s)	(1/0)
33	Playing piece(s)	(1/0)
34	Bone bead(s)	(1/0)
35	Comb(s)	(1/0)
36	Bone fitting(s)	(1/0)
37	Potsherd(s)	(1/0)
38	Pin(s)	(1/0)
39	Iron nail(s)	(1/0)
40	Silver ring(s)	(1/0)
41	Miniature bronze tweezers	(1/0)
42	Miniature bronze shears	(1/0)
43	Iron shears	(1/0)
44	Iron knife	(1/0)
45	Girdle hanger	(1/0)
49	Number of individuals	
50	Neonate	(1-9)
51	Infant	(1-9)
52	Child	(1-9)
53	Adolescent	(1-9)
54	Young adult	(1-9)
55	Mature adult	(1-9)
56	Adult (unknown)	(1-9)
57	Old adult	(1-9)
58	Male	(1-9)
59	Female	(1-9)
60	Animal	(1-9)
61	Lamb	(1-9)
62	Sheep	(1-9)
63	Cow / Ox	(1-9)
64	Pig	(1-9)
65	Horse	(1-9)
66	Deer	(1-9)
67	Bird	(1-9)
68	Fowl	(1-9)
69	Dog	(1-9)